Drop Dead Gorgeous

YO-EHY-297

Images of Death
Studies on the Social Transformation of Death

Edited by Dominik Groß, Andrea Esser, Hubert Knoblauch and Brigitte Tag

Volume 6

Tina Weber is research assistant at the Technical University of Berlin.

Tina Weber

Drop Dead Gorgeous

Representations of Corpses in American TV Shows

Campus Verlag
Frankfurt/New York

This publication has been produced with the financial assistance of the DFG Graduate School "Codification of Violence in Medial Transformation" at the Humboldt University Berlin, the "German Academic Exchange Service (DAAD)" and the Volkswagen foundation research project "Death and Dead Bodies – Transformation of Attitudes towards Death in Contemporary Society".

Bibliographic Information published by the Deutsche Nationalbibliothek:
Die Deutsche Nationalbibliothek lists this publication in the Deutsche Nationalbibliografie; detailed bibliographic data are available in the Internet at http://dnb.d-nb.de
ISBN 978-3-593-39507-4

Printing office and bookbinder:
Printed on acid free paper.
Printed in Germany

This book is also available as an eBook.

For further information:
www.campus.de
www.press.uchicago.edu

Content

Part 1–Introduction

Part 2–Analysis: What is shown and how?

Part 3–Field Research: What is not shown and why?

Part 4—Conclusion

Part I–Introduction

Preface

Death is a sore subject, difficult to discuss. It concerns every one of us, though approaching it often brings conversations to a halt. Yet, the bodies of the dead remain a simultaneous source of fascination and disgust. This interest is especially palpable in television programs. Soon after the TV show *Six Feet Under* aired, I applied for a position at the biggest funeral parlour company in Germany. I witnessed an increasing interest in death amongst the public but also the company's increasing efforts to be more visible in public. I also detected the same interest in art and media. Antje Kahl, Dr. Rolf Peter Lange, Prof. Dr. Thomas Macho and I organised the conference: "The New Visibility of Death" in Berlin in 2005. By then undertakers, pathologists and "death artists" had already shot to fame amongst a growing curiosity driven fan community. I wondered about the reasons for this and started to focus on the increasing amount of new TV shows which were concerned with representations of dead bodies. When I received a Ph.D. scholarship to explore this phenomenon, I had the chance to conduct field research in Los Angeles. L. A. hosts not only the production of most of these new TV shows about the dead; it also has the biggest Coroner's Office in the USA. I visited original film locations; observed filming on set and interviewed people involved in the filmmaking process. At the same time, I undertook an internship at the Coroner's Office, observing closely the work of investigators at the Coroners' Office and medical examiners. Often in the evening I would watch the news and see a coroner investigating a crime scene. Then following this there would be TV shows like CSI, in which their media doubles took over. What I found most interesting about these incidents was the fact that the corpses at the crime scene were covered on the news but the corpses in the TV shows were shown. Moreover, new narratives, settings and roles allowed the fictional dead to be represented in a different, more complex way than ever. The more complex the role on screen became, the less the dead resembled the corpses I had seen at crime scenes or in the pathology department at the Coroner's Office. These new media representations, which shape societies' ideas about the corpse, are the subject of this research.

Acknowledgements

In the course of the last four years, I have had kind and well-meaning support and it is a pleasure to thank those people who made this thesis possible.

I want to express my sincere thanks to my friend and colleague Antje Kahl from TU Berlin for all our discussions and her thoughtful comments. I would also like to express my gratitude to Prof. Dr. Stefan Timmermans from UCLA for his excellent supervision, patience and sense of humour.

This thesis would not have been possible, unless Prof. Dr. Thomas Macho and the Deutsche Forschungsgemeinschaft (DFG) had not supported me intellectually and financially through the graduate school "Codification of Violence in Media Transformation" at the Humboldt University Berlin in 2006–2008. I would also like to thank the German Academic Exchange Programme (DAAD) for the financial support of my research stay in Los Angeles in 2008. Since 2009, I have been a Research Assistant for the Volkswagen research project "Death and Dead Bodies" at the Technical University, Berlin. I would like to thank Prof. Dr. Hubert Knoblauch for his intellectual support and the Volkswagen Foundation for its financial aid.

I would also like to express my appreciation to Romy Bartsch, Zara Morris and Ian Perdue, Patrick Schubert, Nicole Schulz, Stefanie Krämer, Peer Günther and Björn Haase for technical support.

This research would never have been as profound, if I had not witnessed the real world of dead bodies and their caretakers. Therefore, I would like to thank the staff of the Los Angeles County Coroner's Office, particularly Chief Ed Winter, Investigator Steve Nelson, Dr. Louis A. Pena and Dr. Paul V. Gliniecki, and also the Las Vegas Coroner for their trust in my research intentions and unconditional support. Many thanks to my interviewees; Elizabeth Devine (Co producer, CSI), Chuck Bemis (Cameraman, CSI), Matthew W. Mungle (Producer of prosthetics and manikins,

MWM Inc.), Eddi Vargus (Employee of MWM Inc.), Ruth Haney (Special Make-up Artist, CSI) and Joshua Meltzer (Props Manager, Dexter), and those who made the interviews possible, namely Patricia & Melissa Hayden, Steve Dowell, Andree Brennan and Stefan Timmermans.

I am especially grateful for all the support that I have received on the home front from my family, friends and Mister Mueller whilst researching and writing this dissertation. I would like to thank them for their merriment and the warm glow, which I always feel surrounded by. I dedicate this book to them.

.

Introduction[1]

I am a social scientist writing about the representation of corpses in new TV shows of the 21st century. This work is divided into four sections: firstly Theory and Methods, secondly Pictorial and Film Analysis (subtitled: What is shown and how?), thirdly Statistical Research and Interviews (subtitled: What is not shown and why?) and fourthly the Conclusion.

In 2005, a colleague and I in cooperation with Humboldt University Berlin and the funeral parlour company Ahorn Grieneisen AG, organised a conference on the topic "The New Visibility of Death". Papers were given about the developments taking place in economics, art and the media. In 2006, Thomas Macho argued that death, once invisible, has become recently more visible, referring amongst other things to numerous TV shows. Hans Belting, however, argues against a new visibility of death, pointing instead towards an accomplishment of the invisibility of death. He argues that these images do not represent the dead but hide them with substitutes, since there is no real reference point and no dead person being represented, a replacement of death is instead put forth. Belting, explains that humans have produced media masks of those things that they refuse to see since time immemorial. We hide those things that are unwanted and replace them with something more desirable but we are nonetheless aware that this representation of death is fake. Elizabeth Hallam et al., argues in quite the same fashion about sophisticated systems concerning the representation of death with functions that mask its reality. In my work, I aim to analyse the systems of representation in contemporary TV shows and question the validity of the arguments of Thomas Macho and Hans Belting concerning "The New Visibility of Death". I want to combine both approaches of the "New Visibility of Death" and the new sophisticated representation systems of death. My hypothesis is this: when a distinctive

---

1 In my dissertation I will translate German literature which is not published in English. The original quotes can be found in the footnotes.

large number of new and consistent images of corpses appear in new TV shows, one can then deduce codes of representation, which constitute a new system of corpse presentation. The codes of representation define a rigid field of visibility. My research is therefore concerned with analysing the visibility of certain codes of contemporary representation of corpses in a certain place (daily TV shows), dissociated from paintings and photographs of the dead in past centuries. The analysis of corpse representation in 21st century media will shed light on the contemporary media's ideals of beauty and the conveyed body knowledge about the dead body. Section 1: Theory and Methodology

In the first chapter, I will introduce the theoretical background for the following chapters. I will start with the exploration of (1) the connection between image and death. When writing about death and the representation of death, one has to refer to Maurice Blanchot, Hans Belting and Thomas Macho. Not only because they claim that the dead were the first pictures created by prehistoric man, but also because they state that the experience of death and loss made way for these images. These images changed as the shapes of the bodies of the living changed. Thus the bodies of the living, altered and manipulated by social conventions are the bodies then altered again in death. They change shape over time. The body has become more prominent in sociology due to the attention it has gained in society. Norbert Elias, Michel Foucault and their followers stressed the important role of the body and its transformation from a historic perspective.

I will exemplify the connection of death and images by presenting (2) a historical survey of depictions of corpses. I will highlight the research on the history of changing attitudes toward death and the depiction of death in different centuries. Moreover, I will point to new forms of representation in art, such as death photography or installations and then continue by examining how death is portrayed in audio-visual media. I will contrast this historic pictorial discourse with the (3) first media representation of corpses in TV shows from 1950 until 2000. Before the 21st century, crime shows have always shown the victims at the crime scene. With the turn of the century and the rise of TV shows like *CSI* or *Six Feet Under*, the dead became a constant player in the plot, not only at the crime scene but also in the morgue, in the embalming room or in pathology. Before the turn of the century, there was only one show on TV (*Quincy, M.E.*) that presented a pathologist and corpses. I want to explore whether there are any differences between these recent TV programs and previous ones and if so, how these differences can be characterised. In the following, I would like to outline (4) the new representations of corpses in TV shows from 2000–2010. I will argue that (5) a new sophisticated system of death representations has emerged since the turn of the 21st Century and depict where this description originates from. Subsequently, I will expand on (6) the characteristics of this new representational system.

In the second chapter, I will talk about the methods used for analysis. The research material consists of the shows *Six Feet Under*, *CSI Las Vegas*, *Crossing Jordan*, *Bones*, *Castle*, *NCIS*, *Dead like me*, *Pushing Daisies*, *Heroes*, *Dexter*, *Tru Calling*, *Dr. G*, *Autopsy*, *North Mission Road* and *Family Plots*. These fifteen new shows were all produced in the 21st Century. Additionally, *Quincy, M.E.* as a forerunner show model and the documentary *Autopsy* have been selected. The common criterion for my selection is that the dead figure remains in the centre of the story and turns into an object of interest. I will introduce pictorial analysis followed by film analysis and proceed to expert interviews and finish with statistical research.

For the majority of pictures, I will use a pictorial analysis, which consists of a pre-level, the preparation of prototypes, and actual single case analysis.

For an analysis of the specific representations of the moving dead, I will choose sequence analysis. I will also present interviews with producers, make-up artists and prop makers from *CSI* and *Dexter*. In order to validate my assumptions, I will additionally provide statistical research on the TV shows and disclose general representation restrictions regarding age, gender and race proportions as well as the specific representation taboos regarding the dead body.

Section 2: Pictorial and Film Analysis

What is shown and how?

Chapter 3 (Pictorial Analysis) is concerned with the representation of "pretty corpses in pathology". TV Genres have various possibilities to represent a corpse. Some genres have more possibilities to represent the dead than others, but altogether they represent a current media discourse. The analysis of the discourse will not only provide an overview about all new TV shows but will also reveal what kind of corpse can be shown, when and where. I will introduce and analyse *Six Feet Under* (drama/black comedy), *CSI, Crossing Jordan, Bones, Castle* and *NCIS* (crime series), *Dead like me, Pushing Daisies* (fantasy/comedy), *Heroes, Dexter, Tru Calling* (fantasy/drama) and *North Mission Road, Family Plots* (documentary series). With the help of the presentation of categories and trends of new corpse representations, I will argue that there is a new system of death representations.

Chapter 4 (Film Analysis) will be concerned with "disgusting autopsies in pathology". I aim to analyse the most obvious representational trend, the aesthetic corpse, and will introduce theories about aesthetics. Thereafter, I will apply the theory in the film analysis of *Autopsy–Through the eyes of death's detectives* (documentary) and in the film analysis of *CSI–Down the Drain* (crime). I will argue that there is a massive use of aesthetic media techniques representing the dead in fictional TV shows by comparing and evaluating the representation codes.

Section 3: Statistical Research and Interviews

What is not shown and why?

In chapter 5 (New representations and new taboos), I want to specify what is not shown and why. I will introduce socio-cultural theories on taboos regarding representation of the dead in media. Thereafter, I will contrast the new representations of the dead in a documentary soap with the representation of the dead in a drama/black comedy show. I will distinguish between general representation restrictions and specific representation taboos regarding the dead body. I will argue that there are specific constraints, which can be distinguished from general taboos in television.

In chapter 6 (Field research: The representation of corpses under constraints) I want to reveal the broader context of the production and effects, which generate and shape restrictions on the pictorial discourse of dead bodies in contemporary television. I will ask how the context of the pictorial discourse is organised and argue that officials, producers and recipients alike influence the shape of media representation of the dead body.

Section 4: Conclusion

In chapter 7 (Conclusion) I will summarize my research results and explain my hypothesis in connection with my findings. I will then explore why the new systems of death representation occurred with the turn of the 21st century and why the representation codes are shaped the way they are. I will argue that changing genres and changing body images might contribute to the emergence of these new representations. As a suggestion for future research, I will highlight representations of death in other audio-visual media such as YouTube.

1. Theory

In this chapter I want to introduce the theoretical background for the following chapters. I will start with the introduction of (1) the connection between images, death and the pictorial discourse. I will then exemplify the discourse with (2) a historical survey of the depiction of corpses. Afterwards I will contrast this historic pictorial discourse with (3) the first media representation of corpses in TV shows from 1950 until the year 2000 and then sketch out the actual research subject, (4) the new representation of corpses in TV shows from 2000–2010. I will argue that (5) a new sophisticated system of death representations has emerged since the turn of the 21st century, I will show where this description originates from and amplify on (6) the characteristics of this new representation system.

1.1. Image, death and discourse

What is an image? Hans Belting (2001) answers this question with the help of visual anthropology. He argues that images are not disembodied, rather they rest upon a medium, a picture carrier. He states that the connection between images and death is an essential characteristic of representativeness. According to Belting, images are the outcome of personal and collective symbolism. Everything that we see is an image or can be transformed into an image. He further states that we are surrounded by images in our daily lives, and that we understand the world through them. (Belting, 2001, p. 11) He concludes that the cultural history of pictures reflects the cultural history of the body because transformations in bodily experience are reflected in changing pictorial representations. (Belting, 2001, p. 23) Like Jean Baudrillard, Belting interprets a symbolic exchange where the deceased person exchanges their lost body with an image thereby remaining among the living.[1] Yet, unlike Baudrillard he does not refer to the symbolic exchange as a crisis of representation but as a crisis of reference. He expresses a profound doubt about references. He claims that the reality of bodies is no longer visible. The symbolic exchange of the dead body for an image has changed. The image replaces a body with a hyperreal and virtual figure. (Belting, 2001, p. 108) The concept that images need a medium is based on the idea that people use their own bodies as a means to create internal images (like the imagination) or receive external images (like visual experiences). (Belting, 2001, p. 29) Like Thomas Macho, Belting describes the enigma of an image as an inextricable connection of a paradoxical presence and absence[2]: We see the medium, but we cannot see the absence of the original. In the dead, we see the biological material of an absent person.[3]

This is how depiction started, he argues. The experience of death and loss made way for depiction. (Belting, 2000, p. 10) People wanted to replace this unbearable absence of a loved one with an image, which holds a place for the dead person amongst the living. When a person dies and is no longer a physical actor in social interaction, there is a need to give the dead a place to keep them in society—a symbolic place and a symbolic body to maintain social connections. (Belting, 2000, p. 144) People stand up against the loss of personhood. (Belting, 2000, p. 145) Belting argues that death urged people to set up depictions (Belting, 2000, p. 134). Referring to

---

1 "Das Medium besitzt im Totenkult ein uraltes Paradigma. Der Tote tauschte seinen verlorenen Körper gegen ein Bild ein, mit dem er unter den Lebenden verblieb. Nur im Bild ließ sich der Tausch mit der Präsenz des Toten einlösen. Sein Medium vertrat den Körper der Toten ebenso, wie es für die Körper der Lebenden existierte, die den symbolischen Tausch von Bild und Tod vollzogen. So war es in diesem Falle nicht nur Medium zwischen Bild und Betrachter, sondern ein solches zwischen Tod und Leben" (Belting, 2001, p. 29).

2 "Das Rätsel, das schon die Leiche umgibt, ist folgerichtig auch zum Rätsel des Bildes geworden; es liegt in einer paradoxen Abwesenheit, die ebenso aus der Anwesenheit der Leiche wie aus dem anwesenden Bild spricht. Damit eröffnet sich das Rätsel von Sein und Schein, das nie aufgehört hat, die Menschen zu erregen. Solche Gedanken mögen den Menschen erst gekommen sein, wenn sie entdeckten, dass sie im Bild nur ein neues Rätsel erfanden, als sie mit dem Bild auf das Rätsel des Todes antworten wollten. Das Bildermachen war dabei wohl wichtiger als das Bilderhaben, weil man damit aktiv auf eine Störung in der Lebensgemeinschaft reagierte und gleichsam die Naturordnung wiederherstellte: man gab toten Mitgliedern einer Gemeinschaft einen Status zurück, den sie für die Präsenz in einem Sozialverband brauchten" (Belting, 2001, p. 145).

3 "Der Leichnam ist ein Bild seiner selbst, ein unsicheres Bild, das stets schon verloren ist, und sich schließlich dem wahrnehmenden Begreifen entzieht" (Belting, 2000, p. 145).

Maurice Blanchot (2007) Macho argues that death is the generative impulse of the first images. (Macho 2008, p. 11) At the beginning the dead person was the first pictorial counterpart of a person. According to Thomas Macho (1987, p. 188), death can only be described with metaphors, since one cannot "experience" death.[4]

We cannot experience our own death. Therefore we are limited to the death of others. Following Macho (1987, p. 195), the confrontation with the pure presence of death allows the experience of unique resistance.[5] However, since contemporary society rarely provides possibilities for the individual to materially experience the presence of dead bodies, television fills the void with visual confrontations. Nowadays the TV screen is the dominant medium where visualisations of the dead can be found. (Belting, 2001, p. 30) We can watch actors, who died a long time ago, claiming their vivid presence amongst the living through the medium of moving pictures. Movies can create the impression that pictures are internal images. The viewers imagine themselves in an imaginary situation, as if they were there in the picture. (Belting, 2001, p. 75) At the same time, Belting asks about the meaning of the picture. All pictures are made at a certain time, but timing can change the effect of a picture. Pictures can also carry timeless

---

4 This is why Thomas Macho transfers Hans Blumenbergs concept of the "absolute metaphor", which is not connected to experiences. (Macho, 1987, 185) "Grenzerfahrung und Tod. In dieser Spannung sprechen wir auch über den Tod. Wir verwenden Bild und Symbole, 'absolute Metaphern', um die Unsagbarkeit dieses leeren Begriffs, dem keine Anschauung korrespondiert, auszufüllen" (Macho, 1987, p. 187). The term death is an absolute metaphor for inexpressible experiences. (Macho, 1987, p. 188) "Der Todesbegriff ist eigentlich ein leerer Begriff, ein Begriff, dem keine Anschauung korrespondiert; ein 'flatus vocis' für ein Ereignis, das wir nicht verstehen und niemals werden verstehen können. Nach der Bedeutung des Todesbegriffs gefragt, müssen wir schweigen. 'Tod' heißt alles und nichts; es bleibt nämlich offen, was alles gemeint sein kann, wenn vom Tod gesprochen wird" (Macho, 1987, p. 181).

5 "Was wir nämlich an Leichen erfahren, ist ihre nachdrückliche Resistenz gegen jede soziale Verbindlichkeit. Die Leiche sieht uns nicht an, ihr Blick ist von merkwürdiger und strenger Distanz, ein 'böser Blick', der gefürchtet wird, weil er uns 'durchschaut', als wären wir gar nicht anwesend. Die Leiche spricht nicht mit uns, und ihre Miene bleibt verschlossen. Sie bewegt keinen Arm und kein Bein. Dennoch haben die Leichen Augen; dennoch haben sie Münder und Zungen; dennoch haben sie Gesichter, Muskeln, Arme und Beine. Die Leiche ist ohne Zweifel ein Mensch; aber sie verhält sich ganz und gar nicht wie ein Mensch. Sie ist menschlich und unmenschlich zugleich: ein Wesen, das eigentlich im Universum sozialer Existenz nicht erscheinen darf" (Macho, 1987, p. 198). The paradox of the corpse, a person's absence and presence at the same time, generates another paradox: the media representation of the dead by a living person. The living 'imagine' themselves as dead and 'perform' the dead.

questions. According to Belting people have made pictures of themselves long before they started writing about themselves. Today people film and photograph themselves throughout all different stages of their life. These depictions show bodies, but actually mean to show individuals. (Belting, 2001, p. 87) The natural sciences depict bodies as well. In both cases, depictions either correspond to the current discourse or become obsolete. Belting describes how bodies, in particular, the superhuman beautiful and virtual body in the media, manipulate the viewers and how this has occurred through time. Historical pictures disciplined the respective viewers. Different eras represent the same body differently and present different ideas about bodies. That is why Belting claims that the history of depiction mirrors a history of the body. (Belting, 2001, p. 89) Furthermore, the history of depicting human beings is a history of the depiction of bodies, yet the bodies are carriers of social beings. (Belting, 2001, p. 89) The history of depiction shows historic dynamics and the inherent instability of bodily depictions across time. Referring to Günther Anders (1956), Belting defines an addiction to pictures as a new climax of pseudo communication.[6] The simultaneous consumption of pictures and the satisfaction on the consumers' side convey the idea of a common and shared world. All Live- and Reality TV shows compensate for the loss of experiences in the real world. (Belting, 2000, p. 237) Anders (1956) invented the term "Ikonomanie", the human addiction to images which causes people to feel shame about their own lives by watching television. When humans try to duplicate themselves in pictures through technical productions, the perfection of technical producers creates a shame in their viewer since the viewer is not able to be as perfect and diverse as what is presented to them on TV. Witnessing the post-industrial transformation, Belting goes further and stresses that now society produces fewer things but more information. This development causes a shift from "the thing" to the picture and so the production of pictures becomes the most important social good. This process results in events becoming socially important only once captured in pictures. This spares the viewer from reading about the event. Belting

6 "Die 'Bildsucht', von der Günther Anders einmal sprach, ist der bisherige Höhepunkt einer Pseudokommunikation in der neuen Masse, die alle direkten Formen der Kommunikation verliert. Der simultane Konsum derselben Bilder vermittelt das Gefühl, in einer gemeinsamen Welt ohne soziale und kulturelle Schranken zu leben. Das Zusammenspiel von Produzenten und Konsumenten ist schwer durchschaubar, weil die Produzenten nur die Wünsche der Konsumenten befriedigen, die die bei diesen vorher selber erzeugt haben" (Belting, 2000, p. 273).

writes that if an event becomes socially significant as a picture, then not only the difference between reality and appearance is lost[7], but the depiction becomes more relevant than the content of the pictures. At this point, Baudrillard's term simulacrum can also be applied.[8]

In "Symbolic Exchange and Death" (1976)[9] Baudrillard defines Western civilisation as a system of simulation, and predicts the death of reality. The central thesis refers to signs and their missing reference points. Without reference, signs replace reality instead of depicting reality, which is most obvious when it comes to depictions in the mass media. Baudrillard claims a rupture in the political economy as the signs start to augment and lose their reference points in reality, but produce at the same time a new hyperreality. Baudrillard, however, sees death as the last veritable occurrence in a senseless world destroyed by capitalism. Consequently, he argues for a "symbolic exchange" which is supposed to resist the capitalist logic. The "symbolic exchange" stands for an alternative to capitalist production and exchange. He assumes an incompatible relation between capitalism and human nature, claiming capitalist thinking, such as monetary profit and capitalist values of utility, is against human nature. Baudrillard applies the capitalist exchange and the system of values to death and society. He concludes that the human body in this new relationship of "political economy and death" turns into biological capital. The aging human body loses its value when it turns into a deficient and ineffective body. While in other societies the elderly might be the most respected, the appreciation of experiences of life does not take place within the capitalist system. Death has

---

7 "Wenn ein Ereignis erst 'als Bild sozial wichtig wird, ist der Unterschied zwischen Sein und Schein aufgehoben.' Dann muss 'das Original sich nach seiner Reproduktion richten', für die es nur noch die Matritze liefert. Wo wir 'die Welt in effigie' erfahren, dort ist das Ereignis das Bild selber. Die Zweideutigkeit dessen, was sie übertragen, macht die Bilder zu Phantomen, deren Natur wir nicht mehr durchschauen" (Belting, 2000, p. 276).

8 Elisabeth Klaver refers to Baudrillard's "[…] notion of hyperreality where the real disappear completely under the image. Watching an autopsy on television or in the movies, then, would better be described as watching the substitution of the image for the real, the scene of an autopsy whereby an actor or dummy stands in for the dead body. Indeed, even when a real dead body is used, […], the mediating apparatus of television works to sanitize the event. This may once have been a real cadaver and a real autopsy, but now it is a video, iterable only as long as the videotape lasts. In fact, I honestly did not realize how much the substitution effect of mediation sanitizes an autopsy until I attended the real thing" (Klaver, 2006, p. 134).

9 First translated in English in 1993.

lost its symbolic value of exchange value, was denied in modern society and finally expulsed. The economy and the urge for cleanliness overtakes the traditional idea of death and mourning.

"Our whole culture is hygienic, and aims to expurgate life from death. The detergents in the weakest washing powder are intended for death. To sterilise death at all costs, to vanish it, cryogenically freeze it, air-condition it, put make up on it, 'design' it, to pursue it with the same relentlessness as grime, sex, bacteriological or radioactive waste" (Baudrillard, 1993, p. 180).

According to Baudrillard death became embarrassing.

"It is not so worrying that the dead man is made beautiful and given the appearance of a representation. Every society has always done this. They have always staved off the abjection of natural death, the social abjection of decomposition which voids the corpse of it signs and its social force of signification, leaving it as nothing more than a substance, and by the same token, precipitating the group into the terror of its own symbolic decomposition. It is necessary to ward off death, to smother it in artificiality in order to evade the unbearable moment when flesh becomes nothing but flesh, and ceases to be a sign" (Baudrillard, 1993, p. 180).

Just like Tony Walter (1991), Baudrillard claims death to be the new taboo after sexuality.[10] The denial of death leads to a taboo, the anonymity of the dying, and increasingly artificial funerals.[11]

In general, it can be stated that Baudrillard describes in "Symbolic Exchange and Death" and in his subsequent work "Simulation and

---

10 "Speaking of death makes us laugh in a strained and obscene manner. Speaking of sex no longer provokes the same reaction: sex is legal, only death is pornographic. Society, having 'liberated' sexuality, progressively replaces it with death which functions as a secret rite and fundamental prohibition. Today the opposite is true. But all 'historical' societies are arranged so as to dissociate sex and death in every possible way, and play the liberation of one off against the other/which is a way of neutralising them both" (Baudrillard, 1993, p. 184).

11 "Here, it becomes a question of the dead retaining the appearance of life, the naturalness of life: he still smiles at you, the same colours, the same skin, he seems himself even after death, he is even a little fresher than when he was alive, and lacks only speech (but we can still hear this in stereo). A faked death, idealised in the colours of life: the secret idea is that life is natural and death is against nature. Death must therefore be naturalised in a stuffed simulacrum of life. In all of this there is on the one hand a refusal to let death signify, take on the force of a sign, and, behind this sentimental nature-fetishism on the other, a great ferocity as regards the dead himself: rotting and change are forbidden, and instead of being carried over to death and thus the symbolic recognition of the living, he is maintained as a puppet within the orbit of the living in order to serve as an alibi and a simulacrum of their own lives"(Baudrillard, 1993, p.181).

Simulacra"(1981) the profound break between modern and postmodern societies. While modern societies rest upon production and consumption, postmodern societies rest upon simulation and simulacra. The characteristic of a simulacrum is the impossibility to distinguish between original and copy, i.e. between reality and imagination. Media images become independent. With a reference point missing, copies of copies without originals are made, i.e. media images of the dead have no origin. The consequence of representing images of corpses without origin is that they fail to correspond to reality. Due to the lack of experience with real dead people, these representations are the only source the audience has. (Baudrillard, 1978, pp. 7)[12]

Media representation of the dead always creates an impasse–"a dead end"–, since no real dead people can be used for the representation. Hence, actors, who are more qualified to represent the living, simulate something of what they assume looks like death. This assumption in turn originates most likely from earlier media representations of the dead since at present people see the dead on television rather than in their family homes or other intimate social environments. (Elias, 1985) So actors, in fact, simulate what they have already seen in other representations of the media, i.e. it is not a simulation of a dead body, but an imitation of other actors imitating other actors imitating death. This process connects with Baudrillard's ideas of copies without references. The act of imitating is another copy, and copies of copies have been made since the first corpse appearances on TV in the late nineteen twenties, gradually progressing the representation of death with further markers that the body being depicted is dead. So it could be said that media simulation determines for the most part, society's views of death and dead bodies; consequently, the perception of media images shapes the public image of the "dead body".

I would also like to address the association between images, death and discourse but from another perspective. Neither Michael Foucault (1994) nor Reiner Keller (2005) limited "discourse" to theoretical texts. Reiner Keller especially, points out the importance of audio-visual media.[13] Sabine Maasen (2006), also referring to Michel Foucault (1988), states that images

---

12 Cf. Debord, 1996

13 "Angesichts der enormen Bedeutung von audiovisuellen Medieninformationen und -inhalten (Fernsehen, Film, Fotografie, Comics, Werbung) werden sich wissens-soziologische Diskursanalysen zukünftig stärker mit der Analyse und Interpretation solcher Daten befassen müssen" (Keller, 2005, p. 271).

represent the order of a discourse. She asks if a sociocultural order influences pictorial discourses and vice versa. Mayerhausen (2006, p. 82), also seriously doubts that there are reasons to distinguish between textual and visual images.[14] Instead, he finds it plausible to describe pictures as carriers of knowledge, which have a discursive functionality. In this discourse, the media's images of the dead can also be understood as being metaphors of death bound to a film format. These metaphors represent the dead with certain media codes, and the audience recognises these media codes as representations of the dead. These pictorial expressions generate and reflect social reality, which is why certain representations can be seen as discursive practice. In the following chapters, I will question which representations are shown and which are not. I will also examine which codes can be identified, and which are excluded; which functions can be identified, who identifies with them and at what point of time they are produced, consumed and discussed. This work also follows the premise that pictorial elements are essential constituents of discourses. Therefore, this research is a contribution to pictorial discourse analysis. The actual analysis focuses on a time period from 2000 to 2009, but representations from before that time period are taken into consideration as well. Here analysis might turn vague due to the empirical material that originates from other earlier studies which have different approaches. For this reason, I will only briefly outline the history of the depiction of death. This will emphasise these changes, which have occurred in the pictorial discourse of death representation, and will therefore testify to the novelty of the new system of representation regarding death. Hence, my research will also contribute to the sociology of the body. The increasing importance and awareness of the body in contemporary culture, is categorised by Keller and Michael Meuser (2010) as "body knowledge". According to them, "body knowledge"[15]

14 According to Mayerhausen (2006, pp. 81) Foucault determined less strictly what "discursive" means and what it does not. Mayerhausen formulates the corresponding question concerning the exertion of influence. What knowledge is activated by the power to play off the exertion of influence? Which media is used by power systems for the transport of knowledge? Which textual and pictorial contributions are activated for respective public responsive? Here, Mayerhausen states that images are an essential media for knowledge and lists the examples of passports and application photos, CCTV, pictorial products in sciences and especially TV, the Internet and print media.

15 Keller, Reiner & Meuser, Michael 2010: Tagungsbericht: Körperwissen. Eine internationale und interdisziplinäre Tagung [10 Absätze]. Forum Qualitative Sozialforschung/ Forum: Qualitative Social Research, 11(2), Art. 27, http://nbn-resolving.de/urn:nbn:de: 0114-fqs1002277.

relates to the immediate, private and intimate knowledge of individuals about their own bodies, conditions and processes, together with the so-cialised pattern of thoughts including norms, incorporated routines and skills, as well as those experiences, which are not reflected. The authors also add conveyed knowledge that comes from media representations and expert systems, and suggests amongst others, social norms and the medi-cal-technical potential for body design. While there is always the possibility for society to review and correct the image of the body that is conveyed by the media, before its assimilation and incorporation, images of the dead body cannot be, because media discourse appears to be the only source conveying knowledge about the corpse. Only a few people see a dead body in their lifetime, and of course no one can experience their own body as a dead body. This is why I will later focus on descriptions of corpse repre-sentations.

1.2. Historical survey of depictions of corpses

As the return of the body is often heralded in cultural and social sciences (Gugutzer, 2004) I want to introduce the return of the dead body by pre-senting earlier pictorial appearances of the dead body in different centuries. Therefore, I will elaborate on Philippe Ariès' examination of death. Ariès, a French historian, examined not only the history of childhood and private life, but the history of changing attitudes toward death in Europe through-out different centuries (1980)[16] and the history of the depiction of death (1984)[17]. His work utilised written documents and pictures as his primary source material. Ariès detected different, subsequent periods of depiction. In order to explain the different phases, I will first give a short introduc-tion to the different periods he defined. He set up five basic Western atti-tudes toward death, which are:

1) The "Tame Death" (5th–8th century)
2) The "Death of the Self" (12th–13th century),
3) The "Remote and Imminent Death" (16th–18th century)
4) The "Death of the Other" (19th–20th century) and

---

16 Title: Studien zur Geschichte des Todes im Abendland.
17 Title: Bilder zur Geschichte des Todes.

5) The "Death Denied" (20th century)

Egyptian depictions and epitaphs existed prior to the "Tame Death". Between the 1st and 5th century, depictions of the deceased and epitaphs began to appear in Europe, expressing identification and the invocation of the joy of the here and now. The epitaphs were comprised of a name, age and date of death, while the depictions displayed profession, family and facial features of the deceased. These details indicated the drive for depiction of individuals beyond death. By the 8th century, different types of graveyards had developed. In the early Middle Ages the practice of epitaphs and depictions declined. Ariès characterised the decline in "Tame Death"[18] as an urge for anonymity instead of identity. In the high Middle

---

18 Tame Death (5th -8th century), is characterised by the following parameters: parameter 1 (scrutiny of the community), parameter 2 (control through rites), parameter 3 (death as a peaceful sleep), and parameter 4 (death as an inevitable mishap). With parameter 1 (scrutiny of the community) Ariès describes the awareness of human beings of themselves. Death is not seen as a mere individual act, as an occurrence accompanied by ceremonies with the aim to connect the individual with community and confirm the solidarity. The ceremony entails three elements: first, the adoption of an active role on the part of the dying, second, a parting scene, and third, the mourning. According to Ariès, these rites show the scrutiny of the community as the community feels the weakening of the community through the loss of a member. The community confesses the threat, and through the ceremony they restore their unit and the will to preserve the species.

With parameter 2 (control through rites) Ariès continues to describe the threat through the loss of a member of the community and the defence of society against nature. Beyond the threat of weakening the community, the loss of a member also creates a breach in the defence system of a community against nature and wildness. Although death belongs to natural events, society always tried to balance these circumstances with the organisation of a society and moral rules in order to establish a peaceful and safe life within the community. Death, apart from sexuality, forms the weakest part of the defence system and needs to be controlled with particular care. That is why death is embedded in ceremonies and transformed into a public spectacle for the community.

With parameter 3 (death as a peaceful sleep) Ariès describes the belief in a life after death and the ambiguous reaction to dead bodies. Though the end of life is not denied, this end does not match the physical death but with certain circumstances of the afterlife. Every religion offers life after death, even to the end of time. Christianity offers a wait in peace and silence for the resurrection in glory. The wait is preferably performed as a peaceful sleep. Since the early Middle Ages, this peaceful sleep has become a persistent form of Christian mentality.

With parameter 4 (death as an inevitable mishap) Ariès describes a belief in the existence of evil and the taming of death through rites. In Christianity, death was always explained by the original sin as a reaction to the general feeling of a permanent presence of the evil. This became a long lasting myth. One can tame death but one can never experience

Ages ("Death of the Self")[19], epitaphs and depictions appear again. Different graphic depictions of corpses on sarcophagi made prior to the 18th century characterise this new grave iconography. These different types are the grave with epitaph, the grave with Gisant (lying, 11th–16th), the grave with Priant (praying, 14th–18th), and Gisant and Priant coexisted later on. Depictions of the Last Judgement; usually with Christ and the twelve Apostles in a court, supersede depictions of baptism and resurrection from the 11th century onwards. After the 13th century, the first signs of an individual biography become visible through the ars moriendi, the depiction of books of hours. By the 15th century, the late Middle Ages, the Last Judgement depictions have been replaced by depictions of deathbed scenes, death masques, books of hours and the representation of the layout of the scene and the escort of the dead to the church service and burial. By the 15th century the Last Judgment depictions of the previous era have been replaced by deathbed scenes, death masques, books of hours and other sacred images. Between the 14th and 16th century, simultaneously with the

---

death as a neutral phenomenon. These parameters generate a basis and in the following, these parameters will change and define the new attitudes toward death.

19 The "Death of the Self" (12th -13th century) is characterised by a variation of parameter 1 (scrutiny of the community) and parameter 3 (Death as a peaceful sleep), while parameter 2 and 4 remain unchanged. Furthermore, the first attitude, the "Tame Death", exists parallel. The transformation of the second attitude was caused by parameter 1 with an emerging individualism. The development of individualism changed parameter 3 as well, since the development towards individualism led to different ideas of life after death. The body disappeared, provided that resurrection became a dogma, and the idea of an immortal soul took over. The idea of an active soul proved the denial of letting the identity slip into biological and social anonymity. While parameter 4 remained unshaken, parameter 2 faced a transformation which still led to the same outcome. The new individualism, the will to enjoy life and one's own identity, could have affected the relation between the dying and the bereaved, and consequently the ceremony of the hora mortis. Death could have become wild and desperate. Instead, individualism had no affect on the defence of society against nature because new ceremonies embedded the dead. Several new ceremonies like paying one's last respects, church services, funeral services, etc. took place between the deathbed and the grave. More important about these new ceremonies is the fact that the face of the deceased was covered. First, the shroud covered the face. Later, the coffin and catafalque covered the whole body. Not later than the 14th century did theatrical monuments cover the mortal remains. Surprisingly, this phenomenon took place while macabre art started depicting the decomposition of the dead. While the macabre art disappeared shortly afterwards, the veiling of the dead body became permanent. The face of the dead provoked fear, and veiling overcame this fear. According to Ariès, veiling is the most important element in this attitude: Death of the self. The veiling secured the traditional arrangement with death against individualism.

artes moriendi, macabre topics like the *Transi* a decomposing corpse, emerge. Defined as "macabre" they are the realistic depictions of the human body as it progressively decays. According to Michael Sappol this development is accompanied by the emergence of various anatomical illustrations (Phase 1, 1550–1700, Playing with death–Fun with science).

"Early modern representations of the anatomical body took death head-on: the dead mocked the living; the living mocked the dead. The cadaver was an effigy of social types: the courtier, the flirt, the harlequin, the fecund woman, the heathen warrior. At the same time, the cadaver was Death, with a capital D. It served as a reminder of our mortality, our fallibility, our folly–the fragility of human life and civilization. Anatomy cited or parodied or augmented long-established iconic traditions and subjects–natural wonders, the classical ideal, memento mori, heraldy, dance macabre, Christian and classical martyrology–and newer genres such as still life, which featured human mortality as one of its tropes" (Sappol, 2003, p. 12).

In the early modern era of the 16th and 17th centuries, the abstract *Vanitas* depictions emerge in art Ordinary items such as the clock, the hourglass or the skull come to represent death. Clean articulated skeletons replace the depiction of the *Transi*. However, both the corpse and the macabre iconography return later in modern age during the enlightenment of the 17th and 18th century ("Remote and Imminent Death")[20]. In addition, depictions of public autopsies and anatomy paintings increase again. (Phase 2, 1680–1800, Getting real–The new aesthetics of scientific illustrations).

"Between 1680 and 1800, the convictions, meanings, audience, and uses of anatomical representation shifted. Anatomist began to develop new criteria for what constituted acceptable scientific illustration. Play and the pursuit of truth became incompatible. The cadaver was no longer made to pose and dance. The artist was no longer asked or permitted to embellish the background, to provide fantasy architecture and landscapes for the anatomical figures to frolic in. The reader was no longer asked to mediate on human mortality. The high spirits and intoxicated

---

20 The "Remote and Imminent Death" (16th–18th century) is characterised by profound transformations which only existed in the world of the imagery, while the characteristics of the "death of the self" carried on until the 18th century. The profound transformations became visible in the new depiction of death, which consisted of less familiar and tamed, but wild and frightening elements. In modern age death stressed all alienating/disconcerting and, at the same time, fascinating digressions. After centuries parameter 2 finally started to change–the defence against nature defeated heavy shocks. This period of degeneration occurred simultaneously with scientific rationality, inventions and their technical applications. Oddly enough, this is also the time when death provoked greater anxiety, like for instance the anxiety of being buried alive.

humour of anatomical representation were no longer wanted" (Sappol, 2003, p. 25).

Realistic depictions of corpses as private reminders of individuals emerge while the combined representation of violence and the erotic in connection with death disappears. Physicians become the most trusted medium of belief, and private and public autopsies become popular. During the modern age of the 19th and 20th century, the sweet death, the death of the other, indicates a shift of meaning from the individual to the beloved other. Ariès describes this period as a hypertrophy of mourning: a cult of remembrance. Paintings, sculptures and photographs were made of the deceased in the "Sleeping Beauty" mode, or as Jay Ruby calls it the "asleep not yet dead" mode. (The "Death of the Other")[21] In the 20th and 21st centuries, depictions of the corpse indicate again a return of the visibility of the dead body. In "Death Denied"[22] Ariès unfortunately only lightly

21 The "Death of the Other" (19th–20th century) With the new industrial and agricultural techniques and the new scientific thinking, Romantic movement emerged leading to various reactions. All four parameters are in transformation. When parameter 1 indicated the awareness of the individual about its own death, it now indicates the awareness of the death of the other. The idea of romanticism and the development of privacy and the nuclear family caused a revolution of emotions. The separation from a significant other initiated a dramatic crisis. The anxieties about one's own death emerging in the imagination of the 17th and 18th century now were projected on the significant other. The death of the other, i.e. the pain about the separation from the loved one, generated greater emotional mourning, while the ceremonies became less ritual. Death became somewhat beautiful and emotional. Parameter 4 obviously started changing: Death was no longer associated with evil only. Parameter 3 also started changing since the belief in life after death declined. In the 19th century, the beyond turns into paradise, a place of reunion for the separated ones.

22 The "Death Denied" (20th century): This model continues the basic tendency and structure of the previous one. The ideal of privacy became stricter in its demands, and the exchange between the dying and the bereaved more intimate. Soon after, the ugliness of the disease of the person dying and their hospitalisation poisoned intimacy. Death became "dirty" and was subsequently "medicalised". The "apparent death" attracted fascination for and disgust at death, sublimated by the extreme unction. However, without fascination, people only felt disgust at illness and caretaking. Now, medicine took over the defence against death and locked death into scientific laboratories and hospitals, where there was no room left for emotions. Medical progress was supposed to humanise death and defend society against wild nature. A society of individuals with new compulsions, rules and new taboos regarding death replaced community and solidarity. Shame and denial characterise these new taboos. Furthermore, the outsourcing of death has not eliminated anxiety about death. On the contrary, under the mask of medical progress the old imagination of the wildness of death returned. The unconscious

touches upon film representation and comments even less on photography or art installations. Instead he discusses movement to banish death to medical institutions. He also refers to new funeral rites in America and indicates new attitudes towards death curiously even before publishing his classifications. (Ariès, 1974)[23] It should be mentioned that during these periods certain modes of representation did not always disappear, but coexisted next to the new ones. The periods only mark the beginning of new modes of representation, which can last for decades or slowly vanish again. Of course, such a major work and clear-cut model attracts major criticism. The most serious criticism came from Roy Porter (1999) in "Classics revisited: The hour of Philippe Ariès".[24]

---

person dying in the hospital bed, attached to tubes and wires, provokes more anxieties than the "transi" or the skeleton from the macabre depictions in previous centuries.

23 Ariès refers to the new funeral rites in the USA in two articles in 1974 (American Quarterly, p. 558; The Hastings Center Studies p.15)

24 Porter's first question of many was whether Ariès actually focused on Europe or rather on European Catholicism. He also states that Ariès does not provide as many statistics on death as other French historians do, for instance Pierre Chaunu. He criticises Ariès empiric material as impressionistic and idiosyncratic. Porter also refers to other scientists, when he points out the failures of the third phase, which was particularly criticised by Lawrence Stone: Ariès failed to address the dynamics behind the sequences of phases, because he defined consciousness as autonomous, and not as a mere expression of socioeconomic forces. Referring to other scientists again, Porter also points out how profoundly Ariès' views reflect his religious and political ideas. He then focuses on the reading of the early modern age (the enlightenment), which, in his opinion, caused severe conceptual problems. He claims that the contents of "Western attitudes towards death" (1974) differs from "The hour of our death" as the "remote and imminent death" was inserted in the later version. Porter questions this insertion and doubts Ariès' conclusion about the disposition of the royal and the rich regarding a dazzling departure. Ariès' claim that the fascination for dissection in the 18th century was new was also criticised by Porter. Of course, the "culture of anatomy" developed earlier, but then I could not find a proof that Ariès did overlook the developments two centuries earlier. According to Porter, section 3 also fails to give a fair account of the new attempts to spiritualise and philosophise the afterlife, but unfortunately, he does not elaborate on this point. In general, Porter is right when pointing out the lack of medical aspects. In particular, the developments of anatomy, the changing understanding of the body and the shifts in the medical-scientific attitudes toward the dying are too important. Porter summarises "By largely excluding the medical dimension from his gaze, Ariès gives us but a partial story, and a skewed one at that. He fails to engage with the (medical) reasons why the abandonment of the religious rituals had powerful attractions. Closer integration of the medical aspects of death with its religious, cultural and social dimensions remains an urgent desideratum" (Porter, 1999 p. 90).

In summary, the history of death depiction, according to Ariès' documentation of certain periods, seems to develop cyclic representations. It seems as if the open confrontations with graphic and realistic depictions of the corpse are always only temporarily acceptable. For instance, vivid depictions of death existed in the Ancient World, but were challenged by less vivid depictions in the early Middle Ages. In the high Middle Ages, however, different graphic depictions of corpses on sarcophagi appeared once again. In the late Middle Ages, macabre iconography took over the representation of death. The early modern age, however, is characterised by displacing the realistic corpse representation by abstract *Vanitas* depictions. In the middle of the modern age, the corpse returns with macabre iconography, and even public autopsies are well attended. This trend is again replaced by a sentimental post-mortem photography fashion in the late modern age, which was widespread in both Europe and America. [25]

Recently, the realistic corpse representation in the art of death photography has risen once again through Jeffrey Silverthorne's Morgue work (1972–74), Rudolf Schäfer's *Visages de morts* (1983), Andres Serrano's *The morgue series* (1992)[26], and permanent art installations like those created by Teresa Margolles, or Body Worlds in which plastinated corpses are exhibited. The field of art is by far not the only field where an increasing presence of death representations can be observed. The moving image of the film industry has taken over the lead with a tremendous amount of representations of the dead across all genres, but first and foremost amongst horror, crime and action. We seem to be surrounded by death, yet fail to take an interest in the sudden increase of death representations in daily forensic TV shows. These TV shows seem to indicate the return of the realistic corpse. Yet, the representations can still be trumped by the latest interactive media phenomena. Take the example of the online video platform YouTube on which the execution of Saddam Hussein, the killing of the Iranian Neda or simply entire autopsies were temporarily available. The flood of representations is overwhelming and can no longer be described with a taboo of death. Clearly death is newly visible through the television in a multitude of ways. I want to start with the most visible, accessible and common source of representations of death, the massive

---

25 Great interest is taken in the analysis of these photographs as literature, referring to Stanley Burns (1990, 2002), Jay Ruby (1999), George Batchen (2004) and lately Katharina Sykora (2009), shows.

26 Cf. also Guthmann, 2002

presence of TV shows. This history of the bodily representations of death in the 20th and 21st centuries is cyclical by visual mode; the body appears and disappears. It is at once visible and then obscured.

1.3. The representation of corpses in TV shows from 1950 to 2000

A natural starting place for corpse representations in American TV begins with crime shows. These programs have different themes focusing on detectives, cops or lawyers. Of all the TV shows from the 1950s to 2000

Fig. 1.1.: Quincy, M.E. looking at the corpse

Source: Episode 29

there was only one that revolved around corpses and starred a coroner. The show, *Quincy M.E.*, focused on the crime fighting efforts of the eponymous protagonist, a coroner. It was the only TV show before the turn of the 21st century in which the corpse appeared in every episode as an object to be examined. For this reason alone, the show bears scrutiny. In the following, I will introduce the TV show and elaborate on the early corpse representations as a contrast to the new TV shows representations.

The show *Quincy, M.E.* (Medical Examiner) was created by Glen A. Larson and Lou Shaw and produced in the U.S. from 1976 to 1983. The 148 episodes had a length of approximately 45 minutes, and the first one was aired on October 3, 1976. Jack Klugman played the coroner Dr. R. Quincy who investigated suspicious deaths with his colleagues. The show was nominated several times an Emmy.[27] The plot is relatively straight forward. Usually, a suspicious death occurs and the dead person is then examined by Quincy. He discovers inconsistencies in evidence either at the scene of the crime or during the course of the pathological examination. He then attempts to solve the case. Importantly the corpse is only visibly recognizable at the scene, but hardly ever during pathological examination.

Fig. 1.2.: Quincy examines a hand

Source: Episode 30

An examination of *Quincy*,[28] reveals that 268 corpses were recorded and categorised. These corpses, mostly crime victims, are usually seen for the first time at the crime scene. 152 of the corpses were also shown in the pathology lab. The age range of the corpses covered infants, children, teens, adults, and the elderly. However, there is a clear dominance of corpses between the ages of 30 and 50, numbering 41. The gender proportion also displayed a clear pattern. Male corpses were shown 74 times and female corpses only 37 times. Racially the corpses are predominantly Caucasian (97) with 9 African-Americans, 2 Hispanic/Latinos and 2 Asians. Altogether, the white, male adult is most frequently represented in *Quincy*'s pathology. The determination of age, race, and gender was possible through either the visibility at the crime scene and several times in pathology or could be deduced from the pathologist's speech on screen.

---

27 http://www.imdb.com/title/tt0074042/, access 03.01.2010

28 The Quincy, M.E. film analysis was assisted by Patrick Schubert, student assistant in the VW Research Project "Death and Dead Bodies" at the Technical University of Berlin.

How is a dead person represented?

Fig. 1.3.: Quincy and Sam examine a dead body

Source: Episode 57

In the course of the show's eight seasons, this lack of presence of the corpse in the pathology room changes slightly. Indeed the laboratory changes itself as time progresses. After episode 10, pathology scenes become regular constituent components of the episodes. The dead continue to be represented in quite the same fashion, however, covered in their entirety or with only small portions of their extremities visible.

Fig. 1.4.: Quincy and Sam just finished an autopsy

Source: Episode 21

The most remarkable views were of faces, autopsy procedures or the pathology itself. At first, the face of the dead body is never shown, but in later episodes parts like the forehead or nose can be seen. At the end of the series they began to show the faces of the bodies. This happened in total, only four times. Prior to this however, parts of the face appear when the camera, usually shooting Quincy during the examination from a low angle, is placed next to the table with the corpse. From this angle, the forehead and the nose of the corpse can still be seen at the lower part of the image. In the first two seasons, only two rather explicit and longer autopsy scenes were aired in which Quincy performs some procedures. When Quincy performs autopsy, however, usually no body can be seen. Quincy and his assistant Sam are acting on or with something that is off-screen. One of these scenes (episode 11) is about a demonstration of forensic work for police officers. One shot shows how Quincy acts as if he performs a "Y incision".

Fig. 1.5.: Quincy and Sam examine a hand in a blue-lit pathology

Source: Episode 67

The other shot depicts him holding a trepan, presumably to open the skull of the victim. This action lasts only a few seconds and no assistant is present. You cannot see the corpse because of a green cover and later, when Quincy starts to perform this procedure, the camera angle captures him only, excluding the corpse. In these scenes the cops are either leaving the pathology room or alternatively, collapse in front of the Quincy and the body he is examining. The shot of the collapsing police officer becomes part of the opening for the series, presumably because of its transgressive and humorous nature. An exception to the covering of the body is in episode 15 where the corpse is shown without a sheet but a huge surgery lamp obscures most of the body. After the first few episodes, the pathology room slowly starts changing its design. From various colours like yellow, whitish-grey and blue, the pathology turns into a solely blue operation suite by the end of the season. Silver tables and scientific tools complete the medicalised image.

In season 3, corpses with different ethnic backgrounds such as Asian or African-American become present in the pathology room. Simultaneously the camera angle which previously had been the low angle shifts and becomes a worm's eye view. Now, the back of the head of a corpse becomes visible every so often. In episode 29, a close-up of a wound on a victim's thigh is also shown. With the beginning of episode 60, discrete body parts like feet, arms and hands, as well as the head, can be seen more frequently while the rest of the body is covered. Season 4 and 5 represent, apart from an increasing number of corpses in the scenes, unique shots: Two times the faces of dead boys are shown in pathology.

In season 5, it finally becomes typical of the program to quickly display the face of the deceased. Later the entire torso of a male corpse can be seen on the table, although a picture, held up by Quincy "covers" most of it. As the episodes progress the corpse representations begin to resemble those of later shows like *CSI: Las Vegas*, though the visual practice of obscuring the deceased body remains predominant. The equipment of the pathology room dominates the scene with its diffuse blue light, fluorescent tools behind glass cupboards, and chilled feeling. The typical media codes of TV shows of the 21st century seem to have their forerunner in *Quincy*. The huge difference between *Quincy* and what followed *remains* the nonrepresentation of corpses. While more current shows continue to depict the dead in pathology, *Quincy*, a show 20 years older, mostly omits the corpses' representation. The dominant autopsy procedure was filmed without the corpse.

More current TV shows are based on familiar themes and pictures. However, they have sensational new forensic images.

1.4. New representations of corpses in TV shows from 2000 to 2010

Nowadays the most usual place an individual will encounter the body of a deceased person is through a funeral, an exhibition like "Body Worlds", in art or on television. In the latter arena and nowhere else, experts make specific efforts to present a dead body with a very specific agenda. Nevertheless, the same rules apply for the representation of the media corpse as for the representation of the corpse, at the funeral. The representation of the corpse in front of the surviving relatives at the funeral parlour is characterised by the experience of the ambivalent situation facing the present funeral attendees and their sense of the "absence" of the deceased, who is nonetheless present bodily. The representation of the corpse is characterised by efforts to cover and embellish the dead to present the body as not dead, because the corpse is associated with pollution. Undertakers try to cover the corpse's inability to control the bodily boundaries in front of the living. Through cosmetics and embalming they cover the ugly details of death and turn the corpse into a representation of the beautified former self. The improved appearance or and obscuring of the ugly details of death is the main characteristic of representation of dead bodies in the funeral business.

Fig. 1.6.: CSI-Examination of a dead body in a blue-lit pathology

Source: Episode 905

Besides the obvious difference between the dead being a media product consumed by an audience and a deceased relative in a funeral parlour being represented as a figure of life and memory, both attempt to make the dead palatable to the living. Yet more recent television crime dramas do not always make attempts at beautification of corpses. Occasionally the change to the body is manufactured to specifically index disgust and the abhorrent nature of death. The shows with recurrent representations of corpses that followed *Quincy* include *Six Feet Under, Crime Scene Investigation (CSI Las Vegas and Spin offs: Miami*[29], *New York*[30]), *Navy CIS, Tru Calling, Dexter,*

---

29 http://www.imdb.com/find?s=all&q=CSI+Miami, October 10th, 2009
30 http://www.imdb.com/title/tt0395843/, October 10th, 2009

Bones, Castle, Family Plots, North Mission Road, Crossing Jordan, as well as *Pushing Daisies, Heroes* and *Dead Like Me.* Only the last three shows depict dead people without showing typical autopsy or embalming procedures. However, the corpses do appear in similar settings to those mentioned above. Other less prominent TV shows representing the dead are *Dr. G–Medical Examiner*[31] and *Autopsy–Medical Detectives* [32]. Since these TV shows were difficult to obtain and were not consumed on the level of those previously mentioned, I excluded them from the examination. By 1990 certain programs demonstrate how TV crime narratives were changing. TV shows like *Law & Order*[33] (and various spin-offs: *Law & Order: Special Victims Unit, Law & Order: Criminal Intent, Law & Order: Trial by Jury*) added medical examiners and thus corpse centred plot aspects. *Law & Order* not only introduced the medical examination as part of a TV show plot, it also added a medical examiner figure, Dr. Elizabeth Rogers, to the set of characters. Since her introduction in 1992, she has become a recurring character. Yet she is not a regular cast member. These shows are excluded from examination in this thesis because the representation of the dead in pathology is not as routine as it is in the other TV shows.[34] In all shows analysed from 2000 to 2009, the corpse is visible and present, not only at the scene wherein death occurred but also in the specialised room, particular to the show, where the body was treated. For some this was a pathology lab, for others an embalming room. A typical corpse is represented as an attractive actor or actress who appears to be young, thin or athletic and unsoiled with an unstained skin and hair.

---

31 http://www.imdb.com/title/tt0364314/, July 5th, 2008, Dr. G: Medical Examiner is a show about Dr. Garavaglia and her investigative work at the District Nine Medical Examiner's Office in Florida. In every episode, Dr. G who also explains to the audience the matter of death will examine three authentic cases. The show runs on Discovery Health Channel.

32 http://www.imdb.com/title/tt0430897/, July 5th, 2008, Autopsy/Confessions of a Medical Examiner is a collection of documentary series that airs on the cable television network HBO and is about real crime cases like homicides in the USA. The show is a sub-series of America Undercover documentaries, which presents police investigating crime cases and original footage material from the police. The case is presented by conducting interviews with different eyewitnesses, police officers, and coroners.

33 http://www.imdb.com/title/tt0098844/, Access: 15th September, 2008

34 The newer TV show The Forgotten (2009) deals only in a few episodes with dead bodies in pathology, but not regularly, which is why the TV show is also excluded from examination.

Only the Y incision or the deadly wound might indicate a representation of death and not simply a sleeping person. This typical corpse representation is sometimes challenged by representing skeletons and bloated, partial, decomposing or burned corpses. However, the representation of those rather horrifying corpses, usually without identifiable facial features, still excludes signs of old age. In summary, the media represent a corpse either as particularly attractive or extremely ugly, but avoid any pictorial association between age and death. The media represent predominantly young and middle-aged deceased, reflecting the age of their audience instead of contemporary mortality rates.

The new TV shows introduce new rooms and actions. These actions are, first and foremost, the autopsy procedures like incisions and removal of organs. But included in this genre are touches or reanimating contacts made by certain special characters. The new rooms include those centred around pathology, the morgue, embalming and murder. Prior to 2000 we saw the dead person at a crime scene, but never in the pathology department. Pathology becomes an important part of the crime show narrative after the 21st century. This is something new in the representation of death. A new field of expertise is opened up. The media's pathology room serves as a transition place. The dead body, which cannot yet be put to rest, has to pass another exam and stage of exploration before moving to its final location beyond the pathology lab. From an ethnological point of view this special room serves as a stage in the body's transition between states. As Douglas explains referring to Arnold van Gennep's explanation of ritual behaviour:

"He saw society as a house with rooms and corridors in which passage from one to another is dangerous. Danger lies in transitional states, simply because transition is neither one state nor the next, it is undefinable. The person who must pass from one to another is himself in danger and emanates danger to others. The danger is controlled by ritual which precisely separates him from his old status, segregates him for a time and then publicly declares his entry to his new status. Not only is transition itself dangerous, but also the rituals of segregation are the most dangerous phase of the rites" (Douglas, 2002, p. 96).

According to van Gennep (1999, p. 27), everyone who moves from one sphere to another, stays in a special spatiotemporal situation which van Gennep calls *liminaire*. Victor Turner, another ethnologist, takes up on these *rites de marge*, the liminal phase of transition which connects the pre-liminal phase of separation and the post-liminal phase of reincorporation.

He elaborates that in uncertain times in the life stage of an individual or community, like that of transition and transformation, rituals are used to generate and restore certainty.

"Liminal entities are neither here nor there; they are betwixt and between the positions assigned and arrayed by law, custom, convention, and ceremonial. As such, their ambiguous and indeterminate attributes are expressed by a rich variety of symbols in the many societies that ritualize social and cultural transitions" (Turner, 1995, p. 95).

According to Turner, "rites de passage" adjust the status of individuals during transformation. In the separation phase, the individual leaves their pre-transformation state and then passes through the liminal phase and, with the help of a ritual, the individual reincorporates into their society in their newly transformed state with a new identity. This new identity is reinforced by outstanding rituals, which create a counterworld. In this counterworld the person does not possess any social characteristics. In the course of the reincorporation the person gains the new status. Thus through these television shows the body is presented in various states. It's potency as an object in transition from individual to dead body and evidence requires various treatments. The corpse in the pathology room and in the morgue serves as evidence used to solve a crime, the corpse in the embalming room serves to offer a projection screen for the emotions of the survivors, and the soon-to-be-dead in the killing room serves the vigilantism of those protagonists who kill people within the plot structure of their program. Bodies within these bounds have a task to fulfil before they are released to be buried. Their presence in these special rooms is marked most noticeably by medical sterility. When the victim's body is found messy, in a dirty environment and in an awkward position, the corpse is cleaned and covered in the almost antiseptic transition room. According to Mary Douglas (2002), dirt is dangerous. Nothing could be more dangerous, in this sense, than a dead body encrusted with dirt. The dual nature of this pollution increases the level of danger. The polluted body at the crime scene has an unclear identity and an ambiguous status. This uncomfortable status is connected with insecurity since it might reveal the actual contingency of everyday life. The search for purity is the attempt to stabilise structures and concepts.

"It seems that if a person has no place in the social system and is therefore a marginal being, all precautions against danger must come from others. He cannot help his abnormal situation" (Douglas, 2002, p. 98).

The transition rooms and their sterility stand for these structures, solutions, and stability. In these special rooms other people smooth the transition and take care of the body as it is propelled into its next phase. In this special transition phase, the counterworld, the dead appears with different characteristics. Like their surroundings the dead are, most of the time, clean and embellished, covered and without movement, stiff and torpid. Even flesh wounds, organs or Y incisions cannot harm the aesthetic dead. This comprises a trend which is becoming manifest in *Quincy*. However, as time progresses, the limits of visibility change and more of the corpse is shown, while other things are covered. The following chapters will elaborate on this.

1.5. New sophisticated death representations

I argue that the media started a process of visualisation by creating a sophisticated system of death representation while the death of the other, using Ariès' terms to describe the real death of a person, remains hidden. In *Quincy* the dead were hardly ever shown in pathology, while today an actor is deployed to re-enact the dead. This new system generated a set of codes on which the current media representation of the corpse is based. This system produces more visible corpses and simultaneously, hides the death of the other. The death of the other remains invisible while more copies of the same representation mode are produced for not only one TV show but also genre-crossing TV shows. In the following analysis, I will present a description of where this "sophisticated representation system" originates from.

Macho (1987) describes the dead and their emphatic resistance against any social obligations. The dead person cannot look at, speak about, move towards or respond to any trial of interaction, but instead withdraws from any social commitments. The withdrawal from social commitments also includes the control of one's own body. The dead body gives off an unpleasant smell and bodily liquids leak out. This leads to a major issue of how to deal with human remains. According to Macho, the body of the dead can be characterised as a thing, but the dead person cannot be considered as a thing. The simultaneousness of humanity and inhumanity is the problem, which Macho calls paradox of the dead. The peculiar characteristic of the dead is the presence and absence of a human being: the simultaneousness of an identity and its absence. Therefore, an ambivalent atmosphere determines the presence of a dead person, which causes familiarity and unease at the same time. (Macho, 1987, p. 219) Furthermore, Hallam, Howarth, and Hockey describe in "Beyond the body" (1999) the frailty and vulnerability of a corpse as follows:

"As we shall see, witnessing or experiencing the body in decline through death or decay forms a potent reminder of frailty, vulnerability and mortality. The passage of time and the inevitability of physical transformation become powerfully evident. They provoke anxieties about the integrity of the body as it faces destruction. When emphasis is placed upon control and the regulation of the body as a prerequisite for the maintenance of self-identity, the dying body and the dead body acquire terrifying qualities. The bodies render visible the processes which are denied in the pursuit of an ideal which rest upon the control of bodily boundaries [...]" (Hallam, Howarth & Hockey, 1999, p. 21).

The ambivalent experience, facing the presence and absence of a person in a dead body, is accompanied by the reminder of frailty, vulnerability and mortality. Nowadays the dead body, in particular the soon-to-be-embalmed dead at a funeral parlour, is still a screen upon which the reflection of former social preoccupations of life are projected. The authors argue:

"[...]that in modern Western societies, preoccupied as we are with the living body and its property of vitality, there continues to be tremendous difficulty and fear entailed in confronting the dead body as material entity which abrogates the powerful cultural drive for the body beautiful, healthy and youthful"(Hallam, Howarth & Hockey, 1999, p. 140).

As the authors conclude from their ethnographic field trips to funeral parlours they continue to state that the dead person is perceived as physically polluting by survivors:

"As such, the dead body, once a symbol of natural order, now has a destabilizing effect on social order. Since the nineteenth century, and the recognition of the link between disease and hygiene, the corpse has increasingly come to be perceived as polluting. The modern concern with public health, coupled with the science of pathology, has led to the establishment of a link between decomposing bodies and disease" (Howarth, 2001, p. 120).

That is why the undertaker aims to shield clients from contamination and tries to reconstruct the dead. The reconstruction entails the maintenance of the visual outlook of the former living person and of the bodily boundaries.[35]

"As the material reality of death, the body is also symbolically threatening as it represents discontinuity, disorder and mortality. At an individual level it signals loss of identity. When living bodies fail, there are attempts, either by the individual, professionals or carers, to revitalise their physical functioning and to restore order and stability to dishevelled or disorderly flesh" (Hallam, Howarth & Hockey, 1999, p. 140).

Similar to these authors Mary Bradbury, who focused on the survivors' response to the dead as an object, pointed out that:

"The symbolic value of the decomposing corpse holds the key to understanding why we behave as we do when someone dies [...] The corpse, human and yet non-human, has an ambiguity made even more threatening by its decay. The unfamiliar corpse is an object of both ritual and secular power. Classifying the cause of death, manipulating the appearance of the corpse, arresting its decay by embalming it and then destroying it altogether in the cremator are all attempts to gain human control over a natural event. The corpse's capacity to be used as a symbol system allows it to be harnessed to express many things, acting as a metaphor in this modern rational-scientific society, articulating traditional cultural norms, such as patriarchy, as well as playing out age-old beliefs regarding death and rebirth into the world of the ancestors" (Bradbury, 1999, p. 138).

Hallam, Howarth and Hockey refer to Gittings (1984) stating the same about individualism and anxiety of death, which Ariès also already noted in 1981: Anxiety about death is caused by individualism, so as to avoid the horrifying idea of physical decomposition the dead must be hidden in coffins. The disposal of death had already started in the early modern age. They also note:

"[...] that the elaboration of the cultural devices used to conceal the body in death, actually worked to draw the eye towards it. [...] a proliferation of imagery centring on the dying body which effectively maintains its social presence" (Hallam, Howarth & Hockey, 1999, p. 22).

---

35 "The perception of the corpse as a threat to public health has reinforced a view of the need to acquire the services of an expert, a professional skilled in negating the corpse's power to contaminate. Morticians have thus been employed to render the corpse harmless to the living. Indeed, the handling of the dead body is usually subject to public health regulations and these rules guide death-workers in decisions pertaining to the appropriate location and sanitization of the corpse. As a signifier of pollution and a symbol of death, bereaved families in contemporary Western societies normally concede custody of the body to the funeral director" (Howarth, 2001, p. 120).

Like Baudrillard, Ariès or Belting, the authors point out that the dying and dead body has been removed from the public and replaced with "sophisticated systems of representation". (Hallam, Howarth & Hockey, 1999, p. 23) They quote Ruby by saying that contemporary media exchanges the real death with fictionalised pictures, which only emphasises people's distance from death.

"Although we may talk of denial or a disappearance of death, a focus on the role of visual representations reveals more complex processes at work. Moreover, these are processes which operate in a variety of ways and reflect a diversity of social, moral and political agendas" (Hallam, Howarth & Hockey, 1999, p. 23).

Just like Belting or Macho beforehand, the authors observe that death can only be approximated and challenges the survivor with the interplay of presence and absence. However, the authors also elaborate on the dead body and effects on the spectator during the process of representation. Though the body is made visible, the reality of the embodied death is still masked and fixed in the form of an image.

"Despite the apparent 'otherness' of the body in death, and the extent to which representations have become 'fictionalised', they retain a potency which provides them with significance in the cultural formation of self and social identity" (Hallam, Howarth & Hockey, 1999, p. 24).

Referring to Jay Ruby (1996), they stress the role of visual cultures when it comes to ideas about the dead and self-concepts, because the visibility has changed historically and the perspective is also influenced by different cultures.

"Relationships between spectator and image are complex, given that a multiplicity of interpretations might be derived from a single image and that their meanings are likely to shift over time. In addition, representations are produced, used and circulated in a variety of ways" (Hallam, Howarth & Hockey, 1999, p. 25).

Referring to Mellor and Shilling (1997, p. 5), the authors point out that the discursive or textual analysis can bring out the construction patterns of a body depiction which shows how the body is seen and portrayed. In Christian societies, the need for the appropriate disposal of the corpse has traditionally been associated with the resurrection of the body. The dissection of the corpse at the hands of anatomists and surgeons during the nineteenth century was considered to be the most horrific fate limited, officially, to the cadavers of executed criminals. In practice, following the

Anatomy Act of 1832, this fate was extended to the destitute.[36] Hallam
agrees with Bronfen (1992) and Ariès (1977) when describing the ambivalence of the fascinating and repulsive image of the dead:

"[...] such images variously associate the body with notions about the social, the
sacred, the political and the erotic, depending upon their positioning within wider
image repertoires and historical contexts" (Hallam, 1991, p. 26).

The ambivalence is caused by the European cultural politics of the body,
they mask and conceal something that is too frightening to be openly discussed, and, at the same time, too fascinating and curiosity-arousing to be
repressed successfully. (Hallam, 1991, p. 28) This image of the body was:

"[...] produced in the context of religious devotion and ritual. The ritual disposal
of the corpse removed it from the direct gaze and it was replaced by a range of
representation which effectively preserved the social presence of the dead"
(Hallam, 1991, p. 33).[37]

Howarth states that an increasing separation of the dead from the living
took place late in the nineteenth century and that by the early twentieth
century corpses were less visible than before.

"In this way the corpse has come to be seen not simply as a by-product of death
but as a source of disease and a symbol of mortality. In modern societies, therefore, the dead body is seen as highly polluting: both physically and symbolically.
Physical pollution stems from the fear of contamination by disease and decay;
symbolic pollution from the far of mortality and bodily decay, of which the corpse
is a signifier. This view of the dead body as polluting is common to many societies" (Howarth, 2001, p. 120).

---

36 According to Howarth, this belief has been undermined since Reformation, the loss of
Purgatory, and with increasing secularisation. Evidence of this lies in the now common
practice of people leaving their bodies to medical science and the willingness to be an
organ donor after death. (Howarth, 2001, p. 119)

37 "For example, it was not until relatively late in the nineteenth century that one source of
cholera was located in the drinking water drawn from London's graveyards. Throughout
this period, and in keeping with other strategies for dealing with social problems, the
dead were increasingly separated from the living, so that by the early twentieth century
corpses were often removed to a public mortuary or chapel of rest. In this way the
corpse has come to be seen not simply as a by-product of death but as a source of disease and a symbol of mortality. In modern societies, therefore, the dead body is seen as
highly polluting: both physically and symbolically. Physical pollution stems from the fear
of contamination by disease and decay; symbolic pollution from the far of mortality and
bodily decay, of which the corpse is a signifier. This view of the dead body as polluting
is common to many societies" (Howarth, 2001, p. 120).

Moreover, the representations, as Ariès pointed out, carry certain messages so as to prepare for afterlife or rebirth or the last judgement. The dead body was installed for different moralising, spiritual, political, and scientific discourses. Social hierarchies were presented in these depictions and maintained a close relation between the dead and the survivors, which was formed by these pictorial discourses. (Hallam, Howarth & Hockey, 1999, p. 41)

In this chapter, I have introduced the theoretical background for the following chapters. I presented the connection between the images and death and the pictorial discourse, gave examples of the discourse with a historical survey of depictions of corpses. Afterwards I contrasted this historic pictorial discourse with the first media representation of corpses in TV shows from 1950 until 2000 and then sketched out the actual research subject, the new representations of corpses in TV shows from 2000–2010. I have argued that a new sophisticated system of death representations with certain codes and topoi have emerged since the turn of the 21st Century and revealed the origin of this description and justified the use of these specific terms.

To sum up, in this research I aim to focus on the contemporary part of the historic discourse regarding the pictorial representation of death. The sophisticated representation systems consist of codes which result in specific topoi. By analysing these topoi I aim to prove that the previous decade of television shows utilize a very specific representation system for death.

2 Methodology

My research includes a variety of analytic tools to explore the representation of dead bodies in current TV shows. As previously mentioned, discourse research should not just be reduced to the analysis of text alone, but should be inclusive of pictures, especially in an explicitly pictorial medium. According to Keller (2005), contemporary discourse theory is based on a variety of approaches, which deal with the term discourse. The most famous approach is Michel Foucault's[1], and has become the foundation of "social constructivism" which, according to Keller (2005, p. 96), underlines the constitution and construction of reality in these discourses. Amongst many other theorists, Keller notes that in various respects Foucault's concept of discourse remains unsatisfactory for sociological research, proclaiming that discourse analysis from a sociology of knowledge perspective would accommodate it better. (Keller, 2005, p. 96) Therefore, Keller connects the hermeneutic sociology of knowledge with discourse research in order to establish an independent "wissenssoziologische Diskursanalyse".

He "[…] argues for a grounding of discourse theory and empirical discourse research in the sociology of knowledge, especially in the German-based Hermeneutische Wissenssoziologie, which follows the Berger and Luckmann approach to knowledge"(2007).[2]

Referring to several deficits, he claims that they can be balanced by shifting from a concentration on knowledge and interpretation of individuals in everyday life, towards an analysis of the discursive processes of the genera-

---

1 Michel Foucault used the concept of discourse mainly in his earlier work such as "The Order of Things" (1970) and "The Archaeology of Knowledge" (1972).

2 Keller, R.: Analysing Discourses and Dispositifs. Profiling Discourse Research in the Tradition of Sociology of Knowledge. Forum Qualitative Sozialforschung/Forum: Qualitative Social Research, North America, 8, may. 2007. Available at: http://www.qualitative-research.net/index.php/fqs/article/view/243. Date accessed: 06 Jul. 2010.

tion, circulation and manifestation of the collective stock of knowledge. Keller's approach of discourse analysis in the sociology of knowledge is therefore based on discursive construction. Keller defines discourses as structured and associated practises, which constitute subjects and social knowledge politics. The discourse analysis focuses on the mechanisms of the formation of discourses, as well as the relation between discourse and practice, and the discourse performance of social protagonists. (Keller, 2005, 181f)[3] In my research, I will follow the possible questions, which arise from a sociology of knowledge discourse analysis, which is concerned with the process of discourse development, the location, practises and resources of the production and reproduction of a discourse, the instruments and strategies used, and the generation and distribution of knowledge (interpretation and problem solving). (Keller, 2005, 257f)

I already provided information on the development and location, and I will now focus on a precise and detailed analysis of pictorial representation, in order to reveal the production of representation codes.[4] Thereafter, I will move on to practises and resources of production, to eventually offer suggestions for the generation of knowledge regarding interpretation and problem solving. Other important perspectives like audience, reception and consequences will, in favour of a precise and discerning analysis, not be taken into consideration (i.e. protagonists, responsible for the reproduction and the effects of the reception are not part of my research). Another variant would only affect the fundamental criterion of my research

---

3 "Die Diskursperspektive richtet sich auf die Ebene der gesellschaftlichen Wissensformationen und -politiken, deren Konturen, Genese, Entwicklung, Regulierung und Folgen ('Machtwirkung'). Sie versteht sich als empirisches Forschungsprogramm: Diskurse werden auf der Grundlage entsprechender Datenmaterialen untersucht. Die einzelnen Äußerungen werden nicht als singuläre Phänomene analysiert, sondern im Hinblick auf ihre typische Gestalt als 'Aussage'. […]Die Diskursanalyse interessiert sich für die Formationsmechanismen von Diskursen, die Beziehung zwischen Diskursen und Praktiken sowie die strategisch-taktische Diskurs-Performanz sozialer Akteure." (Keller, 2005, 182).

4 "Foucault fragt danach, welches Grundmuster des Wissen ('Episteme') in spezifischen historischen Epochen den unterschiedlichsten wissenschaftlichen Klassifikations-prozessen zugrunde liegt. Verschiedene Epochen lassen sich durch die Prinzipien beschreiben, nach denen sie quer zu den disziplinären Grenzen von Einzelwis-senschaften die weltlichen Dinge ordnen. Foucault schließt von empirisch beobachtbaren Regelmäßigkeiten in wissenschaftlichen Texten auf eine Regel, einen Code des wissenschaftlichen Deutens. Seine Vorgehensweise gilt ihm als 'Archäologie': Er gräbt die Wissensordnungen vergangener Zeitalter aus, ohne Stellung zu deren Wahrheits- und Sinngehalten zu nehmen" (Keller, 2005, p.129).

because I am pursuing a narrowed analysis of pictorial representations and not of texts. Hence, in contrast to Keller, I will not include terms such as "audience" or "addressee" but "producer" (instead of protagonist). Instead of "messages" (Aussagen), I will use the term "codes" for typical pictorial messages, which can be tied to topoi, and instead of "utterances" (Aeusserung), I will also employ the term "representation" for every visible materialisation of signs. Discourse, therefore, will be the clear definable entirety of representation with common structure, rules, resources and practises. Dispositifs, or practise and fields of practise will be described in Chapter 6, as the material and ideal infrastructure of discourse. Thus my discussion of some restrictions, rules and confinements, which have had an impact on these fields of practice will be analysed later.[5]

The research material consists of the shows *Six Feet Under, CSI Las Vegas, Crossing Jordan, Bones, Castle, NCIS, Dead like me, Pushing Daisies, Heroes, Dexter, Tru Calling, North Mission Road* and *Family Plots*. These thirteen shows and additionally the documentary *Autopsy* were produced in the 21st Century. Again, *Quincy* is utilised because of its status as a forerunner model. The commonality between programs being explored is that the dead figure remains in the centre of the story and remains a constant object of interest. To thoroughly analyse the extent of the material, I will introduce firstly pictorial analysis, secondly film analysis, thirdly expert interviews and fourthly statistical research. It is necessary, however, to briefly examine television's role in represent the dead and shaping social ideas about death.

2.1. Analysis of TV shows

Very few of us have ever been inside a pathology lab, yet, most of us could describe one if asked. Where do we so frequently see the dead in our daily lives other than through media? Funeral homes offer viewings for significant others, hospitals offer services for brain dead patients and their significant others, yet few people will experience these life altering moments, and certainly not with weekly frequency. Additionally these possibilities for encounters with death are inexorably bound to a morass of emotion, pre-

---

5 Further terms listed by Keller such as discourse regime, discourse strategies etc., are generally left out because I am focusing on pictorial representations.

dominantly grief, which is an experience almost uniformly absent during television viewing. For the public, who are broadly curious and interested in death, the most easily accessible visual resource is the television. There, the availability of representations of the dead in mass media are unlimited. Every day during prime time, millions of viewers can visually experience various parts and sights of the corpses presented to them. These representations are shaped partially by censors and censorship negotiations. Television, therefore, represents a subjective perspective on the dead. It also guides viewers into areas of death to which they previously had no access. Thomas Luckmann (1992) argues that the assimilation of media experiences turns into experiences which stand side by side with the real experiences of the lifeworld (Lebenswelt). The perception of reality in movies provides the foundation for everyday communication about death. (Schmidt, 2002) Since the viewer can "follow" the camera into the hospital, pathology lab or funeral home television has become the main source that provides visual knowledge about the dead to individuals. Stephan Schwan (2005) states that the immediate experience of reality leaves the individual unsatisfied. This dissatisfaction generates a need for media-based narrative representations.[6] The special functions of movies such as the simulation of various spatial, temporal and personal experiences cannot always be covered by immediate experiences of reality. Another function is the conscious influence of one's own mental state through film based upon the availability of experiences. Schwan (2005: 463) also adds that the externalisation of social interaction rehearsal and the customisation of the representation to the viewer's mental state are mentioned as other functions, as well as the support and easing of cognitive processing.

2.2. Pictorial Analysis

Due to the specific research material, none of Keller's suggested analytic tools, such as interpretative framework, classification, structure of the phenomena or narrative structure, have proved to be appropriate. My research therefore starts with pictorial analysis in order to provide a comprehensive and detailed review of all the TV shows and different types of

---

6 Schwan even argues that there is a psychological need for media narratives. (Schwan, 2005, p. 461)

representation. The structure of pictorial analysis will be applied to film, generating a film analysis. Since one would expect a comprehensive film analysis, I want to point out the importance of pictorial analysis for this TV show research before I proceed with its structure.

According to Hans Belting (2001), people generated images of themselves long before they started writing. Taking pictures was a privilege of professionals when the camera was invented, while today pictures are taken by everybody from birth to death.[7] Pictures, however, are not produced solely for private consumption. The natural sciences have benefited immensely from this by generating and distributing body images, thus perpetuating the practice of taking photographs to capture or fix reality. Markus Buschhaus (2005) demonstrated that knowledge of the body has always been based on anatomical examination. Belting connects the alternation of body perception with the alternation of picture perceptions. According to him the cultural history of the photograph has always been reflected by the cultural history of the body. The history of the image of humanity has therefore been dynamic and unstable over time.[8] The body remains the same; contemporary art, however, represents the body in a fluid and dynamic fashion. More precisely the medium of pictorial representation of the dead has changed. In the past a diverse set of materials and mediums presented death such as death masks, effigies, sepulchral sculptures, paintings, and more recently, photography and media images.

To examine the more current representations I take screen shots from TV shows and analyse the representation of the dead as stills.[9] Hans

---

7 "Die Menschen haben von sich Bilder gemacht, lange bevor sie damit begannen, über sich zu schreiben. Das war bis zur Erfindung des Kodak-Systems vor über hundert Jahren ein Privileg der professionellen Bildermacher, doch heute photographieren und filmen wir uns gegenseitig von der Wiege bis zur Bahre. Wo immer Menschen im Bilde erscheinen, werden Körper dargestellt" (Belting, 2001, p. 87).

8 "Der Wechsel der Bilderfahrung drückt auch einen Wechsel der Körpererfahrung aus, weshalb sich die Kulturgeschichte des Bildes in einer analogen Kulturgeschichte des Körpers spiegelt [...] Die Bildgeschichte, die uns die Menschheit in den erhaltenen Bildzeugnissen hinterlassen hat, bietet eine einzige Beispielsammlung für die historische Dynamik des Menschenbilds, die dessen Instabilität beweist. Körper erscheinen in solchen Bildern, weil sie eine aktuelle Idee des Menschen verkörpern" (Belting, 2001, p. 94).

9 In the case of the moving image and enactment of the dead by a living individual the dissolution of the figurative dead in the picture actually leads to a double paradox. The living represent themselves as dead. Since they probably lack any experience with the real dead they have recourse only to the existing stock of visual knowledge: another representation of a dead body on television performed by an animate actor.

Belting (1996) quotes Maurice Blanchot (1951), asking what we learn about death and pictures when we look at them together. He answers, referring again to Blanchot that in both cases we look at something that is absent. The picture presents something that can only, due to its absence, be presented in a picture. The dead body is already a picture, which only resemble the former self (Belting, 1996, p. 94).[10] The difference between a film image and a photographic image arises out of the motion of the former.[11] According to Knut Hickethier, the photographic image is the originator of the film image and at the same time stands between the visual arts and the moving image. The photographic image shows the stillness of illustration, the fixation of the moment (See Hickethier, 2001, p. 44). Representations of the dead, whether in a picture or in a movie, have certain characteristics in common. Conventional forms of representation provide the possibility to distinguish between representations of the living, the sleeping, or even the comatose body and the dead body. Dead bodies are not moving, not responding and do not interact. The passivity as a stereotypical pattern makes it therefore possible to analyse the dead not as a person, but as an object.

Media representations of the dead on film can be captured with screen shots and turned into photographic images. Thus the relationship between photos and film is interconnected. The selection of possible shots of dead bodies were reduced to those shots that represent the dead when they are most visible and in context-rich environments. By this I mean those scenes that take place significant spaces mentioned previously: the pathology room, the embalming room, the morgue, or the room in which killing is performed. The screen shot material consists of approximately 5000 images of dead representations taken from the selected TV shows.

Stefan Mueller-Doohm is one of the first sociologists who took an interest in the preparation of tools for sociological interpretation. His aspiration to systemise methodological tools for pictorial hermeneutics was begun by questioning how cultural sociology could possibly understand the world of images (Mueller-Doohm, 1997, p. 83). In his first paper about

---

10 "Wir bekommen paradoxerweise in beiden Fällen etwas zu sehen, das dennoch gar nicht da ist. Das Bild findet seinen wahren Sinn darin, etwas abzubilden, was abwesend ist und also allein im Bild sein kann. Es bringt zur Erscheinung, was nicht im Bild ist, sondern im Bild nur erscheinen kann. Das Bild eines Toten ist also unter diesen Umständen keine Anomalie, sondern geradezu der Ursinn dessen, was ein Bild ohnehin ist" (Belting, 1996, p. 94).

11 Cf. Keppler, 2006

visual understanding (1993) he criticises the lack of cultural sociological research on the fact that the presentation of reality takes place more frequently through the medium of pictures. According to him, cultural sociology misses the modern transformation from a textually based society into a pictorial society. This implies not only the increasing quantity of visualisation, but also the domination of subjective perception through pictures (Mueller-Doohm, 1993, p. 439). In 1994, W.J.T. Mitchell, following Erwin Panofsky, described the cultural transition as the "Pictorial Turn". At the same time, the lack of preoccupation with an adequate science of pictures (Bildwissenschaft), comparable with general linguistics, is criticised by Gottfried Boehm. Boehm classified the transformation as the "Iconic Turn", in reference to the linguistic turn whilst Horst Bredekamp (1997) argued that society was pictorially illiterate. By this he meant that there was an increasing inability to interpret pictures despite their ubiquity. Hubert Burda claimed as well in 2004 that the turn of the century was marked by pictures not by text and a "return of the pictures" in the course of a shift from verbal to visual information. These first issues are concerned with the definition pictures and their uses.[12] Instead of proceeding to sketch the outlines of a budding yet unintegrated Bildwissenschaft (Bildwissenschaft means "image science" which can be understood as Visual Culture)[13], I want to identify appropriate possibilities for image interpretation thus finding a method of analysis.

Mueller-Doohm[14] connects hermeneutic and structural interpretation in order to combine an analysis of sense and meaning. While Mueller-Doohm tested his case analysis on text and pictorial messages, I aim to analyse only

---

12 "Die Frage 'Was ist ein Bild?' zielt in unserem Falle auf die Artefakte, die Bildwerke, die Bildübertragung und die bildgebenden Verfahren, um einige Beispiele zu nennen. Das 'Was', das man in solchen Bildern sucht, lässt sich nicht ohne das 'Wie' begreifen, in dem es sich ins Bild setzt oder zum Bild wird. Es ist zweifelhaft, ob man im Falle des Bildes das 'Was' im Sinne von Inhalt oder Thema überhaupt bestimmen kann, so wie man eine Aussagen aus einem Text heraus liest, in dessen Sprache und Textform viele mögliche Aussagen enthalten sind" (Belting, 2001, p. 12).

13 By mentioning the underlying developments within the "Bildwissenschaft" it, however, should have become clear that the "Bildwissenschaft" provides various methods since the "Bildwissenschaft" includes art history, philosophy, psychology, anthropology, social sciences, media and communication sciences.

14 "Kultursoziologische Bildanalyse ist Bildinhaltsforschung, die folglich nicht in erster Linie auf Stilkritik und Quellenanalyse abzielt. In ihrem Mittelpunkt steht vielmehr die Rekonstruktion der sozialen Mitteilungsgehalte, der manifesten und latenten Deutungs- und Orientierungsmuster visueller Präsentationen" (Mueller-Doohm, 1993, p. 443).

the pictorial messages, i.e. I will introduce a pragmatic shortened pictorial analysis. Mueller-Doohm's analysis model was inspired by Erwin Panofsky's "Method of Iconology" (1975), Max Imdahl's "Ikonik" (1980) and Barthes's "Semiology" (1957). Imdahl explains his method as an extension of the hermeneutic designed iconology of Panofsky, which more precisely captures the density and structure of pictorial representation. Barthes, however, deals exclusively with the deciphering of the denotative and connotative messages of pictures. In a schematic overview, Müeller-Doohm demonstrates that these three approaches resemble each other in a "three-phase process of analysis" (Mueller-Doohm, 1997, p. 98), which mainly serves to detail the complex content of the picture analysis. Mueller-Doohm attempts to generate a cultural-image analysis and to overcome the difference of the classical-hermeneutic and the structural oriented interpretation, thus resulting in a three phases: the description of the analysis, reconstruction analysis and the interpretation of analysis. Mueller-Doohm first aims to describe and then reconstruct the relations in which social phenomena are expressed. He seeks to understand the constitution of their significance as a function of a particular syntactic order. (Mueller-Doohm, 1997, p. 99) According to Mueller-Doohm the hermeneutic oriented approach includes inaccuracy in that one attributes isolated meanings to elements dissolved from their context. This failure, however, can be dismissed in the structural-hermeneutic method by reassembling the isolated elements into their former relations. Hence a systematically hermeneutic symbol interpretation is based on a prior structural analysis of meaning. (Mueller-Doohm, 1997, p. 100)

What justifies the approach of a structural-hermeneutic symbolic analysis of pictures in this work? I begin with the fact that the pictures of dead people have always been equipped with symbolic content, because they had to be adjusted on account of the unlearnable experience.[15] Pictures are usually contextualized, i.e. they are produced by somebody for somebody during a certain time and for a certain purpose. (Blum, Sachs-Hombach & Schirra, 2007, p. 7) This means that pictures of the dead refer with differ-

---

15 "Das Bild selbst entstand in der Lücke, welche die Toten hinterließen. Im Sinne Baudrillards kann man von einem symbolischen Tausch zwischen Körper und Bild sprechen. Das Bild gab dem Toten ein Medium zurück, in dem er den Lebenden begegnete und von ihnen erinnert wurde. Der Bildkörper gehörte als Tauschkörper dem abwesenden Toten"(Belting, 2000, p. 10).

ent forms to different codes in different social discourses.[16] Mueller-Doohm (1990, p. 28ff) refers to Roland Barthes, who classifies pictorial messages as both perceptive, non-encoded pictorial messages and as symbolic, encoded pictorial messages. The encoded pictorial messages illustrate the area of the pictorial connoted significatum, because pictorial elements are not only denotative, but also unfold a metalanguage by way of chaining and visual order. (Mueller-Doohm, 1997, p. 101) The reconstruction of the connotation system depends on its readings. Mueller-Doohm points out that not every connotation system can be analysed, but that the semantic organisation of the field can be. When it comes to demonstrating pictorial analysis, Mueller-Doohm inserts a pre-level concerning the preparation of prototypes[17] for single case analysis.

The pre-level starts with the first step: the classification of the pictorial message–the first impression, respectively the primary message. The second step comprises of the recording of the represented objects and people. The third step includes the collection of the distinguished style of representation and the fourth step consists of the making of the staging. These steps allow a classification of the material regarding the "family resemblance". If any resemblance exists, the pictures can be summarised into categories. These heuristically developed categories provide examples, which serve as prototypes for single case analysis.[18] Summarised into a schema, the levels can be arranged as follows:

---

16 "Die Tatsache, dass Bilder immer wieder in eine historische Situation eingebunden sind, obwohl ihre Fragen über jeden zeitlichen Kontext hinausweisen, bestätigt nur den Grundsatz, dass sich der Mensch nicht anders als unter historischen Bedingungen ausdrücken kann"(Belting, 2000, p. 8).

17 The term prototype is used for the typical exponent of a category. The exponent consists of the main characters of one category. The attribution of others is based on the family resemblance to the typical exponents' characters, which also structure the category. (Cf. Kleiber, 1993)

18 "Zweck der Ersteindrucksanalyse ist die Sichtung des Materials im Hinblick auf 'Familienähnlichkeiten'. Solche Familienähnlichkeiten liegen vor, wenn sich die markante Botschaft […] zu einem Klassentypus zusammenfassen lässt. Aus den heuristisch so gebildeten Klassen lassen sich die Beispiele gewinnen, die als Prototypen Gegenstand der Einzelanalyse sind" (Mueller-Doohm, 1997, p. 102).

1. Analysis of the first impression	a. The primary message b. Recording of objects and people c. Recording of distinguishing styles d. Recording of the making of the staging
2. Hypothetic generation of categories	a. Summary of the analysis of the first impression b. Review within a research group c. Family resemblance
3. Generation of categories	a. Classification of the material into the categories b. Selection of a prototype (including most of the characteristics of the perspective category)
4. Single case analysis	Pictorial analysis based on a three stage model of interpretation

Tab. 1: Pre-levels of analysis

Source: Mueller-Doohm 1997

The guide for the subsequent pictorial interpretation contains all three levels of analysis: description, reconstruction and interpretation. The description puts visual elements into words in a methodically controlled manner which allows an accurate and complete record of all pictorial elements, which might stand as the constitutive elements of the symbolic pictorial message. Therewith, a holistic data structure can be reconstructed and interpreted. The second level of is reconstruction, an analysis of the already described elements for their symbolic meanings. Reconstruction is a tool for the development of these individual elements and their structures of meaning. The third level of analysis is socio-cultural interpretation. Here, the reconstructed symbolic meanings are attached to expressions of cultural patterns of meanings. According to Mueller-Doohm, this structure

1. Description	2. Reconstruction	3. Interpretation
A. Analysis of pictorial elements:	*A. Analysis of pictorial elements and connotation:*	The interpretation starts with the synthesisation of reconstructed meanings as cultural expressions of meanings.
- Description and Configuration of objects and people	Configuration of objects and people	
- Scenic relations and situations	Scenic relations and situations	
- Relations of action	Relations of action	
- Additional pictorial elements (logos or detail shots)	Additional pictorial elements (logos or detail shots)	
B. Room/Space:	*B. Room/Space:*	In this work I also want to compare the contemporary cultural expression of meanings to previous media representations, in order to demonstrate how certain ideas of the dead can change with certain historic conditions.
- Pictorial format (also pictures within the picture)	Pictorial format (also pictures within the picture)	
- General perspectives: Foreground / background, lines of flight, partial spatial perspectives etc. planimetric conditions (lines, centrality, geometrical figures, faces, etc.)	General perspectives: Foreground / background, lines of flight, partial spatial perspectives, etc, planimetric conditions (lines, centrality, geometrical figures, faces, etc.)	
- Separate perspectives of arrangements	Separate perspectives of arrangements	
C. Aesthetic elements:	*C. Aesthetic elements*	
- Light and shade conditions	Light and shade conditions	
- Styles: eg. naturalistic, artificial, harmonious, disharmonious, static, moving, etc.)	Styles: e.g. naturalistic, artificial, harmonious, disharmonious, static, moving, etc.)	
- Style contrasts / breaks		
- Graphic / photographic practices (eg. filtering, perspective, motion...)	Graphic / photographic practices (e.g. filtering, perspective, motion ...)	
- Colours, contrasts, nuances	Colours, contrasts, nuances	
D. Impression in total:		
- Overall impression in terms of "mood"		

Tab. 2: The Guide for Pictorial Analysis

Source: Mueller-Doohm, 1997

will generate a solid foundation for cultural interpretation, which is based on dense description and systematic reconstruction.

These pictures are screen shots from movies. The "weakness" of this methodology therefore, lies in the fixation of moving images and, to a certain degree, the arbitrary selection of those screen shots. However, for any forensic work performed on a dead body, I will provide a film analysis. Another "weakness" is the transition between description and reconstruction. I will describe the facsimile "dead" as a human body first. I will, however, refrain from describing a recognisable table as a table and not as an object in detail.

2.3. Film Analysis

The richness of the research material makes it difficult to analyse the representations of the dead with methods from film studies. Taking samples with a customised film analysis would therefore not serve the purposes of this study. Thus for this work, the moving image becomes important. When the "dead representation" cannot be captured in a still image, i.e. when somebody moves the dead body or body parts or the dead move they are subject to film sequence analysis. These scenes are exceptions to the usual modes of representation. The interdisciplinary development of film analysis since the 1960s, has created a complex variety of methods and a heterogeneous set of film theories (Kuchenbuch 2005, Hickethier 2001, Silbermann, Schaaf & Adam 1980, Bignell 1997, Metz 1974, Metz 1982, Mersch 2006) which aimed to explore film's complex order of representation. (May & Winter 1992) There are numerous approaches in film theory to film analysis. (Hickethier, 2001, p. 27) Therefore, for analysis of the specific representations of the "moving dead", I can choose from a variety of methodological possibilities. An overview, however, shows that for these short sequences, a Sequence Analysis is most appropriate. In order to keep a similar structure of interpretation, Sequential Analysis will follow the three level structure of Pictorial Analysis and will therefore also include the areas of description, reconstruction and interpretation. The level structure will also guarantee that all necessary visual elements are described in detail and reconstructed as constitutive elements of the symbolic meaning. Hence, just as for the Pictorial Analysis, the interpretation will not take place before the itemisation of all visual elements, in order to search for cultural patterns of meaning. The description and reconstruction takes place on a visual and audio level. The visual level consists of the categories "light design", "camera", "setting", "room space relation" and "storyline". Angela Keppler (2006), describes movies as a combination of acoustic and visual movement. The importance of the acoustic dimension is determined by the dialogue, sound effects and background music. The audio level consists, therefore, of the categories "transcript", "noise", "music" and "atmosound". The division of both levels is necessary to not confuse the description. However, in the description table, the visual storyline is found next to the audio elements. I have selected the categories' content from a variety of suggestions on how to accomplish a sequential analysis. In particular, Thomas Kuchenbuch (2005), Knut Hickethier (1993), Nils Bostnar, Eckhard Pabst and Hans Jürgen Wulff (2008), James Monaco (2000), Herbert Zettel (1995) and Lothar Mikos and Claudia Wegener (2005) were very helpful authors in completing the sequential analysis protocol, which I will now introduce.

I will first explain the categories in the protocol. On the visual level, the light design is concerned for instance with hard or soft light. Colours can be natural, luscious or unsaturated. Special effects are considered as all post production modifications. The camera category will be divided depending on the cut (e.g cross dissolve), its movements (panning shots), and its movement into different perspectives (high angle, low angle, bird's eye view) and the shot itself (medium shot or close ups). The setting and room space relation is concerned with all visible objects within the frame. I will divide the visible objects into corpses, their (medical) context, the living and objects of work. The description of the storyline entails the entire acting within one shot. For the audio level, the description comprises of the transcription of communication, noises like the cut, music and the Atmosound (surround sound).

The protocol schema for the reconstruction basically looks the same. Instead of the description within the categories, I will reconstruct possible meanings of the described elements within the categories.[19] The interpretation will synthesise and summarise its meanings and connect contemporary cultural expressions of these meanings to previous media representations.

---

19 Example: The Description includes four wheels, body, windows, steering wheel, signs and hallmarks. The reconstruction concludes on certain characteristics that a Maybach Limousine is shown.

It is the nature of an exhaustive media research that not every audiovisual element that contributes to a film experience can be measured. Research methods are cut in order to cover the research object and the research question. The composition of the protocol is, therefore, new but contains categories, which are proven to be reliable in other research studies.

Desciption					
Protocol Nr:					
Title:					
Season: Episode: Length total:					
Camera Set Nr.:	Time	Visual level		Audio level	
		Camera and Composition	Setting and Storyline	Communication	Atmosound, Music, Noise
		Light Design Light quality Key light Shadows: Colour Special effects *Camera* Cut Movement Perspective Shot	Setting Room- Space rela- tion Storyline	Transcript	Music Atmosound Noise

Tab. 3: This is the protocol schema

2.4. Interviews

To supplement and validate the research findings, oral interviews have been conducted. Each interview used a topic guide for consistency and thus all other forms of interviews were inadmissible. The interview guide supplied a structure to the conversation and served as a checklist. It is possible to change the wording and sequence of questions, and to ask supplementary questions thus interviews provided fast access to the field to obtain specific information. (Schnell, Hill & Esser, 1999, p. 355) Siegfried Lamneck (2005), distinguishes between six different interview types. Uwe Flick (2007), on the other hand, subdivides them, under the category "Guided Interviews", focussed, semi-structured, problem-centred, ethnographic and expert interviews. I selected the guided expert interview because the participant is chosen due to their attributed expert status in a particular field. Their status for this research is thus representative of a group. The expert's professional function in the field requires a guided interview because of time constraints. In an expert interview, the interviewer has a fixed framework of themes. The interview, however, is fairly open for bringing up further questions as it takes place, allowing a conversational communication. The goal of the expert interview is to obtain information and insights on specific issues not limit the questions to a rigid set of ideas.

The interview type used in this research was a mixture of an explorative expert interview and a systematising expert interview. They covered technical knowledge such as management procedures, process knowledge (e.g. routines) and explanatory knowledge, such as subjective interpretations of ideas, routines and decision processes. (Meuser & Nagel, 2005)

The guided expert interview consists of three parts. I started with general questions about their position and job practices. The main part of the interview consisted of questions about dead body presentations and finished with prepared statements, read by the interviewer, about dead bodies, soliciting the expert's opinion.

The interviews took place in the respondent's everyday environment to encourage a natural situation and to obtain authentic information during the interview process. Since the interview setting influences the information obtained, the schedule of the interview was aligned to the interviewee's schedule.[20] Each participant had the process explained to them and were given the option to not consent to being recorded. I conducted two pre-test interviews to eliminate possible misunderstandings.

The analysis was done according to the standards of Michael Meuser and Ulrike Nagel (2005, p. 80ff). Therefore, I audio recorded the interviews and then transcribed them, depending on the quality and content. The transcription was carried out by writing out the actual spoken text and then by paraphrasing it. Omissions were completed by summarising; I also left out non-verbal communication. I identified different themes and thoughts[21] in separate paragraphs and gave them headings.

I applied a sociological conceptualisation throughout, i.e. developing categories with the goal of systematise relevance, generalisations and patterns of interpretation (Meuser & Nagel, 205, p. 88ff). Last but not least, I attached the theoretical generalisation. The most probable practical problems were approaching experts, time constraints and in dealing with sensitive subjects such as death, gender and race representations.

2.5. Statistic Research

A descriptive study was used in chapter 6 for the exploration of new representations of death and (new) taboos. Therefore, I simply compared a non-fictional TV show with a fictional one. In order to validate my thesis, I provided statistical research about the TV shows and disclosed general representation restrictions regarding age, gender and race proportions and also the specific representation taboos surrounding the dead body. I obtained basic descriptive statistics using SPSS 16.02 (Statistical Package for the Social Sciences). I used two data files containing 63 episodes of the TV

---

20 The selection of some interviewees resulted from personal contacts at the LA County Coroner Office (Steve Dowell). An actress (Melissa Hayden) and my supervisor (Stefan Timmermans) also brought me in contact with interviewees and once I was at the TV set I approached more interviewees. Usually the personal contacts would first approach their contacts for me and then I contacted them via phone or email. I explained my affiliation, the function of my research and the time span of the interview (thirty to forty minutes).

21 E.g.: typical experiences, observations procedural rules, interpretations and constructions, standards of decision making, value attitudes, positions, maxim of action, concepts in the context of functional exercise

show *Six Feet Under* and 16 episodes of the TV show *Family Plots*. I entered these files into the SPSS data editor, defined variables, and completed the two data files. Thereafter, I compared the results.

2.6. "Genre"

From a methodological point of view a brief discussion of terms is useful. "Genre" and "Topoi", for decades, have been connected to various discussions. They have also different meanings in English and German. Therefore, it is necessary to discuss the different terminology, disciplinary usage and translations; however, it is not necessary to illustrate the content of each of the three attached concepts. Thereafter, I will introduce and explain the terms used in this research "genre" and "topoi". "Genre", "Gattung" (Family) and "Topoi" are terms, which refer to coherent structural features, if one wants to demonstrate the coarsest common denominator. According to Steve Neale genres:

"[…] are not to be seen as forms of textual codifications, but as systems of orientations, expectations and conventions that circulate between industry, text and subject" (1980, p. 19).

Steve Neale declares that "genres are instances of repetition and difference" (Neale, 1980, p. 48). He adds that "difference is absolutely essential to the economy of genre" (Neale, p. 50): mere repetition would not attract an audience. As an example, Neale refers to westerns, gangster and detective films:

"In each case too, therefore, the discourse mobilised in these genres are discourses about crime, legality, justice, social order, civilisation, private property, civic responsibility and so on. Where they differ from one another is in the precise weight given to the discourse they share in common, in the inscription of these discourses across more specific generic elements and in their imbrications across the codes specific to cinema" (Neale, 1980, p. 21).

A forensic crime series, for instance, shows dead bodies as forensic objects. In comparison, black comedy/drama series shows individualised representations, as well as unconventional deceased body representations and dead bodies as bodies of projection. "Generic specificity is a question not of particular and exclusive elements, however defined, but of exclusive and particular combinations and articulations of elements, of the exclusive and particular weight given in any one genre to elements which in fact it shares with other genres" (Neale, 1980, p. 22f).

Still, Neale points out a few years later:

"Genre can mean 'category' or 'class', generic can mean 'constructed or marked for commercial consumption'; genre can mean a 'corpus' or 'grouping', genre can mean 'conventionally comprehensible'; genre can mean 'formulaic', generic can mean 'those aspects of communication that entail expectations'; and so on" (Neale, 2001, p. 3).

David Chandler summarises the problems of defining the genre:

"The classification and hierarchical taxonomy of genres is not a neutral and 'objective' procedure. There are no undisputed 'maps' of the system of genres within any medium (though literature may perhaps lay some claim to a loose consensus). Furthermore, there is often considerable theoretical disagreement about the definition of specific genres"(Chandler, 2000, para. 4).

In German media studies, the genre definition is much more pragmatic. Hickethier draws a distinction between the literary "Gattung" and the cinematic "Genre" by stating that a genre is labelled as a product group when social or geographic location, specific milieus, character constellations, structures of conflict, specific story plots or special specific emotional or affective constellations are recognisable. (Hickethier, 2003, p. 151) Media studies defines "Gattung" and "Genre" as not being synonymous, but using "Gattung"[22] for the mode of presentation. (Hickethier, 2003, p. 151) According to Hickethier, genre theory is a definition of genre, which describes and systematises narrative patterns of genre. It also provides a description of the visual stereotypes and standards, and represents the relationship between ideology and history. Furthermore, it examines the relationship of genre and its context of industrial production and the relationship between genre and authorship. (Hickethier, 2002, p. 69)

While researching the subject of how television constructs historical, social and cultural presence through the variety of its genres Angela Keppler (2006) argued, on the contrary that "Gattung" and "Genre" are

---

22 "Der Unterschied zwischen 'Genre' und 'Gattung' lässt sich an einem Beispiel veranschaulichen: Das Krimigenre wird durch das Vorhandensein wesentlicher Handlungskonstellationen (Verbrechen und Aufklärung des Verbrechens) definiert. Dieses Genre kann in unterschiedlichen Filmgattungen (Spielfilm, Animationsfilm) vertreten sein" (Hickethier, 2003, p.151).

equivalent. She sees television as a part of reality, while also shaping reality. The product configures itself as a "Gattung" and their variations are associated with markers that, for instance, distinguish the real from the fictitious, the present from the past, and seriousness from unserious. (Keppler, 1006, p. 9) According to Keppler the question: "how does television shape social reality?" depends on the answer to the question: "how does television present itself within the diversity of its 'Gattungen'"? This conclusion is similar to what Knoblauch describes as a communicative genre, namely, those communicative processes that have entrenched themselves in society. According to Knoblauch, a "Gattung" is a framework for the production and reception of communicative acts. They differ from spontaneous communicative processes by the fact that people orientate themselves in a predictable manner typical of prefabricated patterns. Therefore, "Gattung" analysis is fundamentally interested in the consolidation of communicative forms and patterns. (Knoblauch, 2000, p. 539).[23] In addition, Knoblauch refers to structural individual characteristics and their degree of consolidation within the internal structure of a "Gattung". Audio-visual "Gattungen", therefore, include motives, topoi and certain outline characteristics. (Knoblauch, 2000, p. 542) Knoblauch refers to Curtis, who understood topos as an established mode of speaking, with constant motives and ava-

---

23 "Gattungen bilden somit Orientierungsrahmen für die Produktion und Rezeption kommunikativer Handlungen. Gattungen unterscheiden sich ihrer Form nach von ›spontanen‹ kommunikativen Vorgängen dadurch, dass sich Menschen in einer voraussagbar typischen Weise an vorgefertigten Mustern ausrichten. […] Die Gattungsanalyse zielt also nicht nur auf diejenigen kommunikativen Formen, die als prototypische Gattungen in jeder Hinsicht verfestigt sind und eine situativ, funktional und prozedural deutlich bestimmte Struktur aufweisen […].Weil sie sich grundsätzlich für die Verfestigung kommunikativer Formen und Muster interessiert, behandelt sie auch schwächer verfestigte und kanonisch nicht festgelegte kommunikative Formen […]" (Luckmann & Knoblauch, 2000, p. 539).

ilable and stereotype-thinking models. (Knoblauch, 2000b, p. 655) The audio-visual media representations, which I will analyse in this study, also show established and conventionalised representations. I will, therefore, stay with the term "genre" when I refer to the description of the TV show by the producer and use the term "topoi" for the specific representation codes of dead bodies.

Part 2–Analysis
What is shown and how?

-

3 Pictorial Analysis: Pretty corpses in pathology

In this chapter, I want to introduce television shows that have drawn on the model created by *Quincy, M.E.* With these more current programmes I will develop a general categorisation of the new manners in which corpses are depicted. The categorisation will not only provide a background orientation to the research material, but will also prove that there is in fact a new system of death representation. Therefore, I will use the pre-level analysis, which consists of classifying the pictorial message, recording the represented objects and persons, and distinguishing the orchestration of the representations. For each TV show, I will provide pictorial prototypes in order to exemplify the modes of depiction. Therefore, I divided the chapter into three parts: (1) the introduction, in which I will present the characteristics/features of the television show depiction models, (2) a list of all examined TV shows and the respective prototype pictures with a description and (3) a summary of the findings.

3.1. Introduction

Ariès demonstrated changing behavioural patterns in previous centuries by analysing depictions of the body. I want to continue to deduce behavioural patterns by comparing present day depictions of bodies with those past since the media has exhibited a tremendous amount since the beginning of the new millennium. According to Ariès, death has turned from denial into a rather spectacular object.[1] I assume that if attitudes towards death have

---

1 Ariès divided his analysis into five attitudes towards death. The last pattern, "Death Denial", is characterised by Ariès as shameful. Society saw death not only as a genuine error of social performance but also as dirty and indecent. Before and during the nineteenth century, death was made beautiful by pleasant and embellished depictions,

changed over time from denial to a period of rapprochement or even taming, a corresponding discourse of images on television can be identified. Through this analysis I have found four consecutive models of image representation[2] which indicate a corresponding pictorial discourse from denial towards domestication:

1) The Simulation of the Authentic (images of real decedents)
2) The Traditional Depiction (no images of the dead or covered dead)
3) The Modern Depiction (plain images of aesthetic corpses)
4) The Breach of Style (abstract images of corpses)

The simulation of an authentic depiction encompasses efforts to depict either deceased individuals or images of deceased individuals. Hence, the scenery is usually the real environment and the original personnel can be seen, i.e. the first depiction model is characterised by authentic corpse representations. In previous modes of depiction, fictional narratives sometimes include the representation of the corpse; however, most of the time the corpse is covered or invisible. Representations of corpses in *North Mission Road* belong to this category, as do those mentioned previously in *Quincy M.E.* belong to that category. Current depiction can be characterised by representation codes, which belong to a fixed representational system. The four depiction models are consecutive and feature:

---

though the contradictory awareness of illness, suffering, and agony was still present and ubiquitous. Nevertheless, according to Michel Foucault the medicine of the twentieth century almost eliminated physical suffering and turned death into a medical issue. (Foucault 2003, p. 159) From then on, medical care centres have isolated and hidden death. This institutional "outsourcing" of death also affected the great pictorial sequences from previous centuries, which still existed in the twentieth century but from then on attenuated and degenerated. (Cf. Ariès, 1988) The death denial thesis is widely spread and still on everyone's lips. Ariès again argued that there are signs of change concerning the representation of death during the last quarter of the twentieth century. He described them as hesitating performances of symbolic representations typical for new cultures. "Death is now becoming what it had ceased to be since the very end of the Romantic era, the subject of an inexhaustible supply of anecdotes/a fact which would lead one to suspect that the newspaper-reading public is becoming interested in death, perhaps initially because of its seemingly forbidden and somewhat obscene nature"(Ariès, 1975, p. 135f.).

2 In "Six Feet Under: Die Domestizierung des Todes" (Weber, 2008) one can find an initial draft of the depiction models.

1) A trend towards aestheticisation, such as the dominance of embellishment of the dead which is a mode that takes great pain to beautify a corpse.
2) A trend towards civilising[3] the dead by depicting sterile bodies: The subtle decay, dirt, and contamination usually considered an inexorable part of a corpse is rendered invisible.
3) A trend towards subjectifying the dead by depicting a dead body with status markers such that the dead body serves as a space for survivors to project their emotions.
4) A trend towards objectifying the dead as an object of anatomical knowledge: A dead body is represented as a place for forensically relevant information.
5) The trend towards violation of the dead. Previously, the dead were untouchable but new representations contain increasingly violent actions against bodies, such as cutting, drilling or breaking skin and bones.

I argue that once the "modern depiction" model and the "breach of style" model replaced the traditional model of depiction, a new representational system of death has emerged in 21st century television shows.

3.2. New TV shows with new representations of death

Since the beginning of the new millennium, new television shows with new representations of death have emerged. The shows with corpses present beyond just the crime scene, are the documentary *North Mission Road* and *Family Plots*, the Drama/Black Comedy *Six Feet Under*, the crime series *CSI*, *Crossing Jordan*, *Bones*, *Castle*, and *NCIS*, the Fantasy/Comedy *Dead like me*, *Pushing Daisies*, and the Fantasy/Drama series *Heroes*, *Dexter*, and *Tru Calling*. Availability was a primary selection criterion for including a TV show in my research. Availability is one measure of popularity as those with greatest reach were most accessible. The spin-offs of the originals like *CSI:*

---

3 I will use the term civilising referring to Norbert Elias. Although Elias (1939, p. 477) speaks of a internalized self-control which cannot be pursued by a dead, I will still use the term "civilising" for a television representation that displays the dead body as a "civilised living" who seems still capable of action regarding the hygiene. The corpse's inability to take care of its own corporality is only seldom shown.

Las Vegas, were not included, since the representations of death between programs resemble the original with only slight modifications. The narratives between shows provide different plots, rooms, and figures. I analyse the new corpse depiction in pathology, i.e. not representations of figures that just passed away at crime scenes. Hence, the following images, with few exceptions, display the corpse mostly in pathology, in the morgue and in embalming rooms. Some exceptions are *Dexter* and *Dead Like Me,* which will be expanded later. The representation of the corpse as supine on a table in the center of a room predominates views of the body on television and as such is similar in most episodes. Therefore, those shots which showed most of the corpse were selected as prototypical images for analysis.

3.2.1. Documentary

North Mission Road[4] and Family Plots[5]

The documentary genre, considered in this section, differs from other genres in many respects. (Cf. Creeber, 2001) Documentaries aim to present "[…] images and sounds to provide an exposition or argument about the real world" (Corner, 2001, p. 125). Hence, the shows selected create a specific approach to depicting the dead as centered in objective reality, through the conventions of realism[6] used in current media.

    North Mission Road—the first to be considered—is a documentary about the Los Angeles County Coroner's Office and their investigation and examination of crime victims and the scenes of their deaths. As in *Autopsy* and *Dr. G* the cases are presented in interviews and through scene footage. *Family Plots*—also under consideration—is a documentary about a family-run mortuary in San Diego. The show concentrates on the work and private life of the employees of the mortuary. The embalming work, the cosmetic alterations and the dressing of the dead are depicted more rarely than in other shows.

---

4 http://www.imdb.com/title/tt0381788/, July 5th, 2008

5 http://www.imdb.com/title/tt0407390/, July 5th, 2008

6 "The specific conventions of 'realism' in television drama are always changing (which is why the idea of 'realism' is sometimes to be preferred). The particular ways of relating the viewer to the real in documentary are changing too, and the rise of popular factual entertainment […] has increased the rate of change" (Corner, 2001, p. 127).

Documentary	NMR	Family Plots
Production	2003–2008	2005
Idea	Court TV	A&E
Episodes/length	155/30min	16/30 min

Tab. 4: Documentaries

North Mission Road produced only two DVDs with selected episodes. These episodes display a balanced proportion of female and male dead bodies, mostly Caucasian adults.

Family Plots is available with two complete seasons on DVD. *Family Plots* is presently the only TV show about a funeral business to ever utilise real dead bodies in filming. The corpses presented belong primarily to elderly people. This uniquely contrasts to every other television show on record, and while these bodies are mainly Caucasians, the representation of female and male elderly presented is almost balanced.

The documentary soap shows dead bodies in many different ways. Sometimes the show avoids displaying the decedents' identity and faces are covered by using visual effects. Other times the faces can be seen, for instance, during the make-up or viewing. Additionally, the mourning relatives give information about the identity of the decedent as part of the narrative. In *Family Plots* the decedents are depicted in very short shots which is not the case in a show like *Six Feet Under*, which deals with a similar setting of an undertaking business. Different embalming methods are seen on screen, but the camera never stops for a longer shot. Instead, it focuses up on the funeral parlour employee performing the embalming or cleaning tasks. *Family Plots* is the only show in which the most revealing scenes are shown right at the beginning. The degree of detail declined soon after the broadcasting of the initial episodes, and the show was eventually cancelled.

Family Plots

The Simulation of Authentic

This image (Fig 3.1) shows a room with a person standing in the foreground next to a coffin and a corpse tied to ropes fixed at the ceiling hovering horizontally above the coffin. In the background cupboards and

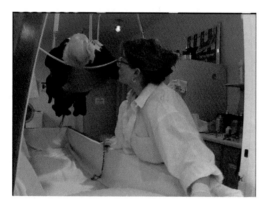

Fig. 3.1.: Family Plots–Mortuary employee moves a decedent into the coffin

Source: Episode 1

different tools can be seen. The dead body is dressed in a black suit, which is cut open at the back. The exposed portions of the anatomy are covered by means of visual effects. The same scene without visual effects is shown immediately afterwards.[7] The worker is about to adjust the coffin underneath the hanging corpse. The individual wears a white coat and gloves. The camera perspective is shot from an observer's position in front of the open coffin. The source of light in the scene consists of a single bulb at the ceiling and a diffuse light in the background behind the camera. The dominant colour is shaped by this light, which is yellowish in the background and white-pink in the foreground. A specific camera style is not recognisable. The overall impression, based upon similar scenes, is that this show presents the dead differently to other shows. The image most likely provides the first television depiction of a dead body in motion, literally hanging in the air, without a comedic context. Though *Six Feet Under* also

---

7 However, the following scene is divided into two images within one frame, so the naked back and the diaper is not visible to the naked eye due to the downsizing of the images.

depicts corpses in a funeral parlour, a corpse in motion was never shown. In summary, the documentary drama differs from other television shows due to the use of real corpses and the depiction of various funeral operations. The pictorial discourse includes many new images, which are not present in other TV shows. *Family Plots* is an exception in that they not only represent corpses of decedents in a San Diego funeral parlour, but that they reveal funeral operations which hitherto were never aired. Because of this, *Family Plots* serves in chapter 5 to contrast the fictional funeral parlour based show *Six Feet Under*. *Family Plots* was cancelled soon after being first broadcasted. Though the cancelling of programs on television is subject to many influencing factors and its depictions cannot be cited as one of these reasons, in this research the show stands out for breaching the limits of contemporary pictorial discourse about dead bodies. It is therefore categorized as an authentic simulation depiction model.

North Mission Road

Traditional depiction model

In the documentary *North Mission Road*, dead bodies in their entirety are not shown, but body parts like fingers are present on screen. Photographs are also used to display the entire body or body parts. Usually the pathologist

Fig. 2.2.: North Mission Road–Medical Examiner

Source: Episode 11

is depicted from a worm's eye view so that the table and the pathologist can be seen, but not the corpse.

Though the Los Angles County Coroner's Office is equipped with glaring ceiling lamps, the image as seen on screen is predominantly bluish and dark. No source of light is directly visible. The show adapted the bluish lighting from forensic crime shows and moved from the original autopsy theatre, a large and loud pathology hall, to the calm VIP-style small pathology room. The camera work is fast, restless, and swaying whenever it comes to the corpse, regardless of its position within the theatre or crimescene. When authentic police video tapes are used, the dead bodies at the scenes are not within the picture frame. In summary, just like the TV show *Dr. G: Medical Examiner* this documentary TV show is about the cases of medical examiners in the LA County Coroner's Office. However neither shows the main part of the medical examiner's work, the eponymous medical examination. Instead, the pathologists are shown only while they report on the case or handle different pathological and technical devices above the table where the corpse presumably rests. The same camera work and actions are shown in *Dr. G: Medical Examiner*, with the exception that when a supposed dead person was shown, the scene was clearly marked as re-enacted by subtitles. All available episodes from the TV-show *Autopsy*, on the other hand, worked with photos of the decedents instead of re-enactments. In chapter 6 the *North Mission Road* TV show will be further discussed. Here the image demonstrates the traditional depiction model of a corpse which is not shown but referenced.

Summary

The *North Mission Road* documentary style depicts original medical examiners and autopsy suites but no dead, only body parts. It is unclear if the body parts actually belong to real decedents. In contrast, the dead-body-in-motion (though dressed and with the face hidden) and embalming procedures are depicted in *Family Plots*. Still noticeably absent are the crucial markers of the dead such as nudity, the biological processes of gross decay and contamination, and detailed autopsy and embalming procedures. The dead body is never depicted on its own, dissected and laying on a messy pathology table. The previously described trends towards aestheticisation, civilising, objectifying, subjectifying or increasing violence cannot be seen, since the corpse is either missing or real decedents are presented. Hence, the documentary images cannot be classified as a traditional, modern, or breach of style depiction model, but only as an authentic simulation depiction model. The show *Family Plots* is a noticeable exception. In summary, the documentary genre complements other genres with additional depictions. Yet, the new images have not become a constant part of the pictorial discourse.

3.2.2. Black comedy and drama

Six Feet Under[8]

Six Feet Under presents the audience with a narrative about a family and their work in a funeral business. In every episode someone dies at the outset, and the pilot episode starts with the death of the funeral director Nathaniel Fisher Sr. on Christmas Eve. His sons Nate and David fight from then on for control of the family business against competing corporate companies. Nathaniel Fisher's widow and his daughter display vastly different attitudes towards the presence of death and their daily problems than his sons. The complex relationships of the protagonists structure the series' plot and allow the depiction of the work funeral business in a rather casual manner. (Akass & McCabe, 2005) *Six Feet Under* was commissioned by the HBO network and produced from 2000 to 2005 by Alan Ball. The show contains elements of drama and black comedy and was first broadcasted on the third of June, 2001 in the US. Five seasons with a total of 63 episodes, each with a play length of approx. 60 minutes were produced. Numerous awards like three Golden Globes and seven Emmys were given to this series and speak to the extremely high quality of the series. What is so special about this show is the fact that we can find modern and breach-of-style-depiction features.

Six Feet Under is the first TV show of the 21st century that represents dead bodies and funeral rites. Some of the corpses are very authentic latex figures made by the LA MastersFX studio. Other corpses, without major injuries, are presented by actors. Obvious ocular movements or respiratory movements are removed in post-production with digital technologies. Certain rules of etiquette determine the contact of the mortician with the dead bodies. Most of the time, the actions performed on the corpses are

---

8 http://www.imdb.com/title/tt0248654/, June 17th, 2008

carried out as if the corpses could "wake up" any minute to express disapproval with their insensitive treatment. Irreverent actions such as un-
covering a corpse are rarely shown. And if these seldom displayed depictions do occur they are mostly followed by a counter-representation, which
offsets the unpleasantness of the representation immediately thereafter and
often refer to a satirical elevation. Scenes in which the corpse is carelessly
and roughly treated are hardly ever shown. However, if this does happen,
then it happens for a higher purpose or is done by non-protagonists, which
would provoke immediate rejection by other figures on screen. Deference
is also given to the dead by the characters. Age, gender, and class attributions of the corpses are shown with different dress codes. The content of
most scenes in the embalming and viewing room of the funeral business is
arranged to represent the dead body as the former self. The undertakers
endeavour to restore the corpse in such a way that the continuity of the
meaning of the identity of the deceased is guaranteed.

Modern depiction

This image (Fig 3.3) illustrates the modern depiction model. It shows a
person standing in the middle of a room behind another person, who lies
supine on the embalming table. Another embalming table is placed behind

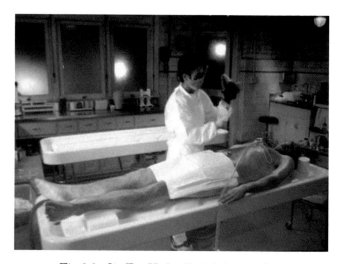

Fig. 3.3.: Six Feet Under–Embalming procedures

Source: Episode 1

the standing person and all around the edge of the room half-high cupboards with materials placed upon them are depicted.

The standing person is dressed in a protective suit, with a mask and gloves on, and holds a camera. The naked corpse is covered with a towel over the genitals. The face of the individual is shown with injuries. Tubes are attached to the chest and between the legs. The upper tube in the chest is flesh-coloured; the lower tube is red. The person on the table in the foreground directs all attention to herself. Different sources of light are responsible for the bright but diffuse atmosphere. The colours in the image are not luscious and crisp, but greyish. Due to the bright lighting conditions and the disharmonic arrangement of the material, the picture leaves a rather restive and chilly impression. The camera perspective is a mid shot from the position of a third person who stands in front the person on the table. The reconstruction of identity and status after death follows attributions, e.g. the unsaturated colour, different dresses and the arrangement of the individuals, as well as objects and space. Because of the severe injuries to the face and the embalming tubes attached to the body, the person is clearly identified as dead and the dressed person as an undertaker; one can see how a live actor is being portrayed as dead. The space can be identified as an embalming room of a funeral business in a cellar vault. The undertaker is busy taking pictures of the dead. The undertaker wears protective clothes against perceived contamination caused by the dead body. The dominating grey tone symbolises fatigue. The grey colours constitute a dreary, cold atmosphere. The depiction belongs then to the modern depiction model, because it shows the dead as an object on a table. Controlled violence against the dead body in the form of embalming or forensic treatments is a common characteristic of this mode. The dead body serves as both an object for cosmetic concerns and a subjectifying object onto which projections of the relatives, in this case the sons, are placed.

Breach of style depiction

The second image (Fig. 3.4) shows the undressed upper-body of a person whose chest is sewn shut. The seam appears red and straight like the seam from an organ donation. A white plastic cover surrounds the figure. On the left margin of the picture, a hand is shown in gloves. The figure lying on the table fills the whole picture. The head is wrapped in a bandage above

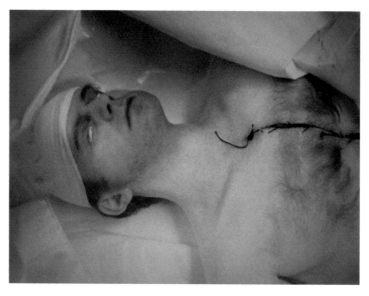

Fig. 3.4.: Six Feet Under–Organ donor

Source: Episode 61

the eyebrows. The eye balls are missing. The lids are open; instead of the eyeballs white material fills the space between the lids. The vanishing line leads into the head of the figure. A light grey colour dominates the picture. The red seam, the red lips and the white material in the eyes contrast somewhat the dominating grey tone. The overall impression of the picture radiates artificiality because of the white-grey colour tone. The reconstruction of the description of the image suggests that a dead organ donor is shown.

The corpse was one of the series' protagonists. As a main character, his fear of death was predominant. By the staging of the death of a main figure, the writers create a "Leichenparadox." This refers to the simultaneously absence and presence of a person as a paradox that strikes most survivors. The 'person' is still physically there, but ignores the environment and additionally dares to detach themselves from important social obligations like interaction and self-control. (Macho, 1987) In the image, the unpleasant representation of the dead is staged even more strikingly, because the eyelids are open, and corpses with open eyes were never depicted in the show previously. Furthermore, instead of the eyeballs only the white of the cotton in the eye socket is seen. The eyes of the character were very often shown through close shots to reflect the inner agonies during interactions with other characters. Certain linguistic idioms link the whiteness of the eyes with fear since people react similarly to frightened facial expressions throughout the world. As a result, the anxiety depicted in the familiar face of a dead person substantially tackles the cultural urge for a peaceful death. The depiction is disturbing, because the main character "died" and his facial expression leaves an impression of fear and alienation instead of silence and peacefulness like those in traditional depictions. The comfort of the illusionary "asleep, not yet dead" images is not given. The rather domestic codes of the modern depiction features are powerfully violated, which is why the image belongs to the breach of style depiction models.

Summary

In the comparison of the representations, the following common characteristics can be ascertained. All corpses are shown in a supine position on the embalming table. The corpses appear as objects of interest and, though they are not accessible and inactive, they are never depicted on their own. Depending on age, sex, and localisation the dress and lighting changes and underlines the transitional stage (Van Gennep, 1986) of the dead.

Six Feet Under displays two depiction models. Modern and breach of style depictions appear without chronological order.[9] No corpse is

---

9 Already in the second episode a special scene about picking up a body from the nursing home is shown. While lifting the old man's corpse from the bed onto the gurney, the blanket covering the corpse slips and bares the erected genitals of the dead body. The picture is shot in a close up. In a later episode, the same naked representation is used again on a different corpse, though with a piercing present. Yet, representations like the "angel's lust", as one of the figures explains, are only conceivable on a television channel like HBO on which these depictions are not censored. It illustrates not only two strong taboos, death and sexuality, but also establishes a connection between both taboos. "Angel's lust" is therefore another example of a breach-of–style representational mode. Only a few sequences later, as the corpse is transported in the hearse, typical noises of a decomposing corpse, which suggest a leaking of liquids and gases, are heard. Yet, these biological processes are not depicted. The explicit depictions of certain biological circumstances on the one hand and the omission of other biological circumstances on the other hand reveal additional structures of the discourse, namely the procedures of inclusion and exclusion. The combination of the representation of sexuality and death is perhaps less of a taboo than the representation of the combination of dirtiness and death. Thus, for instance the character of the baker Romano, who dies accidentally in the bread

"moved" uncovered, as for example on the embalming table or from the embalming table into the coffin. Corpses are moved only when they are covered by a body bag. Hence, the question in the end is whether this is owed solely to theatrical-technical reasons that neither protagonists nor the latex imitation can deliver a convincing representation. Corpses of infants or old-aged people are also represented with restrictions. Though one would expect mostly elderly dead in a funeral home, the age of the depicted dead bodies was mostly estimated to be between 20 and 60 years. This might lead to the idea that the combination of very young and very old age and death is not an entertaining arrangement. However, another breach of style deals exactly with that restriction. The image "laughing child corpse" (Fig. 5.9) which will be analysed later on, shows a young girl who broke her neck falling from the bed laughing. The laughter stays as a frozen facial expression in her face. Usually children are only partly shown and their faces are never depicted.

Though destroyed bodies and some cosmetic work are shown, not one older decedent with explicit signs of degeneration and decay is depicted. Biologically decomposing processes are only rarely shown. Status attributions are carried out via the dead body representations.[10] Femine and masculine attributions are shown through different clothing styles. Most female corpses are shown only with the upper part of the body covered or only from the shoulder thus recapitulating modesty taboos. On female corpses, the Y incision is seldom sewn and severe head injuries are seldom seen. The physical ramifications of these destructive acts are only shown on male corpses: one cleaved by a lift and the other shot in the head as the victim of a burglary. Yet, the covering of male corpses varies mostly with age, status, and attractiveness prior to demise. The more attractive the decedent the less he is covered. In addition, the contact with corpses is

---

machine. The body bag with the remaining body parts is treated inappropriately during the transport. As the bag opens, a background noise implies the leaking out of body liquids onto the floor, but the actual scene is not shown. Mess and disorder just like dirtiness in combination with the dead is obviously a strong visual taboo.

10 Thus, for instance the figure of the Hispanic decedent Paco, who, of course, is a gang member and littered with tattoos, while figures like the white decedent porn actress Viveca are shown undressed with silicone enlargements. In comparison Hatti, an older black lady, is shown only quickly and covered even on the embalming table. Several times explicit social and political subjects are demonstrated via corpse representations. Dead soldiers from the Iraq war are shown with their physical disablements or victims of crimes while dealing with themes like homophobia. Also topics like death penalty, suicides, or euthanasia are presented via the dead.

different. The treatment of the dead resembles the deferential interactions between living people. Though the genitals are at some point uncovered, these areas will never be touched on screen by a character. After all, the pictorial discourse determined by producer and audiences excludes two authentic sides of death. The trend towards aestheticisation like the dominant depiction of the embellished dead is clearly recognisable as well as the civilising depiction of dress codes and the sterile presentation of the dead. The trend towards objectifying and subjectifying can be seen in the embalming room where most of the dead become a piece of artwork for the undertaker and a projection screen for the Fisher family. The trend towards more violence shown against the dead, when previously the dead were untouchable, can be proven by the increasing depiction of these embalming scenes.

3.2.3. Crime

CSI[11], Crossing Jordan[12], Bones[13], NCIS[14], and Castle[15]

Similar to *Six Feet Under* the television shows about crime begin with a death. The finding of a dead body is usually linked to a crime. The audience follows the plot based on the "Whodunnit principle" and accompany the investigative team during the crime scene investigation, the processing of evidence, the reconstruction, and inquiry into the motive of the crime. These newer crime shows differ from earlier crime shows where the focus was on psychological motives behind the crime. In the newer programs the focus is on biochemical and physical processes driving the search for clues. The new shows even differ from previous forensic crimes shows such as *Quincy, M.E.* where the dead are shown not only at the crime scene but also in pathology. This new type of investigator runs the investigation processes not only on scene, but also in a test laboratory where physical and ballistic experiments, biochemical tests, questioning rooms, pathology rooms, and courtrooms are present. Additionally, most of the shows use simulations, 3D animations and extensive police archive software with the most mo-

---

11 http://www.imdb.com/title/tt0247082/, June 15th, 2008
12 http://www.imdb.com/title/tt0284718/, June 15th, 2008
13 http://www.imdb.com/title/tt0460627/, June 15th, 2008
14 http://www.imdb.com/title/tt0364845/, June 15th, 2008
15 http://www.imdb.com/title/tt1219024/, January 5th, 2010

dern but fictional audio and video technology. With the help of computer simulations a fatal bullet trajectory including the penetration of skin and organs can be shown in slow motion and in microscopic detail. The television depiction of forensic science becomes an infallible method and suggests that despite the crude murder there is a higher justice, because at the end of almost every episode the case is solved.

CSI (Crime Scene Investigation) started in the USA in 2000 on CBS. The show consists of a team of investigators who examine crime scenes and solve homicide cases. The show is still very popular and has been awarded many Peoples' Choice Awards and several Emmy Awards. Both spin offs of the original, *CSI: Miami* (2002) and *CSI: New York* (2004), also ran very successfully. Since both spin offs display the dead body with the same representation codes as the original I will only present the original in analysis.

Crossing Jordan has a similar structure to *CSI* but concentrates on forensic medicine. The protagonist, doctor Jordan Cavanaugh, and her team of scientist are paired with a detective to solve homicide cases. The show was broadcast from 2001 to 2007 on NBC. The series received several nominations and awards like the ASCAP award, but was cancelled in 2007.

Bones is a similar crime series that concentrates on forensic anthropology. The central figure is forensic anthropologist Dr. Temperance Brennan aka "Bones", whose work concentrates on the identification of skeletal remains, often archaeological in nature but occasionally from mass graves and genocidal wars across the world. As the show progresses however, the institution for which she works "The Jeffersonian" coerces her to assist the FBI in order to create good press for them. The series began on FOX in 2005.

Castle is another of the typical whodunit crime shows. The central figures are detective Joanna Becket and the writer Richard Castle who solve difficult crimes together with the help of two other officers, a pathologist and, often enough, Castle's family. The crime scene, which quite often opens the show, stands out due massive aesthetic arrangements. The victim is depicted in either a creative, embellished, or an abstract manner accompanied by special music. The show began in 2009 on ABC.

NCIS (Naval Criminal Investigative Service) is another whodunit crime show and resembles those previously mentioned. However, in this case, the team of special agents conducts criminal investigations only for the

Marine Corps and the U.S. Navy. The show started in 2003 on CBS. A spin-off, *NCIS: Los Angeles*, was broadcast for the first time in 2009.

	Production	Idea	Length Episodes seen
CSI	2000–2008	Anthony Zuiker	40–45min till ep. 924
Crossing Jordan	2001–2007	Tim Kring	40–45mintill ep. 222
Bones	2005	Kathy Reichs	40–45mintill ep. 425
NCIS	2003	Donald P. Bellisario Don McGill	40–45mintill ep. 406
Castle	2009	Andrew W. Marlowe	40–45mintill ep. 204

Tab. 5: Crime Series

The *CSI* shows have higher ratings than *Crossing Jordan, Bones,* and *Dexter* together. Furthermore, only two seasons of *Crossing Jordan* were released on DVD. Similar to *Six Feet Under*, the crime shows *CSI, Crossing Jordan Bones,* and *Dexter* depict predominantly white adult Americans between the ages of 30 and 50. Twice as often they use dead males than females. *Dexter* is exceptional in this regard, since the gender displays are almost completely balanced.

CSI

Modern depiction

This image consists of two bodies, one who stands next to the table and one who lays stretched out on it. The head of the horizontal body lies on a head rest. The upper chest is naked and shows a Y-incision scar. A towel is

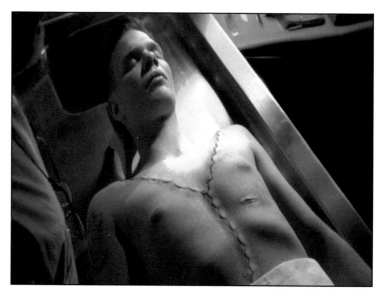

Fig. 3.5.: CSI–Dead body in pathology

Source: Episode 703

seen below the upper part of the body. The body lies in the centre of the picture, while the table below the body shapes the background. The structure of the body shapes the vanishing line leading to the vanishing point, the top of the shoulder. The surface of the table seems smooth, while the smoothness of the skin in the foreground is interrupted by the scar. The camera perspective is relatively medium up-close shot from the position of a third observer. The lighting is diffuse and reflected on the table. All represented objects and persons seem to be overlaid with a bluish tone. The neon lighting resembles the fluorescent glow of luminol. (Luminol is a chemical which makes invisible blood traces visible and is familiar to the audience of these shows.) The colours and objects are harmoniously arranged. The bluish lighting supports a cold, clean, and calm atmosphere, only the red Y scar interferes. The balanced tension between the artificial bluish atmosphere of safety and the disturbing coloured organic dissection marks generates the special feature of crime shows. Ugliness, repellent and frightening, such as mess or the moving of a dead body is not depicted. As in all other new forensic shows the dead look like young models, in good shape, without decomposing signs, or as an unidentifiable decomposed or skeletonised object. The intensified use of specific colours, embellished bodies lifted onto clean metallic tables, and high-tech aesthetic environments constitute the characteristics of the modern depiction model. The orchestration of tension in these aesthetic images such as traces of violence on the vulnerable body, and the display of dissected bodies and viscera will be discussed in chapter 4. The aestheticisation through the embellished dead, the civilising through dress styles and sterile presentation, and the trend towards objectification for research matters can be seen in this image. The trend towards more violent actions against the dead will be further discussed in chapter 4. The following description will be less comprehensive so as to avoid repeating the recurrent components of the scenes in the pathology department.

Crossing Jordan

Modern depiction

The depiction consists of two bodies in a supine position on tables. The first one is seen in the foreground, while the second one behind the first is hardly recognisable. The head of the first body rests on a headrest. The table seems smooth, clean, and illuminated. The camera perspective is a medium close-up shot from a high angle. The lighting is diffuse. As in the *CSI* shows, the skin and hair is dry and clean but the chest displays a Y incision. Both bodies are covered with sheets to the pectoral line. The overlaying bluish tone in this depiction generates the same cold, clean, and calm atmosphere as already described in the previous screen-shot. The aestheticisation or dominant depiction of the embellished dead, as well as

Fig. 3.6.: Crossing Jordan–Dead bodies on tables

Source: Episode 70

Fig. 3.7.: Crossing Jordan–Medical Examiner at work

Source: Episode 70

the civilising depiction of the covers and the sterile presentation of the dead is clearly recognisable. The trend towards objectifying is noticeable in the depiction of the dead as a source of information. The trend towards more violence against the dead will be shown in the following image. *Crossing Jordan* and *NCIS* display more often than *CSI* graphic autopsy scenes.

The second image (Fig. 3.7) displays the same room and the same figures only during the autopsy. Here the two bodies are displayed with open chests while pathologists are performing procedures. *Crossing Jordan* and *NCIS* display more graphic autopsy scenes than other shows.

Bones

Modern depiction

This image (Fig. 3.8) shows three characters standing beside a table on which a skeleton is placed, interacting. The skeleton on the illuminated table and the people behind the table dominate the foreground. The came-

Fig. 3.8.: Bones–Forensic Anthropologists at work

Source: Episode 1

ra perspective is a mid shot from an observation point facing the characters. The background displays a wall storage facility with other bones behind softly lit, milky white glass. The light source is behind these glass cupboards and the illuminated table. A screen next to the characters shows the deceased female tennis player. Sheets or towels do not cover the skeleton. The bones are depicted as clean and without organic remains. The arrangement of the bones approximates the structure of the human body. Like the previous depictions, this one is also dominated by a bluish colour, which seems to be a representation code emphasising a certain kind of atmosphere that is stereotypically associated with medical, in particular, forensic science. The bluish colouration, the clean examining tables with clean dead bodies or skeletons characterises all the selected shows as crime shows with a forensic context. The most interesting part about the skeleton depiction, though, is the fact that the skeleton as a dead body without flesh, blood, and skin is not covered with regards to the genitals. No matter what sex, the skeleton is usually shown as a neutral object, which raises a question about when exactly the gender identity of the skeleton becomes a neutral object.

In summary, it can be stated that the modern depiction of the dead in this show is the arranged ensemble of aesthetically pleasing bones, decomposed objects or dressed dead represented lying in a supine position on illuminated tables, surrounded by a high-tech aesthetic, sterile environment in a dark, bluish light. The trend towards aestheticisation, as well as civilising and objectifying is recognisable in the depiction.

NCIS

Modern depiction

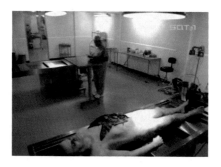

Fig. 3.9.: NCIS–Dead body

Source: Episode 19

NCIS also belongs to the modern depiction category, since it displays typical settings and positions, as mentioned in other TV shows, as well as typical trends such as aestheticisation, civilising and objectification. *NCIS*, like*Crossing Jordan*, only differs from the previous TV shows in that they display scenes which are more graphic. The open chest is shown more often, for instance. Another difference is the bright light, which obscures the taboo genital region, rather than sheets as in other shows.

Breach of Style

NCIS also generates images, which belong to the breach of style depiction model. In the following image, a main character of the investigation team dreams of an autopsy performed on her body. The transition from modern

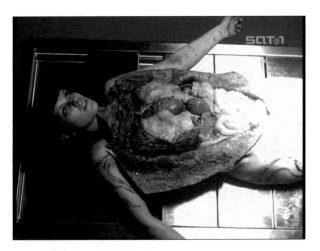

Fig. 3.10.: NCIS–An employee's nightmare: lying on an autopsy table all opened up

Source: Episode 16

depiction to the breach of style is accomplished by staging a living character as a corpse displaying her without covers, with an open upper body and open eyes. The luscious red colours of her viscera contrast with the unsaturated greyish background and turn the image into artwork.

Castle

Modern depiction

The cop-drama *Castle* started in 2009 and adopted the pathology depictions from previous shows. In the image, the corpse lies in a supine position in the foreground on a clean metal table. The table is surrounded by standing persons and medical tools are seen throughout. While two persons behind the table are dressed with causal street wear, the individual in front is dressed with tight blue scrubs. As in the previous TV shows, the corpse is not dressed, but covered by sheets. Apart from the setting and arrangement, the camerawork, lighting, and colours also resemble these previous shows. Just the lighting seems slightly brighter than in previous shows. Aestheticisation, civilising and objectifying trends are clearly visible.

Fig. 3.11.: Castle–Medical examiner explains cause of death

Source: Episode 13

Summary

The dead are shown with covers while skeletons without organic remains or unidentifiable objects are shown without a cover. The skin and organs mark the difference when it comes to the dress code for corpses. The more the dead body resembles a living person the more the dead body will be covered, thus applying living standards to the deceased. Dead bodies are not touched by the investigators without using gloves. This represents a social barrier between the pathologist and the corpse, which is necessary because of contamination but also modesty. The intimacy of the pathologist's touch is detached by the use of gloves. The corpses are rarely ever presented on their own, unless in spiritual or comedic situations. In contrast to *Six Feet Under,* the dead are depicted solely as autopsy objects in the other programs. Occasionally, the eyes are open, and body parts, organs, bones or the process of dissection are shown. The shows provide close-ups of the dissection and exceptional "insights" into the viscera through new visual effects. Furthermore, the simulation of the killing, the process of dissection, and the viscera are depicted even more lusciously and colourfully through various special effects. These new representations will be discussed in a later chapter. The depictions of the pathological environment can be traced back to the 16th and 17th century where depictions of anatomy lectures displayed dissected bodies, anatomists, and even the public audience. (Sappol, 2002) As mentioned in chapter one, anatomy at that time was not just reserved for a small academic elite. According to Ariès, these early paintings combined elements of science, death, and desire, which not only provoked anxiety but also curiosity. (Ariès, 1988, p. 192) The new depiction codes combine elements of science and death with a hyper-stylish, high-tech, icy atmosphere and high gloss aesthetic, which will be exemplified in the following analyses. There has been a trend in audiovisual stereotyping at the beginning of the twenty-first century, i.e. the generation of conventional patterns that reduce complexity such as quality, quantity, dynamic, and presence. (Schweinitz, 2006, p. XI) Hence, in reality, there can be many different forms of forensic environments and different shapes of dead bodies. Typifying this is the classical stretched-out body on a table with closed eyes, Y scar, and covered sexual organs in a bluish, fluorescent atmosphere which dominates the current representation in TV shows dealing with dead bodies. These images are categorised as modern depictions. In the continuous depiction process these images initially seemed to be somewhat new and outstanding and then, through reiterative representations, they become worn out and reduced to bare semantic signals. Therefore, finer characteristics were developed, newer ones invented and others combined with the older codes. For example, the basic atmosphere of a bluish, dark cold remains constant and newer characteristics combine these aestheticisation codes with more colourful elements such as the display of blood, viscera, and bones allowing for an altered presentation. Additional genre elements such as horror or comedy add to the new model, the breach of style. The essential codes of representation changed only modestly and continuously provide the same unique idea about the dead in pathology. The scientific atmosphere in the sterile environment is cold and calm. The pathologists care about the protection of the intimacy of the dead. The objectification of the decedent and the violation of the dead body can be explained and justified with forensic interest and the need to solve a crime. Yet, most conspicuous are the significant blank spaces in this discourse: The dead cannot lose control of their bodily functions. Even facial expressions of the dead are mostly shown as equally controlled and composed.

The modern depiction model contains dead representations, which display the dead as an object of forensic interest. The violent action against the dead in form of forensic treatments appears as a common characteristic, either shown as actions or through traces of actions such as the Y incision. The breach of style depiction model, however, stages the body as an object of art. The trend towards aestheticisation and civilising is seen in the dominant depiction of embellished, dressed, and sterile dead persons. The objectification of the dead can be seen by the use of the dead body as a source of evidence, while the rather subjectifying attributions are caused by the different dress codes. The trend towards more violence against the dead can be seen in the increasing display of pathology procedures performed on the body.

3.2.4. Fantasy comedy

Dead Like Me[16] and Pushing Daisies[17]

Like the previous TV shows, *Dead Like Me* and *Pushing Daisies* mostly initiate an episode with a death. While the dead in *Pushing Daisies* are also linked to crimes, the dead in *Dead Like Me* are linked to fatal accidents. Both series differ from the previous shows through the use of a comedic narrative. The idea for the two series stems from Bryan Fuller, but while *Pushing Daisies* was nominated for three Golden Globes (and then got cancelled due to the writers strike), *Dead Like Me* got cancelled after a year.

	Dead Like Me	*Pushing Daisies*
Idea	Brian Fuller	Brian Fuller
Production	2003–2004	2007
Length	47 min	42 min
Episodes seen	till ep. 215	till ep. 212

Tab. 6: Fantasy Comedy Series

Dead Like Me is a TV show about a group of grim reapers. The main character Georgia, an 18 year old, dies after being hit by a toilet seat which fell down from the de-orbiting space station MIR. She turns into a member of the "external influence" division and is in charge of releasing the souls of people before they die in accidents, suicides, and homicides. She is then charged with ushering them into the afterlife. It rarely, therefore, displays pathological science. Furthermore, the dead are mainly seen before they die, while dying, and as ghosts after they have died. That means in contrast to the other shows the "rites de passage" are rendered significant rather than the place of the corpse in the narrative. In *Pushing Daisies* the main character Ned learns in early childhood that he has the ability to bring the dead back to life by touching them. By touching the reanimated person again, the person permanently "dies forever". Later this talent is discovered by a private investigator who offers Ned a deal to split the reward money for solved crimes where Ned assists by reanimating the dead to question

---

16 http://www.imdb.com/title/tt0348913/, June 25th, 2008
17 http://www.imdb.com/title/tt0925266/, June 25th, 2008

them about their own deaths, most often at the morgue or scene. The depiction of the dead resembles the shows mentioned previously. *Dead Like Me* rather concentrates on the dying and the undead, and the dead are less often depicted in a pathological environment. The show was cancelled after one year, so the analysis is brief and not conclusive. In rare scenes, they adapt the modern depiction model of dead body representations.

Dead Like Me

Modern Depiction

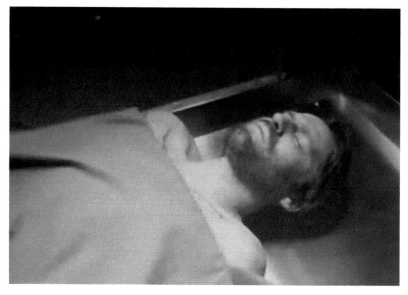

Fig. 3.12.: Dead Like Me–Dead body in pathology

Source: Episode 2

This image (Fig 3.12) shows a dead man on a clean metallic table, covered with a blue towel. Part of a Y scar can be seen. The camera perspective is a medium close shot from the position of an observer. The lighting is diffuse. Hence, representation resembles the forensic crime genre and the black comedy/drama genre. The only difference is the red floor which creates a contrasting, warm coloured background.

Pushing Daisies

Modern Depiction

This next image shows two people standing and a dead person on a stretcher from the cold storage. The corpse is covered with a blue sheet up to the chest. The person standing behind the stretcher is looking down at the body while another person is leaving the room. As in *Six Feet Under* and

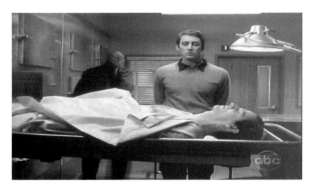

Fig. 3.13.: Pushing Daisies–Dead body before reanimation

Source: Episode 1

Dead Like Me the person next to the corpse wears no medical protective clothing, which can be seen as a distinguishing mark of the forensic context. The dead body lies in the foreground and the mid shot camera perspective is taken from the opposite side of the stretcher approximately at the same height as the stretcher. The unsaturated grey bluish tone, similar to previous shows, covers all objects and figures. The source of light is a lamp above the dead body and the ceiling lights. The image leaves the impression of a cold, dreary atmosphere like in *Six Feet Under*. In the second season this fantasy comedy changes the morgue's look (e.g. the background is rather green and more saturated colours are used) and varies the representations of corpses with more comedic elements.

Summary

To sum up, though the selected images show the classic horizontal stretched-out body on a table with closed eyes, Y scar, and covered sexual organs in a bluish atmosphere, the average dead person in both TV shows is seldom depicted in a pathological or mortuary environment. The dead body is mainly shown at the scene of death. After death occurs, a "personified soul" stands beside the corpse. In contrast to the crime shows, the fantasy comedy genre emphasises the subjectification of a decedent rather than an objectified forensic dimension.

These images are categorised as modern depictions, because the representations in morgues or pathological environments varies only moderately from the other TV show representations. Though we see a warm colour or casual wear instead of protective clothing, the idea about the dead in pathology described earlier remains constant. The dead body is covered and placed in a sterile, cold, and calm environment, and the trend towards aestheticisation and civilising is noticeable. The trend towards more violence is directed against the living rather than the dead. A comedic narrative that removes the harshness of the act of dying covers the more violent homicides and accidents. This comedic narrative can be seen as a form of domestication and will be further discussed in chapter 5.

3.2.5. Fantasy drama

Tru Calling[18], Heroes[19], and Dexter[20]

In this section, three very different shows are classified into one genre, because they follow the same science-fiction narrative, which goes beyond the usual criminal investigation plots. These shows resemble earlier ones with respect to cumulative and detailed depiction of dead bodies as in almost every episode a figure dies.

Tru Calling is a TV show that revolves around Tru, a young woman, who works in a morgue and wants to study medicine. She discovers that she

18 http://www.imdb.com/title/tt0364817/, July 2nd, 2008
19 http://www.imdb.com/title/tt0813715/, July 2nd, 2008
20 http://www.imdb.com/title/tt0773262/, April 9th, 2009

she has the ability to bring back the dead when they beg her for help. Shortly after broadcasting the show was cancelled while more aggressive series like *Heroes*, which include aesthetic depictions of killings, continued. Tru Calling contains elements of the crime genre. A whodunit aspect is present, as is the usage of crime scenes and the morgue as environmental settings in which the narrative of the story plays out. *Heroes* hardly focuses on crime investigations at all but instead on a saga about a group of people with superhuman abilities that could save the world. They are contrasted to the villain with superhuman abilities that murders and takes the brains of the other heroes in order to obtain their superhuman abilities. Usually, the victim and their open skull is seen.

Dexter, while focusing on killing , shows a "likeable" serial killer, who works in the police department as a specialist for blood spatter. During the day, Dexter investigates crime cases and if a criminal escapes justice, Dexter would "solve" this case after work. Indeed, the black humour and the episodic act of a "justified" killing as a form of vigilantism is the somewhat controversial new element, besides numerous images of blood spatters or bizarre dead body installations, which predominate the rare pathology depictions. The series started in 2006 on Showtime.

	Tru Calling	*Heroes*	*Dexter*
Production	2003–2004	2006–present	2006
Idea	Jon Harmon Feldman	Tim Kring (from Crossing Jordan)	Jeff Lindsay and James Manos
Length	40–45 min	40–45 min	50 min
Episodes seen	till ep. 226	till ep. 34	till ep. 312

Tab. 7: Fantasy Drama Series

The basis of the image analysis in this section is different because of the distinct plots. In the previous analysis, the dead body was usually located in a pathology surrounding. A morgue is shown in *Tru Calling*, but *Heroes* hardly ever depicts the pathology department at all. However, it does frequently show corpses with open skulls. Hence, the analysis will consist of a morgue image and an open skull image. The stereotyped depiction regarding age, race, and gender is similar to the previous shows. Both shows present predominantly attractive white bodies, twice as often male dead bodies than female ones within an age range of 20 to 60 years.

Tru Calling and *Heroes* resemble each other in many respects. The crime genre coded aspects regarding age, race, and gender representations are an

example of this. They also resemble each other in terms of the cinemato-
graphic codes utilised, such as lighting and composition. The bluish tone
seems to overlay most of the corpse depictions. These depiction codes are
simple and stringent. Yet, in contrast to the crime show depiction codes,
horrifying elements take precedence to the forensic crime elements. In
Heroes the opening of the skull by a villain reminds one of a dissection by a
pathologist who wants to investigate the brain. Nevertheless, in fact, the
character Isaac dies, because his brain stores the superhuman abilities
which are wanted by the antagonist. In *Tru Calling* the dead wake up and
call for help. The awakening moment is horrific because Tru not only hears
the voices of the dead in her head, but sees the dead open their eyes, beg
for help and sometimes grab her arm. This usually happens during eve-
nings when Tru is alone in the morgue. These scenes are not seen in the
selected images as I analyse the dead not the undead.

Tru Calling

Modern depiction

This figure (Fig. 3.14) shows a female body on a clean table. Her body is
covered up to her shoulders with a white blanket. Her arms are placed on
the blanket. Next to the diagonal table stands a person reading a paper

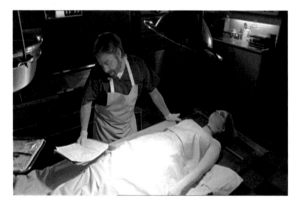

Fig. 3.14.:Tru Calling–Dead body in morgue

Source: Episode 9

while talking on the phone. The person wears blue scrubs, a blue apron, and white gloves. The floor has a red and grey check pattern. In the background a second table and a cupboard with tools can be seen. The camera perspective is a mid shot from a bird's eye view. The source of light is the lamp above the body. The overlaying bluish tone generates the same cold, clean, and calm atmosphere as in other genres. Only the lighting is so bright, that one can even recognise the check pattern on the floor. Besides the less elaborately designed scenery and lighting, all typical codes which mark the modern depiction are displayed.

Heroes

Breach of style

Heroes rarely displays pathology scenes. The two following images show a young cheerleader, who cannot die from her fatal injuries and wakes up in pathology only to realise that her chest has been opened.

Fig. 3.15.: Heroes–Cheerleader wakes up after autopsy

Source: Episode 4

These images are classified as breach of style, since they contain all of the typical features of the modern depiction model of the deceased such as aestheticisation, civilising, objectification, and violence, but they are displayed in a new context. The dead person is alive. Like in *NCIS* an actual living person is dissected.

I selected the TV show *Heroes* because of the emergence of dissected corpses in nearly every episode. While dead victims also appear in other TV shows in crime scenes, the victims in *Heroes* were special, because they all had to suffer surgical operations, i.e. most of the victims are found with open skulls at the crime scene.

The image shows the death of the character Isaac, which is typical of victim presentation. The first image shows a dead person lying on the floor with his head cut in two. The lower part shows the face with closed eyes

Fig. 3.16.: Heroes–Cheerleader wakes up after autopsy

Source: Episode 4

Fig 3.17.: Heroes–Victim killed by villain

Source: Episode 19

and an open mouth. The cranium lies next to the corpse. The body lies diagonally, starting in the middle of the picture covering the right hand side of the picture. The diffuse lighting is reflected on the clothing. The camera perspective is a medium close shot from the position of an observer. The image is tinged in blue. The bluish, pale colouring supports a cold and calm atmosphere. In contrast to the rooms, however, mess and disorder is depicted, which is discernible in a small detail, namely the hairstyle of the victim is messy and bloodstained. Additionally, the dead body is not placed on a table and not embellished in a safe and clean environment. All previous shows described, represent the initial images of corpses in a sometimes bloody or messy environment at a crime scene. However, by the end of the show, the final image of the body is in a cold and calm pathology lab. In *Heroes* the liberating representation of safety, silence, and beauty is missing. The images are classified as breach of style, because forensic crime elements are used for a non-scientific context and additionally, constant recurring comic paintings mark the transition from the modern depiction model to the breach of style depiction model.

Fig. 3.18.: Heroes–Painting of the killing

Source: Episode 118

Dexter

Modern Depiction

In *Dexter*, the environment differs from the other shows as well. Instead of a morgue, pathology or embalming room it is the rooms in which Dexter kills his victims that are shown. The pathology lab is not designed for the

Fig. 3.19.: Dexter–Killing the villain

Source: Episode 201

Fig. 3.20:. Dexter–Dissected body found without blood

Source: Episode 101

plot, since the victim is at the same time the perpetrator who committed a crime. Neither the police nor the law can get a hold of the perpetrator, but Dexter does. The killing rooms are presented in a similar fashion to the rooms in the other TV shows. A table, tools, and a person in a supine position on the table and a standing person next to the table are seen. The person on the table is not dressed, but covered with cellophane, while the standing person wears protective clothing such as gloves and lab coats. The lighting and camera work resembles *CSI*. There is violent action against the body in the name of justice, however. The major difference is, of course, that the body is alive at the beginning of the procedure and show and deceased afterwards.

Breach of style

This image (Fig. 3.20) shows parts of a dead body on the ground. The body parts are separated from one another but arranged like the human body. The parts are placed on a tarpaulin in a swimming pool without water and a blanket is placed behind the upper part of the body. Neither blood nor a head is seen, but bloodless parts of the legs and wrapped up upper parts of the body. In the upper left hand corner of the image, the legs of a person can be seen. The selected perspective shows the body parts from a crouching observer's perspective looking towards the feet. The lighting conditions imitate daylight in a bright, bluish environment. The style of the dead body presentation consists of the combination of separated, lilac body parts and brown, wrapped parts. The environment and the dead body representation differ from previously described images, because the body is not lifted on a table but on a tarpaulin, the colour of the body is lilac rather than blue, the body is dissected into parts and the head is missing. Instead of covering sheets, wrapping paper was used to cover the genitals. This depiction differs from the others because of the distinct narrative, which contains different genre elements including black comedy and mystery. The dissection of the body without any blood splatters or organic remains, is reminiscent of the clean pathology environment. The arrangement of the dead body seems as artificial as the dead body representation in other shows. In summary, besides the lighting and perspective, the image consists of the same representation codes used in the other crime shows. The image is classified as breach of style, because instead of the display of a dead body, an installation, almost a piece of body artwork, is shown.

Summary

Tru Calling displays modern depiction, which consists of the classical body stretched-out on a table in a supine position with closed eyes, wounds, and covered intimate areas. The bluish or grey lighting is constant in all the images. Like in the fantasy genre, the representation codes differ only slightly from the forensic crime TV shows and provide the same idea about the dead being placed in a sterile, cold, and calm pathological environment. The trend towards aestheticisation, civilising, objectifying and subjectifying is clearly seen in *Tru Calling*. On *Heroes* the trend towards more violence against the dead is recognisable, and the actions against the body are not justified by looking for evidence. *Heroes* presents the dead as abstract, horrifying art-like objects. *Dexter* has the same trends and since it is broadcast on a subscription channel, the show is more explicit in its depictions, which lead to these exceptional breach of styles.

3.3. Summary

"Death is now becoming what it had ceased to be since the very end of the Romantic era, the subject of an inexhaustible supply of anecdotes [...]"(Ariès, 1975, p.135f). As Thomas Macho (1987) and Armin Nassehi (2003) commented: Death has became a chatty topic. This talkativeness can be found in the media.

"Indeed, the dead body, especially when represented in visual media, is treated as a highly spectacular object, and the dead body at autopsy becomes the most spectacular. To follow the pathologist behind the closed door, which is not closed so very tightly any longer in contemporary Western culture" (Klaver, 2006, p. 140).

TV Genres have various options for depicting corpses. Some broadcasting stations have more possibilities for depiction of the dead than others do and but together they represent the current media discourse. An evaluation of TV shows revealed a changing attitude towards death from denial to rapprochement or even taming which can, in general, be proven by the large amount of new pictorial material in the media and, in particular, by a corresponding pictorial discourse. I have argued that once the modern depiction model and the breach of style depiction model replaced the traditional depiction model, a new representational system of death emerged in TV shows of the 21st century. The dominance of certain trends has shown that modern depiction models and breach of style depictions have superseded the previous models. With the exception of the documentary all TV shows present actors or mannequins on tables in a supine position surrounded by the living as the ultimate representation of the dead body. Typical biological processes such as excretions are not shown in any TV show. Contamination, exposure, and the movement of the body are not seen. The efforts to hide these processes reveal the strong cultural need for civilising the human body even after death. In genres like drama/black comedy or fantasy/comedy the dead body meets subjectifying attributions through covering and clothing codes or "interactions" with the living. The dead body also serves as a projection screen for different ideas of afterlife or the anxieties about death experienced by the survivors. In the forensic crime genre, the objectification of a dead body is carried out by the representation of the dead body as a source of information revealing crime clues and mediating anatomical knowledge. Depending on the narrative, the status or identity of the dead body oscillates between objectifying and subjectifying. However, especially in the forensic crime and comedy genres scenes containing violent actions against the dead are present. During autopsy, the pathologist performs a constructive destruction of the dead body. This violence against a dead body is hereby justified by law. In contrast to the forensic crime genre, the fantasy comedy genre shows fatal violence against the living as a form of slapstick. The climax of this comedy is usually reached when a figure dies in an unexpected and absurd accident. The comedy genre provides the "justification" of the violence against the body through the comedic narrative. The connection between these trends and the depiction models can be seen in the following table (Tab.: 8).

The number of depictions of corpse representation has risen enormously since 2000 and generated a huge variety of images in different genres of television programs. The variety of depictions encompasses (1) the Simulation of the Authentic with images of real decedents, (2) the Traditional Depiction with either no images of the dead or images with covered dead, (3) the Modern Depiction with plain images of aesthetic corpses and finally (4) the Breach of Style Depiction with abstract images of corpses. This variety supports the conclusion that on the one hand a more open and liberated exposure to death has taken place in the media discourse while on the other hand, depictions of the dead are structured by certain image trends, which replace authentic views of corpses in order to domesticate death.

Depiction models	Simulation of the authentic	Traditional Depiction	Modern Depiction	Breach of Style Depiction
	Family Plots	Quincy M.E., North Mission Road	CSI Las Vegas, NCIS, Crossing Jordan, Bones, Dexter, Six Feet Under, Dead Like Me, Pushing Daisies	Six Feet Under, Dexter, Heroes
Aestheticisation	None	High	High	Extra High
Civilising	None	Low	Medium	Low
Subjectification	None	None	Medium	Low
Objectification	None	Low	High	Extra High
Violation	None	None	High	Extra High

Tab. 8: Depiction models in connection with genres

4 Film Analysis: Disgusting autopsies in pathology

As previously shown corpses in the television shows are usually represented by aesthetically pleasing actors and actresses lying on tables. This, however, is only one facet of the new representation of corpses. The well-known motive of the beautification of deceased females in art and literature, described in Elisabeth Bronfen's work "Over Her Dead Body" (1992),[1] is now not only outnumbered by the altered male dead, but is accompanied by numerous depictions of corpses, which are mutilated, decomposed, bloated, chopped up, dissected, acid-burnt or only extant in pieces. The depictions of various autopsy scenes represent the corpses as disgusting by juxtaposing them to the embellished, pristine and stylish environment. This particular staging turns the image as a whole into an aesthetic image.

What then do "disgusting", "beautiful" or "aesthetic" mean in the context of media representation? According to Menninghaus (2003),[2] the corpse is already the emblem of disgust.[3] For the exploration of disgust he selects the following three fundamental features as a general pre-understanding of the term: "[…] (1) The violent repulsion vis-à-vis, (2) a physical presence or some other phenomenon in our proximity, (3) which at the

---

1 Izima Kaoru "Landscape of corpses" (2008) displays in his work again the old motive of the beautiful female dead. His models are alive and staged as if they were dead.

2 Menninghaus statements are based on his evaluation of several empirical studies (Menninghaus, 2003)

3 "The decaying corpse is therefore not only one among many other foul smelling and disfigured objects of disgust. Rather, it is the emblem of the menace that, in the case of disgust, meets with such a decisive defense, as measured by its extremely potent register on the scale of unpleasurable affects. Every book about disgust is not least a book about the rotting corpse. The fundamental schema of disgust is the experience of a nearness that is not wanted"(Menninghaus, 2003, p. 1).

same time in various degrees, can also exert a subconscious attraction or even an open fascination" (Menninghaus, 2003, p. 6).

All three features apply to the corpse; especially the third. This becomes evident when witnessing the success of horror, crime or action movies, which show representations of corpses, or at least the menace of death through corpses. The corpses are presented through either a living body of an actor, who plays dead, or a latex simulacrum which was never alive and therefore cannot be dead. The actual re-enactment then should not stir up any feelings of anxiety, disgust or curiosity among the spectators. Yet, according to the success of these depictions, they arouse a fascination, which might be connected with the feelings of anxiety, disgust and curiosity. This is the topic of this chapter; namely, how do producers stage the corpses as disgusting objects in an aesthetic way, so that the audience does not turn away in disgust, but rather remains enthralled?

Different genres use different techniques and by comparing a documentary, which aims at being the most authentic form of representation, to a popular TV crime show, I want to reveal how the popular TV show stages the corpse in an aesthetic way; beautiful but provoking a simultaneous disgust. I researched Michael Kriegsman's documentary *Autopsy: Through the Eyes of Death's Detectives* (2000), which presents a complete and uncensored autopsy conducted by Dr. Thomas Noguchi, a former Los Angeles County Coroner at the UCLA Hospital in Los Angeles. I will compare the documentary footage presented with a TV crime show sequence from *CSI: Down the Drain* (2004).

By revealing the media aesthetic techniques used when staging a dead body, I will first argue that the genres produce genre-compatible representations of the corpse. "Genre compatible" means that, for instance, TV crime shows work extensively with media aesthetic techniques and, therefore, the corpse representation will be very different from the corpse representation in the documentary. Secondly, I will argue that the display of the corpse in a TV crime show is not only different, but omits what an authentic documentary displays regarding signs of age, impurity and the lack of self-control. Hence, first, I will elaborate on how the dead are staged with the help of media aesthetic techniques. In comparison to the documentary, I will then subsequently show which details are omitted in this process.

4.1. Media Aesthetics

A common complaint (Schulze 1997, Mueller 1992, Honneth 1992) of the culture critic is the increase of aestheticisation through audiovisual media during the last century. Postmodern theorists claim that audiovisual media has replaced direct confrontation and that aestheticisation has taken over the construction of reality. In this cultural debate, aestheticisation, used in everyday speech, means pretty, beautiful or pleasing. (Schweppenhaeuser, 2007) Wolfgang Welsch (1996, p. 55)[4], rightly, however, detects a tableau of different meanings for the term.

Firstly, there is the aestheticisation of daily life, such as the stylised shaping of our environment and the development of leisure and event culture, as well as economic transformations. Secondly, he discusses the technological and media aestheticisation of material and social reality. This concerns the transformation in the production of material, as well as the construction of reality through media. Thirdly, he identifies the aestheticisation of our moral orientation and attitudes towards life, i.e. the self-styling of the Individual, the aestheticisation of body, soul and mind. In a fourth point, he states that the epistemological aestheticisation is the result of the three preliminary stages. Reality turns into a construction derived from art. Reality is produced, modified and uncommitted. Aestheticisation, therefore, means that a general trend has taken place that is concerned with the aestheticisation of non-aesthetics in all these differently described forms. Something is applied to the aesthetic context, respectively staged within an aesthetic context, which was applied to another context before.

This tableau shows the inherent semantic difficulties of the term "aesthetic", which is according to Welsch as old as the discipline of aesthetics itself. The term "aesthetic" is connected with the description "pretty or beautiful", with staging like "styling or virtualisation" and with an alterable point of reference when it comes to the characteristics of an object, an associate dimension or constructions of reality. (Welsch, 1996, p. 22) At the same time, the aesthetic stimulus satiation can lead to an opposite ef-

---

4 Four forms of aesthetic: 1. Prettifying surface aestheticisation of everyday life (Verhübschende Oberflächenästhetisierung des Alltags) 2. Sustained technological and media aestheticisation of material and social reality (Tiefergehende technologische und medial bedingte Ästhetisierung unser materiellen wie sozialen Wirklichkeit). 3. Sustained aestheticisation of social attitudes (Ebenso tiefreichende Ästhetisierung unserer lebenspraktischen Einstellungen und moralische Orientierung). 4. Epistemological aestheticisation (Epistemologische Ästhetisierung). (Welsch, 1996, p.55).

fect; where everything is beautiful, but nothing remains beautiful. According to Welsch (1996, p. 57) a basic law of aestheticisation says that perception needs not only stimulation but also disruptions and breaks. Constant stimulation provokes blunting.[5] Therefore, aesthetics need interruptions from beautification; otherwise the aesthetic turns into anaesthesia. Nelson Goodman (1995)[6] mentions the same idea and states that the aesthetic also includes ugliness; otherwise a scale for aesthetic values cannot be established. Since such beautiful images are not always pretty but evidently ugly, the term "beautiful" leads only to another deceptive term for aesthetic values. (Goodman, 1995, p. 235)[7] According to Claudio La Rocca (2006), the history of the relationship between beauty and ugliness is quite complex. It is a slow process of monopolisation, which integrates former hindrances of aesthetic experiences, like ugliness into the theory of aesthetics, can be stated. During the nineteenth century ugliness was not part of the aesthetic discourse; though ugly artwork has a long tradition which can be traced back to the ancient world. According to Klemme, Pauen and Raters (2006) the most important phases took place in the eighteenth and nineteenth centuries, through the literature of E.T.A. Hoffmann, Edgar Allan Poe and Charles Baudelaire who presented, for the first time, the ugly, the horrible and disgusting. This trend continues today in art and media.[8] During the nineteenth century, scientists from different disciplines[9]

---

5 "Ein ästhetisches Grundgesetz besagt, dass unsere Wahrnehmung nicht nur Belebung und Anregung, sondern auch Verweilen, Ruhezonen und Unterbrechungen braucht. Dieses Gesetz verurteilt die derzeit grassierende Verschönerungstendenz zum Scheitern. Die Totalästhetisierung läuft auf ihr Gegenteil hinaus. Wo alles schön wird, ist nichts mehr schön; Dauererregungen führen zur Abstumpfung; Ästhetisierung schlägt in Anästhetisierung um. Gerade ästhetische Gründe sprechen also dafür, den Ästhetisierungstrubel zu durchbrechen. Inmitten der Hyperästhetisierung tun ästhetische Brandflächen not. Ästhetische Reflexion wird sich nicht zum Agenten einer Ästhetisierung machen lassen, die in Wahrheit auf Anästhetisierung hinausläuft–auf die Erzeugung von Unempfindlichkeit, auf Betäubung durch ständige ästhetische Überdrehtheit" (Welsch, 1996, p.57).

6 This statement attaches the argumentation of Goodman who applied himself to the definition of aesthetization and the "paradox of ugliness" According to Goodman aesthetic experiences with certain art work can not only evoke boredom but also negative emotions such as anxiety, hate and disgust. These art works can give rise to purify the viewer from held back negative emotions. Art therefore is not only balm but therapy. (Goodman, 1995, p. 227)

7 Cf. Menninghaus, 2003

8 Especially horror movies pull interest to define the actual fascination of the ugliness, which is why Aurel Kolnai, the father of the disgust theory, stated that disgust cannot

started to describe and define ugliness, followed by even more scientists in the twentieth and twenty-first centuries, trying to explain the pleasure of the public in consuming ugliness through art and media.[10] They all faced similar issues. Yet the most important issue seems to be whether ugliness can be measured on an objective scale or only from a subjective perspective.

One can see from this brief explanation that terms like aesthetics or ugliness can only be used with caution for visual examination because of the immediate questions they raise about objectivity and validity. Obviously, a proportionately disgusting detail in a pretty picture or installation can be just another stimulus for its aesthetic value. Welsch mentions aestheticisation as relating to the construction of reality through media. In order to describe the media representations precisely, I decided to use the more specialised term "media aesthetic". Herbert Zettl (2008) for instance works with the term "media aesthetic", which reverses the above-mentioned difficulties:

"Media aesthetics differs considerably from the traditional aesthetic theories. Rather than proffering scholarly arguments about what is beautiful and not, and what is art and not, applied media aesthetics is more concerned with how we, as an

---

only be confined to the phenomenology but also to psychology and aesthetic. (Kolnai, 2007, p. 29)

9 For instance Gottlieb Alexander Baumgarten, Immanuel Kant, Georg Wilhelm Friedrich Hegel and first and foremost Karl Rosenkranz.

10 For instance Gotthold Ephraim Lessing, Moses Mendelsohn and Theodor Adorno and most important Umberto Eco. In contrast to the previous elaboration Umberto Eco (2007) avoids these considerations and claims that one has to take in consideration that ugliness just like beauty has been a cultural conception which has changed over the time. Eco asks if ugliness can continue to be defined simply as the absence of beauty or even as the opposite of beauty. He also asks whether a history of ugliness can be seen as the congruent contrast of a history of beauty. (Eco, 2007, p.16) He then refers to Karl Rosenkranz (1853) and his list of different forms of ugliness and claims, since Rosenkranz detected so many different terms of ugliness, ugliness is not only the opposite of beauty. Eco then works out three different manifestations of ugliness: At first, he defines "the ugliness by itself" which can be for instance a decaying body that elicit strong emotions of disgust. He then defines secondly "the formal ugliness", which for instance entails disequilibrium of proportions. An example would be a picture, which is considered as ugly due to bad handcraft, but the picture does not provoke any passionate emotions. Third, the "artistic representation of both", ugliness by itself and formal ugliness together, which Eco characterizes through the accurate rendition of ugliness which reverses the effect: the artwork represents the emulated ugliness, but through the professional artwork the picture seems beauty. (Eco, 2007, p. 20)

audience, perceive certain aesthetic variables and their combinations in television and film productions. It recognises that the medium is anything but neutral, and that, in moving from idea to image, the aesthetic and technical requirements of the medium determine to a large extent how the message is shaped" (Zettl, 2002, p. 12).

He designed a theoretical framework with five fundamental elements to provide basic criteria for the examination of audio-visual media. These are (1) light and colour, (2) two-dimensional space (area, vectors, and forces), (3) three-dimensional space (screen volume, point of view, and camera) (4) time and motion (motion vectors, editing) and (5) sound (literal, non-literal). (Zettl, 2002) With these elements Zettl covers all media aesthetic techniques used in the production process of a movie. According to Trebess (2006, p. 255), the term media aesthetic encompasses all the design details of technical images, i.e. all the used camera and audio-visual techniques. The examination of these techniques serves: " […] the study of certain sense perceptions and how these perceptions can be most effectively clarified, intensified, and interpreted through a medium, such as television or film, for a specific recipient" (Zettl, 2008, p. 2).

How can I operationalize and measure media aestheticisation? I will describe the use of media aesthetic techniques as used in documentaries and TV crime shows, and then will continue to examine the most evident differences of the use of media aesthetic techniques in the two genres. There are specific issues when it comes to the choice of an appropriate film analysis method. Since the focus of attention is on the representation of the dead body, I had to find an adequate analytic technique for this research object to cover all necessary aspects and at the same time, exclude any redundant information. Eventually after searching through various kinds of analysis schemata, the previously used pictorial analysis from Mueller-Doohm (1997) together with analysis techniques by Thomas Kuchenbuch (2005) and others regarding the visual and audio level,[11] provided a frame that turned out to be broad enough to meet these requirements. The descriptive framework resembles Zettl's five dimensions, which is why I have decided to use that frame for the following examination and add the contextual implication from Zettl in the reconstructive part. The schemata and analysis levels are described in the chapter on methodology.

---

11 Borstnar, Pabst, & Wulff 2008, Hickethier 1993, Monaco 2000, Zettl 1995, Bordwell & Thompson 2003

4.2. Film Analysis: *Autopsy* (Documentary)[12]

The selection of film material is determined on the one hand by the search for documentary that works as little as possible with media aesthetic techniques and on the other hand by the search for a popular fictitious TV show. The aim is to reveal the different representations of an autopsy in these two genres, i.e. to detect the additional media aesthetic techniques used within the visual and audio level in the fictitious TV show genre in comparison to the genre of TV documentary. The range of productions within the documentary genre varies from unaltered documentaries with real life situations to documentaries with re-enactments. The selection of material within the documentary genre was less difficult since there were only two documentations of autopsies available on the market. Michael Kriegsman's documentary *Autopsy: Through the Eyes of Death's Detectives* (1999)[13] was selected because, like the fictitious TV show, it was also filmed in Los Angeles (at the UCLA Medical Centre in cooperation with the Los Angeles County Coroner's Office). Another reason was that it was also produced within the same time span as the crime television show. This documentary contains interviews with pathologists and the filmmaker, which according to the producer; represent a holistic image of the work of a pathologist. The two DVDs have a play length of 100 minutes; the autopsy scene takes approximately 40 minutes. The documentary *Autopsy* consists of three parts with a respective length of 12:29 minutes, 19:50 minutes and 06:50 minutes.

The analysis starts with the visual level (light design, camera, setting/room space relation, storyline). The following describes techniques that are predominantly present. The light is a hard light; the key light is of a normal style with fill light and back light. Cast shadows are present. The colour is natural; no special filter and no special effects are used. The ceiling camera, however, produces a different lightening; less bright and less saturated. Most of the time bright hard floodlights illuminate the scene. The producer has avoided special effects such as filters. The colours of a silver table, pink/white/reddish skin, white towels and yellow/red tissue, are all very saturated and appear at times overly luscious. All objects in the front of the shot are clearly visible. A cross dissolve is used when the ca-

---

12 The description part for the documentation and for the TV show coincides with the respective reconstruction part in order to avoid too many repetitions.

13 www.autopsyvideo.com The video is only available through a website on the internet.

mera cuts to different view-points. Sometimes the camera would move and take panning shots. Different camera perspectives such as a high angle, low angles, and bird's eye view are also used, as were different shots like the medium shot, medium close-up shots and close-ups. The setting consists of a silver table on which a body lies. The body is placed horizontal on the table. The body is a naked, old, overweight woman, who gleams moistly on the damp table. Her face is covered either by a towel or with a visual special effect (VFX). Her genitals are covered in the same manner though pubic hair can be seen. Her nipples are covered with another VFX. Her hair is wet and rumpled. At the end of the procedure the upper chest and head are open, and all her organs have been removed. Other objects in the room include seating, and a little table with medical tools, placed on the silver table. In the background there is an x-ray reader, a TV screen, a room divider, and tiled yellow walls. Further into the procedure, we also see various different people in the background. The three people, two doctors and one technician, wear scrubs and protection suits as well as surgical masks. They move and pull the body around; the body's buttocks and breasts are clearly visible. The clean silver table turns into a working space displaying the wet and gleaming organs, bloody towels, tools, a red tube and a bucket with reddish water, filled up with organs. I divide the autopsy scene into three parts; first the exterior examination and then the interior examination, consisting of both the opening of the upper chest and the opening of the skull. The following storyline describes the exterior examination (Fig. 4.1.):

Fig. 4.1.: Autopsy–Documentary

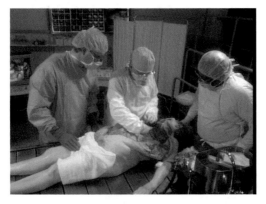

Fig. 4.2.: Autopsy–Documentary

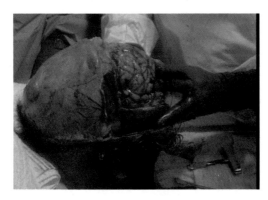

Fig. 4.3.: Autopsy–Documentary

Storyline: The small person in the middle nods to the person on the right side, who then pulls the sheet from the table. He uncovers a naked, overweight body lying on the table. The middle person talks while, in turn,

Fig. 4.4.: Autopsy–Documentary

looking at the left person and the body. The right person puts a towel over the head of the person lying on the table. The middle person holds a loupe above the body of the person lying on the table. He palpates with his right hand over the back of the body while continuing to talk. The middle person with yellow gloves runs his hands over the back of the body, while the other hand holds the loupe. His hand runs down from the back to the buttocks, thighs and lower legs. The person on the right side puts his hands (blue gloves) on the lower legs of the body. The body skin colour is both bright and dark pink. One can clearly see the red coloured spaces above and below the buttocks, as well as wrinkles between the buttocks and thighs. The feet are also wrinkled. The middle person runs his hands back towards the buttocks and lifts the hand of the body. The hand has a pink colouration, but with a darker pink below the fingernails and a yellow-brown colouration in the protruding nail. The thumb has red marks on it. The middle person rubs the fingers. The middle person then bends over the body and lifts up its other hand, while holding the loupe above. He rubs the fingers. The camera moves backwards and a third person becomes fully visible. The middle person runs his hand over the arm of the body, while talking and looking in turn at the arm or to the left person. The left person bends over and looks at the arm. The middle person runs his hands over the head of the body, after the left person has removed the towel from the head of the body. The middle person moves around the table to the top of it. Only the head and the shoulder of the body and the hands of the middle person and one hand of the left person are visible. The middle person rubs the head of the body, while the other hand holds the loupe. The left person moves to the long side of the table. He holds a bottle and puts liquid on the back of the body. The two other people are watching him. The right person puts the liquid behind him on the table. Then he bends over the body on the table and lifts the opposite arm. The middle person puts the loupe on the table and bends over too. The middle person blocks the movement of the right person and puts the arm down again. He looks in the direction of the camera while talking. He then tries to put the right arm of the body on the table beneath the body. The arm moves out again. The right person also tries to move the arm back. The middle person now puts his right arm under the left leg of the body and grabs the right leg, while he pushes the right arm of the body again beneath the body. The arm slips back again. He then pulls the body to the edge of the table, grabs the left shoulder in order to turn the body around. The body slips back to the middle of the table. The right person puts a sponge into the little water bucket next to the tab and supports the middle person by lifting up the head. The middle person tries to move the blocking arms underneath the body and then pulls the arm from the other side. Then they turn the body over into a supine position. The middle person covers the private parts with a towel, as does the right person with the head of the body. The middle person takes up the loupe and investigates the upper body part. He turns the head of the body with one hand while bending over the body with his loupe. The middle person rubs the chest area of the body, the upper left arm, lower arm, lifts the hands and rubs the fingers. The middle person runs his hands over the shoulder and neck of the body.

The exterior examination was accomplished within 02:30 minutes. The camera perspective and lights changed several times. I will now proceed with the interior examination, which is divided into the opening of the upper body part and the opening of the skull.

The opening of the upper body part is as follows (Fig. 4.2.):

The middle person positions the head so that it faces front. He puts his fingers into the mouth of the head and moves them around. He then removes his hand and closes the mouth. The right person gives him a towel so the middle person can dry his fingers on it. The middle person bends over to a little tray on the table and puts back the loupe. Instead he takes a scalpel and leans back. He moves the towel lying over the private parts slightly back. The middle person holds the scalpel in the right hand; the other hand rests on the neck of the body. He inserts the scalpel into the right shoulder of the body and cuts until the middle of the chest, where the solar plexus is. Next he cuts from the left shoulder down to the same middle point. He then puts his hand on this point and cuts down below the navel. This results in a Y incision. The middle person pulls up the skin on the right side next to the shoulder and, with the scalpel, detaches the skin from the adipose tissue and muscles. The close-up shot to the upper body part reveals irregularities of the surface skin. The colour of the fat tissue beneath the skin is lusciously yellow. The soft tissue is red. The colours appear very saturated. The middle person pulls the skin aside while detaching it and the adipose tissue from the flesh with the scalpel on the right side. His hand slips while pulling up the skin. He grabs the skin again and continues on the other side. He cuts a triangle in front of the head. A triangle is cut into the skin, which is pulled in the opposite direction and covers the head. The wax-like skin contrasts with the luscious colours of the soft tissue and the fat tissue. The white towel does not cover the pubic hair, which protrudes out from underneath. The middle person cuts deeper into the skin on the stomach towards the naval again. He yanks at the skin and cuts further on it. It seems as if the skin with the adipose tissue becomes thicker and, therefore, harder to cut through. The face is now half-covered by the skin part of the chest. The thorax, with some soft red tissue attached, is now visible as is the brown and green-coloured viscera. The middle person, using the scalpel, detaches the skin from the flesh. The Y incision opens up while the middle person also strips off the skin. The middle person holds the skin up and strips it with hacking cuts off the flesh. The right and the left person are watching. The skin from the upper body hangs left and right sideways down. The viscera are visible, mostly yellow, red and brownish in colour. The middle person pushes with their hand on the thorax. The middle person cracks the ribs of the thorax with lopping shears.[14] The left person has put his hands on the hips of the body. There is a close-up on the face of the middle person, who works with heavy breathing. The camera moves back down to the body. With one hand he holds the right side of the chest while with the other, he continues cutting into the flesh through the ribs with the forceps. He puts both hands on the pair of forceps in order to crack the rib, and then he moves the pair of forceps jerkily to the left and right side. The middle person pushes the thorax with his left hand again. Then he exchanges tools with the left person, who puts down a towel, a pair of scissors and the scalpels next to the head of the body. The middle person, by making cuts, detaches the upper part of the thorax. He holds up a part while cutting into the tissue. The left person has put his hands on the left thigh of the body and holds the wrist with the other hand. At the same time, the middle person continues to detach the upper part of the thorax. Then the thorax is completely detached, and the middle person passes it to the right person. The middle person digs his hand under the red tissue and moves around inside, whilst looking up to where the side camera is. Next to the head of the body lies the upper part of the thorax. Three sponges swim inside the water basin. The middle person moves his hands inside the thorax. From this angle, the wet legs of the body shine brightly. The blue gloves are now wet and are stained a little red at the fingers. Liquids are to be seen on the left side. The middle person cuts around the heart. He then runs his hands over it, pushing at some points. The water in the basin has turned reddish. A scalpel and a blood-spattered towel are placed to the left of the body's head. Towels, instruments, and organs surround the head. The middle person has the head in his hand and is shaking it whilst explaining. An opened heart, bloody gloves and blood clots inside the heart are to be seen. He cuts open the heart above the thorax. He lays the heart on the thorax, respectively the open viscera, and talks about what is inside. He detaches the clot from the inside of the heart and puts it on a sponge, which is then handed over to the right person. The middle person removes additional blood clot from the heart. The water in the basin has now turned dark red. The middle person bends over, submerges the heart into the water basin, and moves his hand around. Middle Person scratches blood clots away from the inside of the heart. The middle person puts a knife into the heart and cuts it open on the viscera of the body. He pulls clots stings out of the

---

14 Technical terms are used in reference to Dolinak, Matshes & Lew, 2005

heart. He puts them into water and again begins to touch the surface of the inside of the heart. He places the heart in the red water basin. His gloves are now bloody, as is the knife. The middle person continues cutting the heart and scratching the blood off the surface. Using the knife, he pricks the heart's surface. He then cuts it into slices and puts it into the water of the basin. The left and middle persons move over to the towel-covered little table, which lies on the bigger table. The middle person puts the heart on the towel and discusses it with the left person. The right person joins them, bringing with a water tube with, which he cleans the blood from the table. He weights the heart, shaking it up and down. All three laugh about a joke. They return back to the body. The right person, with a scoop, ladles the blood out of the open thorax and dries it with a sponge. The middle person lifts the reddish-pink left lung up and scratches blood off it with the knife. He pulls the lounge up and, with the knife, detaches it from the connecting tissue. He tries to lift the lounge up but it slips. He pulls out some more blood clots strings. The middle person puts the left lounge on the little table again, runs his hands all over it and then starts slicing it into pieces. The right person cleans the table with the water tube. The middle person talks to the left person. He gets the right lounge out of the body, weights it on the table and palpates the organ. He slices this part off the lounge into pieces. He puts a piece of the lounge into a liquid-filled bottle, which is given to him by the right person. They return to the body and, with scissors, detach the liver.

The opening of the upper body part and removal of the organs is completed within 12:29 minutes. The second part of the autopsy includes 19:50 minutes of interior examinations.

The description continues with the opening of the scull (Fig. 4.3.):

The middle person carries the liver over to the little table. On the table is a pan, which is now filled with the heart and lung. The left person cleans the bloody towel with water on the little table. The middle person runs his hand over the liver, whilst explaining about it. He slices the liver in pieces and asks questions about it. He pushes the finger through the liver in order to show how soft the tissue is. Then he puts the pieces of organ into the pan. He returns to the body and moves around the guts, pulling up tissue. He bends over to get the scissors from the little table and uses them to detach the tissue from the body. He moves the guts around. The right person pulls the guts into the thorax area. The middle person detaches the kidneys and places them on the table. The left person transfers them to the

little table, where he slices them into pieces. The middle person detaches
the guts and organs from the body, while the right person pulls them up.
After they are detached, the right person carries the bunch of organs over
to the water basin, which is filled with red water and other organs. Water
runs over the top of the basin, when the organs are added, due to their
weight. He leaves the bunch of organs inside the basin. The middle person
moves his hand into the pelvis of the body and detaches the ovary. The
right person starts to cut around the head (with a scalpel from ear to ear
via the skullcap). The middle person, with a scoop, ladles blood out of the
body into the basin. He then cleans his gloves with a sponge. With jerky
movements, the right person detaches the skin from the skull using a small
scraper. He then tries hard to pull the skin in front of the head and over
the face. The towel slips down, and the face is then covered with its own
scalp skin. He lifts the head and puts an object under the head so that it
remains lifted. He slowly continues to cut between skin and skullcap, in
order to pull the skin further down. Now the right person drills the skullcap open. He holds the covered face with his right hand and drills verti-
cally with the left hand over the face and then horizontally over the skullcap. He detaches the skullcap in the front and back, by inserting the
scraper into the line and turning the scraper around. He then pulls the
skullcap apart from the tissue in between. The middle person takes the
head with the open brain and turns it to the right side. He dries the side
with a sponge. The right person detaches the brain from the tissue while
holding the already detached part in his hand. He hands the brain over to
the middle person. Blood drops from the brain. The middle person carries
the brain to the little table. Holding it up and running his hands over the
surface, he talks about its appearance. The towel is bloody. He then starts
slicing the brain into pieces and explaining the different parts of the brain.
The gloves are covered with brain tissues. All the examiners return to the
head and the middle person detaches the scalp tissues with his hand. The
right person pulls tissue from the inside of the scull with special scissors.
The right person lifts up the upper part of the body and moves the object
to under the back. Next he drills inside the open upper body part and then
alongside the spine. Afterwards he removes the spine by ripping out. He
hands the spine over to the middle person who checks it and puts it down
between the feet of the body. The drilling continues and the right person
cuts some tissue with scissors and then tweezers it out of the thorax. He
continues inside the scull and goes back to the thorax. The middle person,

meanwhile, explains the procedure. He removes the spinal cortex and hands it over to the middle person who puts it on the little table. The liver, heart, kidney, lungs and spine are placed on the little table. The middle person talks for a while. The right person can be seen sewing the upper part of the body together and reconditioning the scull by attaching the skullcap, pulling the skin back into its original position and then finally sewing the scalp together. (Fig. 4.4.)

To summarise, the result of the reconstruction is that the entire autopsy procedure of a dead person is documented, including the exterior examination and the interior examination by two physicians and a technician. The pathologist is hacking, hoisting, cutting, scratching, pulling and lifting organs, tissue and blood. The assistant drills around the skull. In between this, the organs are examined and sliced into pieces on an extra examining table. Meanwhile, the pathologists explain all the steps in a question and answer format with the assistant doctor. All the steps can be seen, even the final sewing up of the body's skin. Specific codes of representations can be found in the different categories. In the light and colour categories, hard light dominates over a normal lighting style; cast shadows and the yellow reddish colours of the corpse are to be seen. Two different cameras (ceiling, crane) provide movements back and forth at different angles (high, straight). The shots differ according to the autopsy procedure, sometimes medium, medium close-up or close-up. The setting consists of a corpse, physicians and technicians, a silver autopsy table and a water bucket. The corpse is placed in the front. The examiners stand behind the table with the corpse. A physician performs the autopsy and talks to the assistant doctor. A technician supports the autopsy procedures. On an audio level, their conversation is to be heard as well as noises from the water bucket, the drill and the breathing of the performing doctor. I will now contrast this documentary display with a fictive crime version.

4.3. Film Analysis *CSI* (Crime)

I selected the crime TV show *CSI* because of its popularity seen through its high audience rating. *CSI* is supposed to be set in Las Vegas, but since the year 2000, it has been produced in Los Angeles. An adequate autopsy scene for comparison purposes was hard to find because one episode has a play length of approximately 40 minutes. One of the longest and most explicit autopsy scenes is approximately two minutes (08:24–10:33). It shows a young scientist, who is feeling challenged by his "first autopsy". The filmmakers in the documentary also described in interviews their "first autopsy" challenge when they were being filmed working. This similar perspective was decisive in the selecting of the autopsy scene in the episode *Down The Drain* (*CSI* Las Vegas: Season 5, Episode 2), together with the fact that this scene represents a typical autopsy scene within *CSI*. I will demonstrate the components of a typical autopsy scene at the end of the analysis.

This episode of *CSI* has a total play length of 42:17 minutes. The lighting and colour design consist of primarily soft light, fill and back light, a brightened low key, with no shadows but uses a special bluish filter colour. The use of soft light induces a diffused atmosphere in the scenery. The diffused atmosphere generates a darkly obscure effect. The use of a brightened low-key style additionally generates a night time atmosphere, evoking loneliness and gloom. Shadows are hardly seen. The filter covers the scene with a bluish transparent colour, so that everything appears in a bluish light of varying nuances. The symbolic meaning of the colour is coolness. It is the colour of distance, rationality and quietness. (Seer, 1992) It is also the colour for dreams. The use of this colour in combination with forensic pathology and corpses seems, in comparison with other episodes, to be a topos: blue pathology. The camera cuts are hard. The camera movement uses zooming and panning shots. The perspectives range from high angles to eye level to low angles. The shots vary from medium shots to medium close-ups to close-ups. Very often, the montage consists of shot-reverse-shot. The producer often uses the shot-reverse-shot montage as the protagonists discuss the manner of death in the presence of the corpse. Close-ups of the faces of the protagonists and also of the corpse are often used. The setting consists of the table on which a seemingly blue coloured body lies horizontally. This body is the corpse of a young man. He lies on the clean, dry table, with only a sheet covering his genitals. His hair is dry and has a side parting. The following storyline describes the examination:

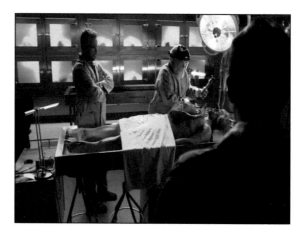

Fig,4.5. CSI–Autopsy

Source: Episode 502

Fig. 4.6. CSI–Autopsy

Source: Episode 502

Setting

The head and shoulder of a person can be seen. This person is wearing special glasses and an apron. The background is not identifiable. As the camera moves/pans to the right side, a head and shoulder of another person becomes visible. This person wears scrubs and gloves covered with red stains and a facial shield. He uses a scalpel. The chest of a male body can be seen. A third person is present. He is also wearing an apron. The room-space relation is as follows: the two people described first are on the furthest side of the table. The body lays on the table horizontally in front of them. The final person stands at the other side of the table, in the foreground of the picture with his back to camera.

Storyline

The person without facial shield looks past the camera. The other person is busy cutting with a scalpel through the skin of a male chest down towards the navel. Red liquid seems to follow the scalpel line. The camera moves over to a third person who turns his head away from the work being done on the body and closes his eyes. The left person looks at this person in the front and back to the body. He smiles slightly. A young person is to be seen with hunched shoulders. Behind the person, next to the wall, is a cupboard with its own source of light, which smoulders bluish-white from inside the cupboard. A desk lamp and a danger warning sign (Danger Ethylene Oxide) can be seen.

The young man who looked away turns his head again back, raises his eyebrows, looks to the right side and then looks past the camera (down onto the body). The open thorax can be seen. The skin is detached from the tissue. Two gloved hands flip the right side skin on the chest to the right side. The colours are tinted with a bluish filter. Nevertheless, the inside of the skin seems slightly yellowish red. The gloves are red with blood. The young man can be seen. He is looking down past the camera, watching the procedure. His facial expression has changed. A pan can be seen. The young man stares at the pan, which is handed from the right person to the left person. The background is now visible, there are, in two rows, refrigeration chambers (2x6) for the storage of corpses. From inside them smoulders a bluish light, which silhouettes the vague forms of the soles of the feet of covered corpses. In front of these is another table. In front of this table are two of the people. Next to the right person is an OP lamp. In front of the two people is the table with the body whose thorax is open. The surrounding skin remains standing straight up in the air. The genitals are covered with a sheet. Behind the table stands a little cupboard with a lamp. In front of the body stands the young man, who is pictured from behind. The right person puts the pan down on top of the table. The young man's face is shown again. His head is not moving but his eyes follow the pan. The camera follows the pan, while water drips. The camera then zooms into a close up of the pan, while water drips from it. The left person with special glasses furrows his brows and cocks his head while looking past the camera (at the young man) and then down (onto the body). The young man looks up (to the ceiling). The left man's facial protector is now in front of his face. He has a drill in his hand, which makes drilling noises. He looks up past the camera (to the young man) and then down (on the body). He moves the hand with the drill down. The young man puts his fingers into his ears, as the sound of the drill becomes audible. He grimaces. There is a medium close-up shot of the middle person. The face of the middle person, who has the drill in his hands, can be seen. He is looking down and moving his arm. A red liquid splashes against his face-shield. The young man still has his fingers in his ears. He is still grimacing. Scissors and scalpels are placed on the sheets. The middle person moves around inside the open thorax, while a drilling noise can be heard. He then lifts the drill, his gloves stained red, turns off the drill and puts it away. The skins (lappets) sway back and forth. The young man takes his fingers out of his ears and opens his mouth without speaking. He looks past the camera (to the man with the special glasses). This person looks past the camera (to the young man) and screws-up his eyes. Red liquids run down the facial shield. The middle person grimaces. It looks like as if he is moving his arm.

Two hands covered by bloody gloves remove a plate out of the open thorax. A plate-like upper chest part is put on a white sheet with red marks. The middle person looks past the camera (to the young man) talks and indicates him with his finger to come nearer. The young man moves closer to the body on the table. From that angle, we see a table with tools next to the head of the body. (See Fig.4.6.)

The sheets over his private parts are covered with medical scissors and the "chest plate". The face of the body appears within the frame. The hair is blonde in colour, as is the inside of the thorax. The face has reddish marks all over it. The middle person holds down the skin on the left side of the body while entering the thorax with scissors. One hand is holding the red tube, while the other cuts the tube with the scissors. It takes a little while until he gets through it. A little blood leaks out of the tube. The face of the middle person is shown. He talks while looking down and up past the camera (at the young man), pointing down. The young man raises his left eyebrow, closes his eyes slowly, opens them again to look past the camera (to the man with the special glasses), and then down (to the corpse). The head is shown in a medium close-up shot. The skin looks blue with violet and reddish parts. The reddish parts on the shin, nose, cheeks and forehead are wounds. The right eye is open. The hair looks a little ruffled but fresh and blonde. The mouth is open and his front teeth can be seen. The skin on his neck looks waxy. The young man's eyes are looking down past the camera (down to the body). He looks further down. The feet of the body are shown. The middle person looks past the camera and talks (to the young man) while looking down, moving his arms. The young man looks down (to the corpse). The neck from the right side is shown. A hand pierces the skin with a scalpel, cutting a slit through it down the throat. The bloody gloves gleam brightly as they reflect a light source. Two cuts are made on top of a throat. The middle person puts the scalpel back on the sheet, while leaving his left hand on the throat. The three people engage in a discussion. The middle person lifts up a heart, at which the young man stares. A medium close-up shot on the face of middle person shows him talking to the young man who looks past the camera. He looks down and then the noise of the drill rings out. The young man steps back from the table, while looking down (at the corpse).

In this reconstruction we see, within these two film minutes, an autopsy being performed on the upper body of a mannequin. The three standing people are supposed to represent a pathologist, a forensic doctor and a laboratory technician. They wear aprons and the pathologist also wears a facial shield. The pathologist cuts and opens up the body. Out of the open thorax, he removes the ribs and the heart. Specific codes of representations can be found here. Compared to the documentary, *CSI* displays a soft light and a brightened low key lighting. A blue filter, unsaturated colours and silver dominate the picture. The camera often uses shot-reverse-shots, panning shots and zooms, high and low angles, medium shots and close-ups. The communication revolves around the cause of death and a possible feeling of sickness. Music appears as an ethereal soundscape and artificial VFX noises are used when the doctor cuts the skin (thorax). During the cut on the chest with the scalpel, an artificial noise is audible (like scratching on paper). This noise is also used during the cut on the neck. The sound of water drops and the sound of the removal of the chest plate are very loud. Other noises are, for instance, the groaning of the pathologist and the men's conversation, which resonates around the room. The artificial noises are clearly associated with disgust, as well as the groaning of the pathologist. The ethereal soundscape and the slightly resonating sound of their conversation induce a surreal, mysterious and sad atmosphere. The setting also differs from the documentary. The corpse always remains in the same position on the silver table, with his private parts covered. Behind the clean and dry silver table, there is a stylish bluish-silver surrounding with cool, glowing chambers and a dimmed surgery light. The corpse is not placed in the foreground but instead between the examiners, who discuss the cause of death, personal matters and perform a few autopsy steps, which are accompanied by ethereal music and various noises. In the following, I will compare both autopsy representations.

4.4. Comparison and Evaluation of the Representation Codes

Which differences exist and what meanings regarding aestheticisation can be drawn from the shows?

It seems as if the media aims to represent an aesthetic corpse, which can be embellished and disgusting, simultaneously. In the two examined genres, the aestheticisation takes place through different aesthetic techniques. These are used on a visual level through certain film methods, such as camera panning, lighting, colours, staged objects, the storyline, and especially on the audio level through noises, atmosphere tones, music and artificial noises. I will now present the most evident differences:

1) First of all, while the documentary showed every single step of the autopsy, the *CSI* TV show showed only approximately two minutes of the autopsy scene. They showed a cut through the skin and the aorta, as well as the removal of the chest plate and the heart. In comparison to the documentary, this representation was not only lacking the visualisation of any kind movement of the body, but also the cutting of the tissue from the skin, cracking the chest bones, the scooping out of blood and the examination of the heart, cutting it into slices. As we will see in the next chapter, the FCC, which controls TV show production scripts in the US, checks for scenes which are too graphic, and vetoes them before the program is aired affects production. If one can actually measure crucial scenes, then the TV show representations lack the

more crucial graphic exposure of an autopsy procedure. Hence, the weighting of certain scenes reveals a selection process or exclusion from the aestheticisation process.

2) Secondly, the content of the settings, such as the embellished corpse on the TV show suggests another aestheticisation effort. The documentary shows what hardly any TV show would represent in prime time, namely an elderly undressed woman. Menninghaus had called this image of woman "Vetula", pointing out that visualising a naked elderly woman was the height of disgust for most of the founding fathers of aesthetic theory. (Menninghaus, 2003, p. 7)[15] The dead woman lies horizontal on a wet silver table. She is naked, old, and overweight and her body gleams with moisture. Her face is covered by a towel, scalp skin or VFX. Her genitals are also covered with a towel or VFX, but her pubic hair is visible. Her nipples are covered with VFX. Her hair is wet and rumpled. At the end of the procedure, she lies on the table with her chest and head open; all organs having been removed. This inconsistent covering of body parts shows the actual issues of how to represent a corpse with propriety. In contrast, the corpse on the TV show is the typical young athletic man placed horizontal on the clean dry silver table only covered by a sheet, which has been placed over his genitals. His skin appears to be blue. His tidy hair is dry and has a side parting. Within two minutes, the pathologist actor has cut and opened the upper body and removed chest ribs and the heart. The corpse displays deadly wounds and some injuries on the face, but not any signs of decay or untidiness. This autopsy sequence from *CSI* characteristically stands for the majority of all other autopsy scenes in this show. Hence, the cast of attractive young actors and actresses is just another example of aestheticisation efforts on the producers' part.[16]

---

15 "[…] the 'classical' authors make use, again and again, of a figure already sanctioned by a long-standing tradition: the figure of the disgusting old woman. She is the embodiment of everything tabooed: repugnant defects of skin and form, loathsome discharges and even repellent sexual practices–an obscene, decaying corpse in her own lifetime. With the single exception of Winckelmann, the disgusting has the attributes of female sex and old age with all the writers treated here. This book about disgust is thus, at the same time, a book entirely concerned with the (masculine) imagination of the vetual, of the disgusting old woman" (Menninghaus, 2003, p. 7f).

16 It might be questionable whether the cast counts in for media aesthetic techniques in Zettls textbook (2008).

3) Thirdly, the environments, which the corpses are in, also differ in many ways. In the documentary, the room is filled with the lecture room seats, tools on the little table on the silver table, an x-ray illuminator, a TV screen, a room divider, tiled yellow walls and later people in the background. It seems busy and somewhat fraught with distracting details. In contrast, the background in the TV show only displays illuminating cupboards, a surgery lamp, medical tools and cool chambers with lights inside, which allow the shadows of corpses to be seen. These few objects never distract from the corpse or the person. Additional setting elements, such as the silver autopsy table, appear to be emblematic objects (Hüppauf & Weingart, 2009) of forensic science in the media, almost supplanting the typical foot tag. The silver autopsy table in the documentary is a working space and therefore wet, covered not only with the corpse's fluids but also with organs, blood and bloody towels, tools, tubes, a basin filled up with reddish water and organs. The silver autopsy table in the TV show is, however, always shiny, clean and dry. Here the dead body is always shown in a safe room, on a clean tidy table and in a sober environment with scientific objects and scientists, where the silver autopsy table plays a major role in narrowing down any possible menace that might spread from the corpse. This clean and stylish silver shining frame of the autopsy table around the corpse suggests another aestheticisation effort.

4) Fourthly, the lighting and colour effects imply different atmospheres. (Seer, 1992) According to Zettl, colour associations are culturally learned. Lighting and the use of certain colours generate moods and atmospheres, which are understood as characteristics of the scene, act or actor. They can also guide the viewer's attention to certain areas and actions. (Zettl, 1973, p. 97) The common three-point lighting technique is used in both genres, its brightness changes the colours in the scene. According to Zettl, the more introverted a scene, the less colourful it becomes. In the documentary, we see luscious colours of yellow, red and white, because the documentary uses floodlighting, a hard, bright light. Everything in the scene can be clearly identified. In the TV show, the colours remain unsaturated because of the use of soft light (diffuse), a brightened, low-key style and a transparent blue filter that leaves hardly any possibility to recognise the other objects or create shadows in the room. Everything appears to be mysterious, vague and blurred. The blue filter enhances the artificiality of the scene. This low-

key style is standard practice for dramatic crime scenes or representations of mysterious actions and scenes fraught with tension. The low-key style is also preferably used to illuminate dark rooms at night, to generate loneliness and a threateningly grim atmosphere. The cool colours of blue and grey are commonly used in media for the illustration of distance, rationality and discipline, calmness and inner contentedness and sometimes for dreams, ecstasy and transcendence. This idio-syncratically staged secrecy of these pathology scenes is the most obvious and recognisable aestheticisation code of the TV Show.

5) Fifthly, on an audio level, the differences between the documentary and the TV show appear in all three spaces of communication, noises and sounds. The communication differs as far as the TV show instils information about the manner of death, as well as the emotional state of the protagonist, while the communication in the documentary revolves solely around the examination procedures and the cause of death. The emotions of the fledgling scientist protagonist are questioned by his seniors, who, as we find out in the episode, fear he will be overwhelmed by disgust, and vomit whilst attending his first autopsy. By staging "the first encounter with a corpse during an autopsy", the producer not only sets up the common visual components for some kind of dark secrecy but also allows the audience to understand, through the protagonists' communication, the disgust of this particular setting. This staged stimulus joins the artificial cutting noises and removal noises. During the documentary, only a few noises of water, drilling and breathing can to be heard. None of them resemble the soundscape of the TV show, where the additional noises used appear especially loud and of course artificial, since no real body is used.[17] According to Zettl, television sound has three functions: "[...] to supply essential or additional information, to establish mood and aesthetic energy, and to supplement the rhythmic structure of the screen event" (Zettl, 1973, p. 330). The ethereal music in the TV show supports the generation of an exceptional atmosphere of surrealism and mystery. To summarise, most of the audio techniques used in the TV show are normally used to evoke fascination and creepiness. The polishedness of the soundscape can, therefore, be clearly recognised as another aestheticisation effort.

---

17 The Y cut for instance is hardly audible in the documentary. The very low sound matches most closely a live wire sound. The Y cut in the fictitious crime show sounds like somebody is tearing a paper apart.

4.5. Summary

I argued that different genres generate different genre compatible representations of the corpse. Therefore, I undertook an examination of two autopsy scenes in different genres. The solitary documentary, which is based on an authentication request, served in this chapter as the contrast to the popular TV show *CSI*, which represents during all their episodes a somewhat limited corpse representation. I demonstrated that in contrast to the documentary, the producers for the popular crime TV show made use of massive media aesthetic techniques on the visual and auditory level. I also argued that because of these media aestheticisation techniques, some characteristics of the corpse openly seen in the documentary, stay covered in the television show, namely, the signs of age, impurity and lack of self-control. In fact, the aesthetically pleasing body is represented as: "[...] elastic and slender contour without incursions of fat, flawless youthful firmness and unbroken skin without folds or openings, removal of bodily hair and plucked eyebrows forming a fine line, flat belly and 'trim' behind [...]"(Menninghaus, 2003, p. 7).

Except in one detail, the attractive corpse actor conforms to this description. The exception is the visible overly large bodily opening of the chest, which belongs to Menninghaus' list of disgusting characteristics:

"Folds, wrinkles, warts, 'excessive softness', visible or overly large bodily openings, discharge of bodily fluids (nasal, mucous, pus, blood), and old age are registered, on the criminal index of aesthetics, as 'disgusting'" (Menninghaus, 2003, p. 7).

Single characteristics of disgust are now merged into the beautified image and turns the image as a whole into an aesthetic one, because the aesthetic image needs interruptions from beautification otherwise aesthetic stimulation satiation leads to the opposite effect: where everything is beautiful, nothing remains beautiful. The bodily openings which evoke blissful disgust, signs of age, impurity and the lack of the self-control as shown in the documentary, are left out in the primetime crime TV shows. Welsch detected three meanings of aestheticisation and I have demonstrated that the second level, the media aestheticisation of material and social reality, which appears with the specific camera angle, light and audio settings used in the fictitious crime setting, is clearly recognisable in five categories. These categories are (1) plot, (2) figures, (3) setting, (4) visual effects and (5) audio effects.

These substantial differences support the hypothesis that a massive aestheticisation effort for staging corpses has taken place in TV shows. These new images shape the audience's imagination of what a corpse is like and form their cultural knowledge. The exception to this cultural formation is through different representations of corpses in the autopsy room in other genres like the documentary or personal experience. In the following chapter, I will elaborate more precisely on the taboos of representation.

Part 3–Field Research
What is not shown and why?

5 New representations and new taboos

In the previous chapter I closely examined the different aesthetic techniques used by the media for the representation of corpses in a documentary TV show and in a fictional TV show. The most striking difference in the documentary was a representation consisting of (1) examiners moving (2) an old decedent (3) on an untidy table. In contrast, hardly any elderly decedents, untidy tables, or bodies in motion were observed in the fictional genre. In this chapter I will extend the examination and concentrate on these three particular findings. I will show that these specific constraints regarding the body's corporality, including its condition and position, are actual manifestations of taboos, and contrast them with general representation restrictions such as race and gender. These taboos serve to protect the classical Western image of the silent sleeping beauty from any harm.

To scrutinise this hypothesis, I will again compare a nonfictional TV show with a fictional TV show. I therefore selected the black comedy/drama *Six Feet Under* and the documentary soap *Family Plots*. As in the previous chapter the authentic documentary TV show serves as a contrast for the fictional TV show. I selected these TV shows because of their thematic similarities; both are about a funeral parlour. Yet, the docu-soap *Family Plots* seeks to reflect the daily routine of Poway Bernardo Mortuary in San Diego while *Six Feet Under* presents a fictional funeral parlour in Los Angeles. To validate my findings, I will provide statistical research results about the TV shows. These results will provide all the necessary information about the distribution of those representation restrictions. The selection of the pictures shown in this chapter serves, however, only to exemplify the results. Before I will present these results I want to introduce the research background regarding death and taboo. Afterwards I will disclose first general representation restrictions in these TV shows and then the specific representation taboos regarding the dead body as mentioned above. I will finish the chapter with an excursus on hospital autopsies and the conclusion drawn from the results.

5.1. Taboo and death

In 1955, Geoffrey Gorer published the article "Pornography of Death" in which he argued that contemporary society was suppressing death as a topic in the manner of the Victorians and sexuality. According to Gorer the topic of death has been tabooed and, "[...] can be vented only in fantasy 'charged with pleasurable guilt or guilty pleasure'–the distinctive mark of pornography. If we make death unmentionable in polite society–'not before the children'–we almost ensure the continuation of the 'horror comics'" (Gorer, 1955, p. 175).[1]

Gorer, not without criticism, referred to publications such as horror comics in order to display that a taboo topic does not simply disappear. According to him, the taboo subject re-appears again as pornography charged with that pleasurable guilt. Since the beginning of the 21st century, representations of dead bodies in the pathology department have found their way into the media and, therefore, into the public discourse. During prime time, these representations became ordinary media elements, along with others. Is death still a taboo then?

It was Tony Walter (1991) who thoroughly challenged the taboo of death by questioning the ongoing debates about whether a taboo really exists.[2] Walter reviewed the strengths and weaknesses of the taboo thesis

---

1 Geoffrey Gorer, "The pornography of death", first published in Encounter (1955). Here quoted after Geoffrey Gorer, Death, Grief and Mourning in Contemporary Britain (London: Cresset Press 1965)

2 "Fifteen or 20 years ago, the jury was out–does our society deny death, or are we morbidly fascinated by it? For some it was the great taboo of our age. And yet in 1979, M Simpson's bibliography, Dying, Death and Grief, began wryly: 'Death is a very badly kept secret; such an unmentionable topic that there are over 650 books now in print asserting that we are ignoring the subject'. The 1987 update added another 1,700 books. In a three-month period in the mid-1990s with no major wars or disasters, my colleagues and I found over half the stories and pictures of Britain's daily newspapers concerned death. It is safe to say that, as far as the mass media are concerned, the secret is now well and truly out: we humans die" (Walter, 2006).
Walter, Tony 2006: Morbid Fascinations–our obsession with death. A Battle in Print. Tony

and tried to resolve the issues by presenting six modifications[3] to the death taboo of which only one can be applied more precisely to the media context of this research, namely the third. The third modification presents the death taboo as limited mainly to the occupational groups of the media and of medicine. Walter states that the two very influential institutions, medicine and media, have unusually strong anxieties about death. These two institutions have also a greater influence on how to interpret death. However, their interpretation should not be confused with those of the public at large. About the media, Walter states that

"Every time there is a disaster, it is not only reported, it is repeatedly reconstructed by the media. I have argued elsewhere that these reconstructions are attempts to make sense of the limits of technology and of power, and to provide images that mediate between the otherwise disparate experiences of death as uniquely personal and death as global. Whatever they are, the media have extraordinary power to interpret death for us" (Walter, 1991, p. 303).

Walter then avers that the media (and medicine): "[…] to which our society has entrusted the interpretations and ritualisation of death […] are, or have been, almost uniquely embarrassed by the subject. It is therefore not so

---

Walter,27June2006:www.battleofideas.co.uk/C2B/document_tree/ViewADocument.asp?ID=266&CatID=42, 7 July 2009

3 1: Tabu plus coda: There was a taboo, but it is now disintegrating. Walter states that there has been a taboo amongst white middle classes. This has been undermined since the late 1960s by a more expressive culture. This has changed attitudes towards death and mourning, which explains the repeated detection of the taboo. / 2: Not forbidden, but hidden: Death is hidden rather than forbidden. Walter states here, that since advanced medical technology generated a low death rate amongst the young, and the dying are removed and handed over to professional care, that modern death is hidden rather than in public. / 3: Limited taboo: The taboo is limited largely to the (influential) occupational groups of media and of medicine. / 4: Disparate frames: The loss of a coherent language for discussing death leads to conversational unease. Walter states that incompatible frames, for instance, in the hospital and during the funeral process within which death is treated, make it difficult to find a common language about death that is understood and accepted by all participants. / 5: The universal taboo: All societies must both accept and deny death, so pundits are able to pick whatever examples fit their thesis. Walter states here that even though contradictory developments have taken place, the acceptance or the denial of death is announced constantly. This is a critique rather than a modification of the death taboo, however, he points to the inevitably of death in any society as being both denied and accepted. / 6: Individual and society: It is the modern individual, not modern society that denies death. Walter finally states that the modern individual rather than the modern society faces a highly problematic relationship with death because of the lack of ritual surroundings. (Walter, 1991, p. 293ff)

much society as a whole, but these two key institutions, for whom death is, or was a taboo" (Walter, 1991, p. 303).

Walter does not specify what this embarrassment is, which is why I defer to Thomas Macho and Hans Belting, who discussed the same subject in different terms in 2006. Macho presented the thesis that the once invisible death has recently become more visible. In the introduction it is argued that death, as a term for a limited concept is neither visible nor invisible. Only the dead can be visible or invisible. In a discussion with Macho, Belting argues against the thesis of a new visibility of death pointing instead towards an accomplishment of the invisibility of death. (Belting & Macho, 2006, p. 248ff.) Belting states at first that contemporary society only witnesses death and dying through television. He also argues that in any case all media images already represent the dead, the soon-to-be dead and the already dead actors and actresses which negates the differentiation between the representation of the living and the dead. Furthermore, Belting argues that these images do not represent the dead, but rather hide the dead with substitutes. Since there is no real reference point, nothing dead is displayed but a replacement of the death is represented.[4] Belting explains that humans have always produced through media, masks of those things they refuse to see.[5] They hide something unwanted and replace it with something wanted[6] Hallam et al. (1999) argue in quite the same fashion:

"The process of representation referred to here is therefore one which allows the dying and the dead body to be made visible, yet at the same time functions to mask the material reality of embodied death and its destabilising effects. The radical disorder invoked by the dying and decaying body is countered by representations which 'fix' this process in the form of an image" (Hallam, Hockey & Howarth, 1999, p. 24).

---

4 "Die Sichtbarkeit des Todes wäre ja nur dann gegeben, wenn Tote für mich eine Sichtbarkeit hätten, die ich im Bild wiederfinde. Wenn ich Tote aber nur im Bild wiederfinde, dann fehlt mir die Referenz von Sichtbarkeit und Wissen. Sehe ich keine Sterbenden, außer im engsten Familienkreis oder im Krankenhaus, dann habe ich zu diesem Thema so wenig Beziehung, dass auch Bilder gleichgültig werden. Sie sind dann alles Mögliche. Sie machen den Toten nicht sichtbar, sondern sind im Gegenteil eine Maske des Todes" (Belting & Macho, 2006, p. 251).

5 Belting elaborated on the relationship of death and images in several books, e.g. "Bildanthropologie"(2005), "Bild und Kult"(2004) or "Bilderfragen"(2007).

6 "Man verbirgt das, was man nicht sehen will, und setzt an seine Stelle etwas, das man sehen will und von dem man weiß, dass es nicht das ist, von dem man ein Bild hat". (Belting, 2006, p. 252).

They continue to argue that historical studies about the diverse proliferation of death imagery prove that the dead body has been replaced with sophisticated systems of representation.

"What is suggested by this complex and extensive domain of images devoted to the visible rendering of the body in decline, is that there is, however historically variable, a cultural apparatus which recovers the disappearing body. Operating through various media and continuing to resonate over time, there has been a proliferation of imagery centring on the dying body, which effectively maintains its social presence. [...] These issues are particularly pertinent in relation to dying and dead bodies in that they have been removed, in varying degrees, from the direct gaze and replaced with sophisticated systems of representation"(Hallam, Hockey & Howarth, 1999, p. 22f).

To sum up, all these authors acknowledge the broad effect of media on representations of the dead, but still associate these representations with avoidance. Belting specifies avoidance by stating that the real dead are hidden by mediated masks while Hallam et al. describe this phenomenon as a sophisticated system of representation. To substantiate this argument they claim that:

"[...] the body in decline through death or decay forms a potent reminder of frailty, vulnerability and mortality. The passage of time and the inevitability of physical transformation become powerfully evident. They provoke anxieties about the integrity of the body as it faces destruction. When emphasis is placed upon control and the regulation of the body as a prerequisite for the maintenance of self-identity, the dying body and the dead body acquire terrifying qualities. The bodies render visible the processes which are denied in the pursuit of an ideal which rests upon the control of bodily boundaries; for example, the passage of organic matter out of the body, the management of movement in limbs and facial muscles" (Hallam, Hockey & Howarth, 1999, p. 21).

I want to take up on the argument and articulate it with the concept of disorder that Mary Bradbury (1999) elaborates on with regards to order, disorder, and dirt. Bradbury refers to Mary Douglas's ideas of pollution and taboo and identifies the dead as "a matter out of place".[7] (Douglas in

---

7 In order to define pollution Douglas approaches uncleanness, as matter out of place, through order. Dirt is something that remains excluded from a pattern. It implies two conditions: a set of ordered relations and a contravention of that order. "Dirt then, is never a unique, isolated event. Where there is dirt, there is a system. Dirt is the by-product of a systematic ordering and classification of matter, in so far as ordering involves rejecting inappropriate elements. This idea of dirt takes us straight into the field of symbolic systems of purity. We can recognize in our own notions of dirt that we are using a

Bradbury, 1999, p. 119) Bradbury identifies the dead as "matter out of place" because of the ambiguity of the presence of the corpse and its symbolic threat as an object of pollution:

"Before decomposition sets in, a corpse can look not much different from a sleeping person. Yet closer inspection can throw an observer into confusion for, in contrast to a reposeful live body, the cold grey corpse is unmoving and unreactive. This object is ambiguous: clearly human in appearance, yet also clearly not human. We can begin to understand how the corpse contains a particularly strong power to pollute. Meanwhile, once the body starts to decompose it further challenges our senses of sight, smell and touch: it is easy to see why this somewhat gross physicality can be threatening to the survivors. The body's remorseless decay can be seen as a symbolic threat to the inner cohesion of a group. Thus, many of the rituals of death and much of the symbolism about the dead are concerned with the corpse's transformation from the 'danger within' into an 'outside' object. In this process, the group has an opportunity of restating its values, hierarchies and systems of belief. All in all, the corpse makes a great ritual object as it has the extraordinary power to surprise, shock or terrify" (Bradbury, 1999, p. 12).

Bradbury follows Douglas by saying that a single comprehensive patterns of taboos are hard to find in contemporary societies, however, "glimpses of pollution" as epistemic fears are traceable, concentrating particularly on areas of ambiguity. Thus, ideas of pollution are not only psychological fears but also social expressions. Referring to nurses and doctors, Bradbury acknowledges that pollution is not so much caused by the physical contact with the dead body as a polluting object but through the attribution of social roles. (Bradbury, 1999, p. 120) While doctors and nurses engage in preserving the life of a person, the undertaker deals with their failure, the dead body. The undertaker endeavours to embalm the dead in order to control the orifices of the dead body and reduce not only the risk of infection but also all other unpleasant side effects of the polluting decomposition process. (Bradbury, 1999, p. 128)

"The act of embalming is not dissimilar to surgery or to a post-mortem. The embalmer works in a room that apes the appearance of a hospital theatre and they make use of 'medical' tools and substances. Thus, in keeping with the dominant ideologies and beliefs of our time, embalming fits nicely into the domain of medical-type interventions. In these terms, tinkering with the body-object is no contra-

---

kind of omnibus compendium which includes all the rejected elements of ordered systems" (Douglas 2002, p. 35). "In short, our pollution behaviour is the reaction which condemns any object or idea likely to confuse or contradict cherished classifications" (Douglas 2002, p. 36).

diction: it is simply another expression of the now familiar and comforting Cartesian model of man-machine, fixable, as long as we have the skill. Embalming can be viewed as a strategy whereby we attempt to attain some kind of mastery over death" (Bradbury, 1999, p. 128f).[8]

Furthermore, Hallam argues that Western societies are occupied with the body in life; its vital, beautiful, and healthy presence and these social standards are transferred to the dead body as well. Christie Davies goes further by claiming that foreign observers often see Americans as being obsessed with personal hygiene:

"For Americans it is as important in life as in embalmed death to suppress all body smells and to achieve a sanitized odourlessness. The greater use of deodorants in America is an expression of the need to be clean, and is not in any sense a means for ensuring good health. [...] Health is important to Americans but the appearance of health and youth is just as important in its own right. Indeed physical fitness is less important to them than attaining and displaying a trim figure" (Davies, 1996, p. 64f).

Davies argues that the American predilection for embalming reveals a general pattern of cultural values and preferences. Since Americans have spent their lives cultivating the body's appearance, the embalming of the body ensures the preservation of these efforts.

As we will see from the American TV show *Six Feet Under*, when it comes to representations of corpses, a cleaned and appropriately covered body in a sanitised environment is the dominant representational mode. The all too visible signs of age and decay cannot to be seen. The real decedents in the documentary soap *Family Plots*, however, contrast starkly with these representations. Erwin Goffman's (1959) informal back stage (embalming room) turns into another formal front stage (viewing room). Since the documenting camera follows the employees into every corner of the funeral parlour, the boundaries between the former separate front and back stage become blurred. An unusual insight into the backstage, where the illusion of the clean sleeping dead for the front stage is in the production process, is given to the audience. Still, in the production process the dead body acquires all kinds of terrifying qualities. Thus, we only see a few and too short shots of the corpses and embalming processes. Nevertheless, even if short and at times blurry, these shots contrast the common corpse

---

8 Bradbury, however, also refers to the death industry benefits: Embalming is yet another way to make money.

representation. My hypothesis for this chapter is based on these documentary representations. The nonfictional documentary *Family Plots* shows that no matter what desolate conditions the corpse has been in before its transfer to the embalming room, in the hands of the professional death caretaker, the ultimate goal is to stop the process of decay and pollution and maintain the body's former aesthetic vision ready for viewing. The fictional drama/black comedy *Six Feet Under*, however, omits all those representations of the embalming process that are connected with pollution and ambiguity. It focuses on the more scientific art of restoration. Therefore, I did not find any detailed representation of embalming work, which does not show the dead as a sanitised decedent. In the embalming room, neither the body nor its environment will ever be represented as untidy. Though it belongs to the essential procedures of an embalmer, the show refrains from moving the uncovered body visibly.

5.2. General representation restrictions

Gender, Race, and Age

In 2007 the casting data report from the Screen Actors Guild[9] showed that television representation does not reflect the demography of the Unites States as Caucasians were predominantly represented on television since the formulation of the survey 15 years previously. In addition, the low numbers of casting data for women and senior performers has remained unchanged.

"Role distribution by gender continues the well-established patterns of prior years, whereby males garnered the lion's share of roles. With regard to age, previous casting trends prevail, with a majority of roles going to actors under the age of 40" (Screen Actor, 2007, p. 55).

Hence, discrimination against women, by race and age is not a novel finding in the television research field. However, it seems important to highlight the fact that this discrimination not only affects the representation of the living actors but also of the dead figures. The most common dead gendered body represented in *Six Feet Under* is a male middle-aged Cau-

---

9 www.sag.org/files/documents/CastingDataReport.pdf, September 5th, 2008

casian. The documentary *Family Plots* differs only slightly and predominantly depicts elderly male Caucasians. In the following analysis, I will disclose the statistical research results of the two shows in these three categories.

In both shows, male dead bodies are represented at least twice as often as female ones. In *Six Feet Under* the male (61.7%) representation outweighs the female one (33.3%).[10] In *Family Plots,* the representation (70%) also outweighs the female one by far (30%).[11] According to David Chandler, who investigated the number of females and males in television: "[…] TV does not reflect observable demographic realities, although it may well reflect the current distribution of power and the values of those who hold it" (Chandler, 2004, p. 2).
In death, the number of males and females on TV obviously reflects the current distribution of power.[12]

When it comes to the representation of race in *Six Feet Under,* Caucasians (74.2%) outweigh African Americans (9.2%), Hispanics (6.7%), Asian Americans (1.7%) and American Indians (0.8%).[13] In *Family Plots,* the representation of dead Caucasians is the only one to be found. According to Herman Gray (2004), this trend is getting even worse:

"Indeed, recent studies by the NAACP that have regularly monitored the distribution of roles, character development, and 'positive' portrayals of blacks, Latinos, and Asians on television continue to give the television industry poor marks and express continuing concern about what they see as the dismal state of minority representation on commercial network television (Elber, 2003, NAACP 2003)" (Gray, 2004, p. xxi).

---

10 Six Feet Under: 120 dead bodies: 6 unidentified, 40 female, 74 male corpses.

11 Family Plots: 20 dead bodies: 10 unidentified, 3 female and 7 male corpses.

12 "Whatever its limitations as a TV research method, content analysis does at least provide us with basic data about the prevalence of gender images on TV. The number of women shown on TV is far smaller than the number of men shown. Men outnumber women in general TV drama by 3 or 4 to 1. 70–85% of those on children's TV are male, and in children's cartoons males outnumber females by 10 to 1. Even in soap operas women can be outnumbered 7:3. There are also more men than women in starring roles; the exceptions are notable only as exceptions. In contrast to this dominance of the screen by men, we all know that in the everyday world, women in fact slightly outnumber men. In this sense, TV does not reflect observable demographic realities, although it may well reflect the current distribution of power, and the values of those who hold it." (Chandler, 2004, p. 2). Television and Gender Roles http://www.aber.ac.uk/media/Modules/TF33120/homepage.html, December 22nd, 2004

13 Six Feet Under: 120 dead bodies: 9 unidentified, 89 Caucasians, 11 African Americans, 8 Hispanics, 2 Asian Americans, and 1 American Indian.

Not only are living characters unevenly distributed, but dead figures are unevenly shown as well. However, when it comes to the allocation of age groups regarding the corpse figures one variation becomes noticeable. Though there is a strong discrimination concerning the age groups in the TV show *Six Feet Under*, it is not entirely clear whether the significant discrimination of elderly is a general discrimination phenomenon or whether it is especially attached to the anxieties about death. This observation bridges the general representation restrictions and the specific representation taboos. Older age groups are generally seldom represented; however, the peculiarity of this is heightened by the show's funeral parlour context.

In *Six Feet Under*, out of 120 directly shown or covered corpses eleven bodies could not be identified. One infant, four children, one teenager, thirteen persons in their twenties, thirty-seven adults (30–50), thirty-five mature adults (50–70), and eighteen elderly adults (70+) died or were dead, and were covered or visibly represented.[14] Although the elderly are underrepresented[15], they are consistently depicted in the embalming room lying on a table, being treated or already finished up for viewing. (See Fig. 5.1.) All of them are dressed, covered by sheets in a supine position on tables or in coffins.

Only two depictions are exceptional. (See Fig. 5.2.–Fig. 5.4.) One elderly person was suffocated by her roommate with a sausage and another one died with priapism in a nursing home. While the decedent with priapism never appeared in the embalming room, the discovery and removal of the sausage out of the throat of the other victim was by violent force on the head. This challenges the previously peaceful depictions of elderly deaths.

---

14 The TV show was produced in Los Angeles and was supposed to play in Los Angeles (Original run: 2001–2005). Funeral homes in Los Angeles, however, deal with a different statistic of death rates. According to the LA County Mortality Report from 2003 the highest death rates in Los Angeles are among the 75+ age group: . http://publichealth.lacounty.gov/wwwfiles/ph/hae/dca/LA%20County%20Mortality%20Report%202003b.pdf, September 19, 2008

15 Other TV shows also underrepresented certain age groups, for instance the crime TV show CSI Las Vegas. The age of the 292 identified corpses in the first five seasons show a clear accumulation of corpses in the adult age group (53.4%–30–50). 13 corpses could not be identifies. Altogether only 3 dead infants (1%), 7 dead children (2.4%), 28 dead teenager (9.6%), 55 young adult (18.5%), 156 dead adults, 29 mature adult (9.9%) and one dead aged (0.3%).

Fig. 5.1.: Six Feet Under–Common representation of the death of an elderly person 1

Source: Episode 25

Fig. 5.2.: Six Feet Under–Uncommon representation of the death of an elderly person 2

Source: Episode24

The elderly dead, while underrepresented in the TV shows, are less often staged in the embalming room, and almost universally covered with sheets or re-dressed. The representation of elderly corpses remains relatively constant.

Fig.5.3.: Six Feet Under–Uncommon representation of the death of an elderly person 3

Source: Episode24

Fig 5.4.: Six Feet Under–Uncommon representation of the death of an elderly person 4

Source: Episode 24

Family Plots by contrast is unique as far as the show represents more clearly decedents in older age groups. Approximately twenty corpses are shown. Since many of them remain entirely covered, the exact number of corpses can only be estimated. However, in comparison to *Six Feet Under* all those

20 visible and recognisable decedents are elderly adults. The decedents are mainly Caucasians, with an equal balance between men and women. Most of the corpses are shown in season 1 right at the beginning. In season two, the representation of corpses becomes less important. Another significant difference is that the show represents at least three corpses of the elderly with clear signs of old age during the first episodes. Medium shots and close-medium shots of the hands of the decedent, for instance, show age spots and decay, wrinkles, and hair. These physical details of corpses never appeared in *Six Feet Under*, though as mentioned before great importance was attached, for example, to certain treatments like the sewing of autopsy incisions. Representational restrictions in *Six Feet Under* concern obviously not only the distribution of elderly persons but also their visual staging.

Fig. 5.5:. Family Plots–Hands of a deceased elderly person

Source: Episode 1

Great concern about the death of children historically set in as the child mortality rate fundamentally declined in the 19th century.(Bideau, Desjardins, Brignoli & Hector, 1997) The intensified and unique mourning for children is known and was investigated with parents (Goodall, 2000 & Videka-Sherman, 1987) and professionals in other studies (Timmermans, 2006). *Six Feet Under* reflects the emotionally greater loss of children by displaying especially emotionally charged story plots. Out of 120 corpses, only five corpses under the age of sixteen are mentioned. Of these five

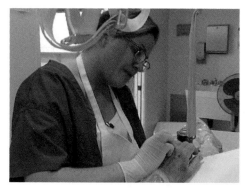

Fig. 5.6.: Family Plots–Deceased with signs of old age

Source: Episode2

corpses only the SIDS infant, a child and a teenager are actually shown. The common medium shot (covering head, neck and chest) is not used when representing the infant and the child corpse, i.e. only the extremities

Fig. 5.7.: Six Feet Under–child corpse

Source: Episode 9

are shown while the face of the corpses stay covered. The following pictures of a child corpse show the character David cleaning and dressing the corpse.

In both cases, the death of a child and the death of an infant, the grief at their death is shared by relatives and professionals. This is particularly true for the character Rico, a professional embalmer, who usually acknowledges

Fig. 5.8.: Six Feet Under–infant corpse

Source: Episode 11

the decedents as artwork and is presented here with an infant death. His explicit avoidance of his usual trope serves to mark the emotional change. The intensity of the emotional outburst he displays is exceptional and presents the otherwise case-hardened professional as emotionally affected. Both representations hide the decedent's face.[16]

Six Feet Under, however, challenges its standard representation and conveys a breach of style by representing a third dead child, whose face is stuck with laughter. This exceptional representation marks the extraordinarily unusual position of the show amongst those similar to it.

---

16 TV shows like CSI Las Vegas started in the same hesitant representation mode. In the beginning, the dead infant was represented fully covered in the pathology department. In later episodes a careful rapprochement towards the common representational style is visible until eventually children's bodies are also exposed to the camera.

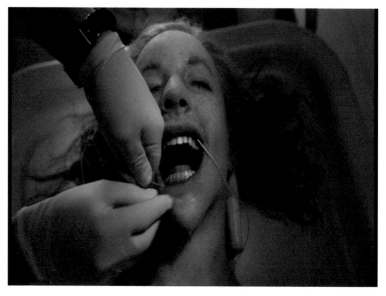

Fig. 5.9.: (above) and Fig. 5.10.: Six Feet Under–Corpse of a teenager

Source: Episode 42

In the story of the laughing girl she fell off her bed laughing about prank calls and breaks her neck. In the funeral parlour, the employees make an effort to turn the stiff, bright laughter[17] into a closed, smiling mouth by sewing the upper and lower jaw together. The staging is unique insofar as the representation of the child corpse includes not only the head but also the head with gleeful laughter. This laughter undermines the ordinary representation of serene death. Thus, the contrasting representation of the young dead girl in *Six Feet Under* demonstrates the common representation of the death of a child. To sum up, two ordinary child corpse representations and an outstanding, unique one are shown in *Six Feet Under*. Thus, children's corpses are still underrepresented, but not static. On the contrary, in "Family Plots" only one infant death is mentioned, but not shown. The background story of the infant death, however, is presented with immense emotional sympathy by the employee.

Summary

The discrimination of certain gender, race, and age groups is not a novel finding. Yet, the discrimination against older age groups, in particular, seems inappropriate for a TV show that is about a funeral parlour. *Six Feet Under* depicts corpses of middle-aged people, most likely mirroring the age group of their audience. (Spier, 1987) Corpses of people of old age are rarely seen, yet if they are shown then they are modestly dressed or covered.[18] No signs of decay, old age or other unfavourable symptoms like

---

17 The expression rictus originated in the 19th century. The rictus is the description of the "[…]Grinsen des barocken Skeletts und gleichzeitig des zahnlosen Greises, des Wahnsinnigen und des von der Leichenstarre befallenen toten Leibes" (Ariès, 1984, p. 192). The grimace developed with the wakening of the macabre iconography in the baroque 16th century in the effigy of skeletons. The macabre iconography was caused by the new interest in anatomy. The grimace is associated with the term sardonic, which expresses "[…] mehr als nur ein Wort, eine physiognomische Kategorie, wenn nicht sogar einen Seelenzustand" (Ariès, 1984, p. 192) This rictus, the sardonic laughter, is usually represented by the jaw torn open of a skeleton but also by the not unusual but rare used movie characters like the grinning, grotesque face of the deathly "Joker" in Batman, Eric Draven as "The Crow", Bates murdered mother in "Psycho" or even Elizabeth Short in "Black Dahlia". (Cf. Weber, 2006)

18 Cf. Klaver, 2006 "The television media censors dictate that the cadaver cannot be shown altogether nude in an autopsy scene, just as a live body cannot be seen nude on-

loose skin are allowed. The low number of children's death represented in the TV show could be explained by the childhood mortality rate, which has declined since the 19th century. Furthermore, people also live longer (Healey & Ross, 2002), but *Six Feet Under* does not reflect the proportion of the population. Tim Healey and Karen Ross referring to the research in the USA since the 1950s focus on the dissonance between the proportion of the population and their corresponding visibility across the television landscape. (Healey & Ross, 2002, 105) They conclude that elderly people are still less likely to be seen on television.[19] Thus, the underrepresentation of the deceased elderly is not necessarily a trope but is caused by a more general discrimination against elderly people on television. Considering that *Six Feet Under* portrays a funeral parlour which in reality, like documentary shows, is usually concerned with the elderly, I would like to argue that an even stronger avoidance of the connection of "death and old age", including typical signs of decay, is clearly noticeable.[20]

5.3. Specific representation taboos regarding death

Death and disorder

On her field observation in a funeral parlour, Bradbury (1999) noted that the embalming room, tools, and substances resembled a hospital setting.[21] She defined embalming as an attempt to control death and identified the corpse as an object capable of pollution. This idea finds expression, for instance, in the protective measures such as the use of medical gloves in funeral parlours that is reflected in their fictitious counterparts. Medical gloves are used in *Six Feet Under* and *Family Plots* to prevent the alleged exposure to infectious matter.[22] However, in contrast to the medical con-

---

screen, even though real medical and forensic autopsies are performed on a completely stripped corpse" (Klaver, 2006, p. 141).

19 They also mention that other research detected the same discrimination with gender, race, and disabled persons.

20 Cf. Weber 2006

21 Cf. Mayer 2005

22 In Six Feet Under all figures wear gloves when in contact with the corpse during the embalming procedures. The embalmer character Rico has the most frequent physical contact with the dead. Usually, he wears gloves and works with embalming tools. Altogether, he touches the corpse directly without gloves only twice. However, if one of the

text, in the embalming context these gloves only serve to protect the undertaker from disease by having contact with the dead body or the dead body fluids. Through the use of medical gloves, the dead body is clearly marked as a polluting object, and the undertaker is exposed to a pollution risk. In order to confine the pollution, the dead body is treated with embalming chemicals which keep the corpse in a sanitised condition stored in a sanitised environment.

In *Six Feet Under,* all corpses in the embalming room are placed in a supine position on the embalming table. There is not one corpse which bends due to being crippled or displays other signs of physical disabilities. The discharge of excretes, mucosal secretions or the seeping of other body fluids remain excluded from the representation of the corpses. Signs of age and decay were almost entirely absent. Blood is only shown occasionally, and usually appears detached from the body it presumably originated in. Most bodies are neatly covered and touched appropriately with only gloves. Thus, the classical image of the dead as asleep is not challenged by any disturbance. The undertaker keeps the polluting object and its environment clean.

In contrast, in *Family Plots* the dead are shown throughout all stages of the preparation process. Yet, no long shots of embalming procedures are taken. Sometimes faces of the decedents or some body parts are covered by means of visual effects. No advanced, aesthetic media techniques such as those in *Six Feet Under* are used, which is why all elderly decedents are seen with plain signs of age and decay. The corpse, in contrast to *Six Feet Under*, however, is never represented completely undraped. The few dead that are exposed are shown without representing their associated body fluids. Still, two decedents are seen in diapers like in Fig. 2. The picture shows a dead person with his suit cut open revealing a diaper, which prevents faecal pollution. The diaper was covered by using visual effects until the very last moment before the corpse was lifted. A "glimpse of the pol-

---

figures works without gloves in the embalming room and touches the corpse directly, the corpse is usually already dressed or put in the coffin for the viewing. That means that no character of the funeral parlour cast touches an undressed corpse figure without gloves during the work in the embalming room. Thus, the direct touch of an undressed corpse in the embalming room without gloves seems to be another representation taboo. This representation equals the Family Plots representation. All undertakers wear gloves when working on the corpse in the embalming room. The head undertaker Shonna is the employee with the most frequent contacts with the corpses. She also always wears gloves. No exceptions were noticed.

luting threat" is visible in the very nick of time. The same efforts to restore order are noticeable when it comes to the corpse's table. The tables in *Six Feet Under* are always neat and clean. They almost never show the embalming table covered with a mess like the ones seen at least four times in *Family Plots*. In contrast to *Six Feet Under,* the embalming table is sometimes covered with tools, paper, and body fluids. Only rarely can blood or tools be seen in *Six Feet Under,* the table is therefore a cleaned frame around which the alleged object of pollution is encapsulated.

In summary, the documentary soap *Family Plots* complements the fictional representations of *Six Feet Under*. In the documentary, the body is often old and shows age spots, the corpse is not always in a tidy condition, and sometimes the tables are also messy. Nevertheless, the efforts to restore order and cleanliness are clearly recognisable.

Death and movement

Standing up straight and still is only one of many complex bodily skills a person has to learn. The complexity of the necessary reflexes can be compared to a railway control system operating with 50 railways at the same time. (Todd, 2003, p. 43) Yet, natural movement attracts no attention unless the movement appears clumsy or out of control. Moving a dead body and revealing the full absence of will and body tension, in contrast, attracts attention, because the movement of a body without life is rarely viewed and breaches serene death conception.[23] Of course, there are abundant examples of how the dead are moved before arriving in these workshop rooms. These are primarily viewed at the scene of death. However, unless the TV show belongs to the comedy genre there will be no corpse in motion in the embalming room, unless the scene is clearly made up to create a comedic element.

In *Six Feet Under* the undertaker transports the corpses either in body bags or in coffins. Head, arms, and hands are seldom moved during the cleaning and embalming. Only once is the leg of a male body lifted. The

---

23 As I have found out in Chapter 4, TV shows like CSI have only limited possibilities regarding the representation of an authentic dead. The actor, actress, or mannequins never move like dead bodies do. If the TV show would focus more on this point, as the interviewed special make-up artist insisted, they could have better representations. The TV show producer, however, stressed that there is not enough money to produce mannequins with authentic movements.

dressing or closing of the eyes or mouth is never shown either. The heaving of the corpse by the undertaker or the movement into the coffin are never shown. In the coffin, the dead person mostly appears untouched. Scenes in which the undertaker pulls a sausage out of the throat of a decedent, where the head of the corpse is tilted back in a bizarre angle are exceptional in this regard. Most common, in contrast, are scenes in which the undertakers sew-up the autopsy incision. All in all, besides the well-known slapstick in which the corpse drops out of the coffin, no uncovered corpse gets lifted, turned around, or is made to sit. A scene in season 3 episode 6 of *Six Feet Under* exemplifies that kind of slapstick. The scene is about the discovery of an overweight decedent who due the coffin slipping apparently fell out of his coffin. After an element of surprise by the employee attempting to move him, family members, and a friend are recruited to help pull the man over. With the united endeavours of family and employees, the deceased can be turned around on a gurney. Their faces are distorted by disgust and strain. The movement of the body by the family members seems to be the punch line as the efforts result in an incongruous, odd situation.[24] Referring to Avner Ziv (1984), Martin Rod (2007) describes taboos which can be represented in a humorous manner without offence being taken:

"Humour can also be used to push the boundaries of social propriety, attack 'sacred cows,' and rebel against social norms. For example, by using obscenities or other types of shocking language in a humorous manner, one is able to violate social norms in a way that reduces the likelihood that others will take offense, since everyone knows that humour is not to be taken seriously. Thus, one is more likely to get away with breaking various taboos, expressing prejudiced attitudes, or engaging in boorish behaviour if these are done in a humorous rather than a serious manner. When carried into the public domain, iconoclastic forms of humour such as satire and comedy can be used to challenge widely held assumptions, expose social ills, and bring about social change" (Rod, 2007, p. 118).

---

24 Manifold theories on humour exist in the academic research environment. Tabooed representations of the dead can be evaded by humorous representations, which weaken the actual taboos. In 2007, Martin A. Rod claims that the perception of incongruity plays a central role in humour. (Rod, 2007, p. 74) He describes the social context of humour and quotes Kane and colleagues (1977) noting "[...] that we are continually exploring our social environments in order to determine the values, attitudes, knowledge, emotional states, motives, and intentions of others. This sort of information is necessary for achieving our goals in interactions with others, whether these are to increase intimacy, obtain desired favours and rewards, or exert influence over others" (Rod, 2007, p. 117).

To support the comedic association of the scene, the rearrangement of the body on the gurney reveals the now damaged and skewed nose of the decedent, which had just been moulded by another embalmer.

Fig. 5.11.: Six Feet Under–deceased on the floor

Source: Episode 32

An extraordinarily incongruous scene is shown here. It can only be so striking because it implicitly refers to the common conception of a body-at-rest. The deceased usually rests statically throughout all episodes while the survivors act. In this scene, however, the survivors manoeuvre the dead which causes the deceased man to have agency again. A breach of this particular paradigm reveals the representational taboo. This breach does not take place in the embalming or pathology room but outside in the final staged room facilitating viewing. It is not shown how the coffin cants over or how the corpse drops, but the final, surprising discovery of the body on the floor is seen. Here humour is used to push boundaries. Social norms such as the peaceful repose of the dead are violated but no one takes offence since the scenes are marked as belonging to comedy and are not meant to be taken seriously. Moreover, these scenes are comparable to the context of Willie Smyths' (1986) Challenger jokes as humour being made of disaster. *Six Feet Under* is always concerned with death, dying, and grief about the deceased. Just like the repetitive coverage of the Challenger tragedy, the omnipresent visual coverage of the grief in the TV shows might be at times too exhausting. The representations turn into touted events requiring humour to provide social release.[25]

Fig. 5.12.: Six Feet Under–survivors move the deceased person back on the gurney

Source: Episode 32

"Media oversaturation of coverage of the Challenger event produced a sense of emotional overkill in many Americans. The same media that brought initial information about the tragedy continued with a relentless barrage of mourning, eulogy, and inquiry. In the face of such a deliberate and persistent intrusion by the media, and the emotional response it demanded from its viewing public, it was perhaps

---

25 "There is no question about it that the news coverage of the disaster was accurate. Indeed, the public interest and need to be informed were more than met by the nation's four major network news broadcasting stations. But, as Nicholas von Hoffman observed, the event became touted as more than a tragedy; it was presented as an occasion for openly promoting patriotic values and ideals [...]" (Smyth, 1986, p. 157).

inevitable that some rebellion would surface. The form that rebellion took was humour" (Smyth, 1986, p. 258).

The Challenger or World Trade Center jokes (Csaszi, 2003) seem to be predictable[26] reactions to the media's omnipresent coverage of death and the emotional response it provokes amongst the viewing public. According to Smyth, the humour of disaster shows how people deal with the over-representation of death:

The Challenger jokes reveal how people distance themselves from the disaster, from intimations of their own mortality, and from the moral posturing of an intrusive media. "[…] These jokes and all the shuttle jokes attack our taboos on talking about and describing death or disaster and attack, as well, the power the media have to shape emotional responses and their ultimate inability to give people more than shallow images of genuine human experiences" (Smyth, 1986, p. 260).

While *Six Feet Under* avoids scenes in which corpses are lifted into their coffins, *Family Plots* show the dead literally hanging in the air. The entire dead body in motion can only be seen when they are covered by body bags or, as described above, in comedic scenes. In the following shot, the body is attached to several strings, hovers in the air, and is lifted into the coffin. This daily routine, lifting the body into the coffin, would only be conceivable in *Six Feet Under* if comedic orchestration embedded the action.

In the second picture, visual effects cover the face and the identity of the decedent. The visual effects also cover the area of the stomach in which the undertaker Shonna (only her hands are to be seen) is bustling with embalming tools inside the body. She restrains the arm of the body to

---

26 At the end of September 2001, just a few weeks after the terrorist attack against the World Trade Center, Bill Ellis reminded his colleagues in the on-line paper New Directions in Folklore that, though no jokes were yet circulating about the catastrophe, their appearance was only a question of days (2001). For the present, he wrote, only political speeches and official memorials dominate the public sphere, but based on earlier comparable situations it was easy to predict that people's repressed spontaneous reactions would emerge in the form of jokes as well. Ellis provided the following prognosis about the foreseeable World Trade Center jokes. After a period of latency, there would be several waves of jokes. Since it took seventeen days for the first jokes to appear after the Challenger disaster and in the case of less shocking events even less time, it was expected that the first wave of World Trade Center jokes would appear in early October and that a second, much cruder wave would follow a week later. The number of jokes would peak approximately one month after the catastrophe, by around the middle of October, after which there would be a rapid decline. By six weeks after the tragedy—that is, by the end of October—they would entirely disappear" (Csaszi, 2003, p. 175).

avoid an agitating the body. During the quick shot, however, the movements can be observed.

Here, identity is not revealed and furthermore, allegedly intolerable scenes are covered. Like the sight of the diaper, these movements are excluded from representation. The obvious urge to avoid too many confusing sights are clearly recognisable in these scenes covered partly by means of visual effects

Conclusion

The association of death with sleep, rest, and silence is as old as Western culture itself. (Ruby, 1995) The corpse therefore is not represented in motion in the fictional TV show and only represented in the documentary

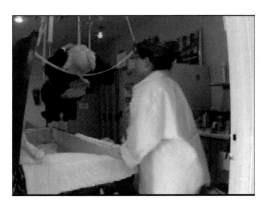

Fig.5.13.: Family Plots–employee moving a dead body into a coffin

Source: Episode 1

temporarily. It is another representational restriction which causes ambivalent feelings. The only way a dead body is consistently depicted as in motion is through humour, which is clearly marked by characters' responses to situations. Other transgressions of this representation of bodies-at-rest come through films like Zombie movies, where the dead are meant to be animated.

Fig. 5.14.: Family Plots–Embalming procedures

Source: Episode 3

5.4.   Excursus on hospital autopsies

There are three different forms of autopsies. In my research I focused on forensic autopsy since this form is most often the type depicted in television shows. Two more forms of autopsies also exist: hospital autopsy, which takes place in the hospital for quality assurance and anatomy autopsy, which takes place in medical faculties for teaching purposes. In comparison to forensic autopsy, hospital and anatomy autopsy have not gained widespread media popularity. The International Movie Data Base (IMDB) search engine provided 323 titles of television shows with medical background. 74 of these TV shows were genuine American medical drama TV shows from 1950 to 2010.[27] Due to the large number of medical drama

---

27 American Medical Drama / Doctors / Nurse / Hospital TV Shows 1950–2010: Scrubs (2001), Medic (1954), Northern Exposure (1990), M*A*S*H (1972), Hennesey (1959s), Breaking Point (1963), Doctor in the House (1969), Bramwell (1995), The Young Doctors (1976), Rafferty (1977), ER (1994), St. Elsewhere (1982), M*A*S*H (1972), The Nurses (1962), Emergency! (1972), Becker (1998), Grey's Anatomy (2005), Ben Casey (1961), Dr. Kildare (1961), The Bold Ones: The New Doctors (1969), Nurse (1981), Nightingales (1989), Marcus Welby, M.D. (1969), Medical Center (1969), Medical Story (1975), The Nurses (1965), Kay O'Brien (1986), Empty Nest (1988), Diagnosis Murder (1993), Birdland (1994), Chicago Hope (1994), Trapper John, M.D. (1979), Nurses

TV shows, an empirical comparison of hospital autopsies with forensic autopsies was impossible. For this excursus, I took a small sample of TV shows, which were and/or continue to be produced in the 21st century and generate high ratings. These TV shows are *ER*, *Grey's Anatomy*, and *House, M.D.*. With the help of episode guides, the search for autopsies was successful, but, at the same time, it did not reveal any additional autopsy scenes, which were not mentioned in the guides. I cannot therefore, verify if there are more hospital autopsies in the shows but surmise that this is not the case due to the findings. The findings were astonishing as only three hospital autopsies were found, i.e. one per TV show. In comparison to forensic autopsies, which are shown in every TV show episode, hospital autopsies only play a marginal role in the medical drama genre. The findings were also astonishing as the representation codes of hospital autopsy (e.g. lighting, setting, and content) resembled most of the representation codes of forensic autopsy. Since I have only three examples from an overwhelming number of medical dramas I will present the three examples without further conclusions.

(1991), MDs (2002), House Calls (1979), Cutter to Houston (1983), Doogie Howser, M.D. (1989), Dr. Quinn, Medicine Woman (1993), Dr. Simon Locke (1971), Strong Medicine (2000), After MASH (1983), L.A. Doctors (1998), Doc (2001), Matt Lincoln (1970), Chicago Story (1982), City of Angels (2000), University Hospital (1995), Trauma Center (1983), City Hospital (1951), Janet Dean, Registered Nurse (1954), Dr. Hudson's Secret Journal (1956), Young Dr. Kildare (1972), Doc Elliot (1973), Doctors' Hospital (1975), Westside Medical (1977) Doctors' Private Lives (1979), Buck James (1987), Hothouse (1988), Private Practise (2007), House, M.D. (2004), 61. Nip & Tuck (2003), Inconceivable(2005), 3 lbs (2006), Saved (2006), Heartland (2007), General Hospital: Night Shift (2007), Private Practice (2007), Three Rivers (2009), Mental (2009), Royal Pains (2009), HawthoRNe (2009), Nurse Jackie (2009), Trauma (2009), Mercy (2009); Source: http://www.imdb.com/keyword/medical/?title_type=tv, February 28, 2010

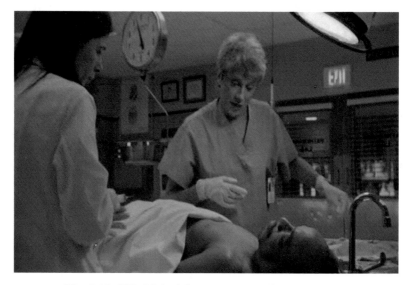

Fig. 5.15.: ER–Medical doctor exercises on the deceased person

Source: Episode 616

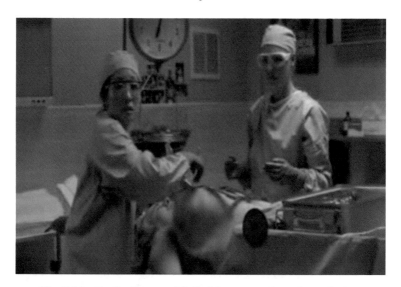

Fig. 5.16.: Grey's Anatomy–Medical doctors examine a deceased person

Source: Episode 9

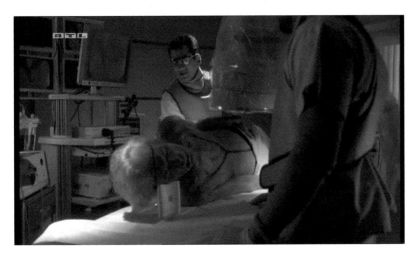

Fig. 5.17.: House, M.D.—Medical doctors examine a deceased person

Source: Episode 88

These findings suggest that there is little incentive for medical television dramas to portray an autopsy for educational or quality control reasons. Instead they are intrinsically linked to the investigative and forensic context. Here one can ask if medical TV shows reflect the retreat of autopsies in hospitals. (Esser, Gross, Knoblauch & Tag, 2007)

5.5. Conclusion on new representations and new taboos

In this chapter, I introduced theories on taboos pertaining to social and cultural sciences regarding the representation of death through media. Afterwards, I contrasted the new representations of the dead in a documentary drama with the representations of death in a drama/black comedy show. I distinguished between general representation restrictions (race, age, gender) and specific representation taboos (untidiness and movements) regarding the dead body. I focused on the difference between non-fictional and fictional representations of corpses. I found general representation restrictions regarding race and gender. Caucasian and male corpses were predominantly shown. I also found that the fictional TV shows omit detailed depictions of the embalming processes that could be connected with disorder and ambiguity. In my research, I found no accurate representation of embalming work in fictional genres. The fictional genre always shows the dead body as a sanitised, tidy, and resting decedent. Furthermore, in contrast to the documentary, the fictional corpse was seldom represented in an old age group and if so, then without any age spots or signs of decay. The dead body as polluting object was mostly represented as a white clean body. In addition, the environment was simultaneously represented as clean and tidy. The greatest restriction, however, seemed to concern the movement of the body. While it appeared appropriate to sometimes move arms, legs, or even the head of the dead, the entire uncovered body was never moved visibly, except for a slapstick scene. These strong restrictions concerning age, disorder, and motion can therefore be seen as actual manifestations of new taboos. Death in Western culture has always viewed death as restful, often in a posture imitating a light sleep. Disorder and motion disturbs this peace. Is this strong classical image being violated by new television representations? These new TV shows provide images of the dead that mostly look like this: a covered, clean and tidy, white, middle-aged man resting on a clean and tidy table in a clean and tidy environment, always surrounded by other figures that seem to care about his appearance. *Family Plots* presented their real dead with fewer restrictions in the first season, and then almost entirely avoided showing their dead bodies again in the second season even though the show was cancelled. I suppose that amongst other reasons the violation of these taboos in the documentary drama might have led to its low popularity and cancelation. *Six Feet Under* on the contrary made it through the scheduled five seasons and won several awards. Their images of the dead were approved by their audience and therefore stayed in the public visual discourse.

6 Field research: The Representation of Corpses under Constraints

The previous chapter focused on the depiction of dead bodies in new TV shows. In this chapter I argue that the representation of the corpse in the pathology department is shaped by various aspects. I aim to reveal the broader context of the production and effects of the representations, which generate and shape restrictions of the pictorial discourse on dead bodies in contemporary TV shows. The question to be examined resembles the questions Graham Murdock asked in his article "Rights and Representation".[1] Adapted to my research field I will ask how the context of the pictorial discourse on the corpse is organised and if anybody's perspective about the dead body is preferred and given particular privileges in terms of space and legitimacy. The chapter consists of three approaches, which will disclose the most significant restrictions. I will argue that the constraints of representing corpses are formed by medical officials in documentaries, but also by producers following film business logistics and by public responses, whereby the public only demands restrictions, but has no measurable influence. The chapter is based on the following order: (1) I

---

1 "The ways in which television addresses itself to matters of public concern, debate and value are inextricably tied up with questions of how programmes are put together as combinations of pictures and speech (Corner, 1995). As John Ellis points out in his contribution to this symposium (chapter 4), forms and genres play a pivotal role in this process. They are devices for converting the fluid conflictual flow of social discourse and resonant imagery into structured and accessible modes of knowing. They may address the field of relevant discourse in a relatively 'open' or relatively 'closed' way. We can assess a programme's degree of openness by asking two basic questions. First, how much space does the programme provide for the range of competing discourses? How far is it organized around the official or prevailing discourse, and how far is it hospitable to alternative and oppositional positions? Second, how is the contest of discourses organized? Is one perspective preferred and given particular privileges in terms of space and legitimacy? Or are competing ways of talking and looking treated in a more even-handed way? Does the programme leave the outcome indeterminate and invite the viewer to judge, or does it close around a particular conclusion" (Murdock, 1999, p. 13)?

will present an interview with a medical examiner from the Los Angeles County Coroner Office who participated in a forensic documentary. I aim to demonstrate the expert view of a pathologist being involved in the screen adaption of his case and show which restrictions are made by the Coroner in filming the dead. (2) I want to present interviews which I conducted with filmmakers, make-up artists, and props' employees. By displaying various restrictions made in the course of a TV show production, these interviews will reveal why certain details about the corpse stay concealed. (3) The third approach revolves around the restrictions demanded on the part of the public. I will reflect the academic discourse on the viewers' response to the new representation. This particular public response will be demonstrated by means of academic articles since a representative examination of viewers would go beyond the actual focus of this thesis.

6.1. Officials: The LA County Coroner TV show *North Mission Road*

As I have noted earlier the documentary genre is broad. The categorisation of the term 'documentary' "[…] always depends on the broader context of the kinds of audiovisual documentation currently in circulation" (Corner, 2001, p.125). I define the *North Mission Road* TV show as a documentary because images and sounds are used "to provide an exposition or argument about the real world" (Corner, 2001, p. 125).[2] The documentary genre is divided into subgroups with different elements. *North Mission Road* includes elements of reality TV, eyewitnesses, 'authoritative' presenters, and expert statements and elements of true crime films, self-description: based on actual crimes. (Dovery, 2001, p. 135) *North Mission Road* excludes elements of the observational documentary, real people in undirected situations (Bruzzi, 2001, p. 129ff), documentary realism, observational realism and expositional realism (Corner, 2001, p. 126f), documentary-soap (ordinary people share ordinary experiences (Bruzzi, 2001, p. 132ff) or documentary-drama (combination of drama and documentary). The distinctive feature of the show is the report of a true crime that was investi-

---

2 "This directness of address to something outside the 'text', this special level of referentiality, is one of the things that distinguishes documentary from fiction, that also points outside itself but much more indirectly" (Corner, 2001, p. 125).

gated by the Coroner's Office in Los Angeles. The show introduces authentic scenes such as the crime scene, the home of the victim, the coroner, and all respective participants like eyewitnesses, forensic experts, and investigators. Some participants have doubles and some scenes are re-enacted. In addition, parts of the alleged victim, respectively the victim's corpse, are shown during the autopsy of the medical examiner. Single body parts such as fingers or photos of body parts are shown as well. In this part, I want to examine the shooting of the autopsy re-enactment with a pictorial analysis. The episode "The Jockey's Demise" is about a jockey's sudden and unexpected death and the resolution of the case by investigators and the medical examiner. I will analyse images in which the medical examiner and the alleged victim are shown. In a second step, I will talk about an interview I conducted in March 2009 with the medical examiner Dr. Louis A. Pena, who was assigned to the case. In the episode "The Jockey's Demise", he was interviewed by the camera team and re-enacted the autopsy scene. I want to complete the report of his experience as part of the investigation and film team with the interpretation of the pictorial analysis in order to answer the main question: Which techniques are used to deal with the aspiration for authenticity in a documentary?

6.1.1. Pictorial analysis of the representation of an autopsy

Fig. 6.1.: North Mission Road–Camera angle during report: Second observer position

Fig.6.2.: North Mission Road—Camera angle during report: worm's-eye view

Fig. 6.3.: North Mission Road—Camera angle during dissection: Close-up on the face

Fig. 6.4.: North Mission Road–Camera angle during dissection: Close-up on the hands

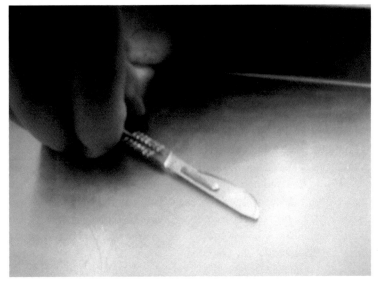

Fig. 6.5.: North Mission Road–Camera angle during dissection: Close-up on the instruments

Fig. 6.6.: North Mission Road–Medium shot medical examiner

The previous images show an identical setting: the autopsy room and the medical examiner. Thus, I will not describe and reconstruct every single image in detail all over again, since only the angles differ while the environment, the lighting, the objects and people remain the same.

Description:

Every picture shows different parts of the same person, e.g. hands, head or upper body. The pictures also show different objects such as instruments and desks. The person is dressed with protective clothing: a pink breathing mask under the face shield, blue overalls, a blue apron, and yellow gloves. The person, or parts of the person's body, is always visible. The technician is also shown working at the desk. While working on a skin coloured object, only little cuts from the object itself can be seen. Depending on the camera angle, the technician is shown from the second observer position (over his head and shoulder), or from the bottom-up. Occasionally, close-up and medium distance shots are taken. The picture frame itself is sometimes shown as a telescoping frame (see figure 6). The light in the room is predominantly diffuse, bright and bluish. In contrast to other scenes, this light appears to be artificially coloured.

Reconstruction:

The reconstruction of the listed elements in the pictures implies that an autopsy room and a forensic medical examiner are being represented. In particular, the arrangement of an individual in protective clothing and gloves holding a scalpel and the environment of a bluish-lighted room with examination tables implies a scientific medical connection. These specific media codes are used frequently for medical contexts on contemporary television. The room and the equipment could also represent a medical operating suite but the medical team is missing, as well as the patient and life supporting machines. The hands covered with gloves hold a scalpel above the skin coloured object and indicate a dissection of a corpse. Picture 4 shows part of the alleged body. The background of the picture is covered by the upper torso of the medical examiner. The front of the picture shows both hands, which hold two silver instruments. On the right side, the left hand holds a silver instrument while the fingers touch the body. On the left side, the right hand points with a silver instrument towards the object. This arrangement implies a cutting of the skin coloured surface underneath the hands. The frame of the picture, however, excludes depictions of the contact between the silver instrument and the flesh-coloured surface.

Interpretation:

The show places the dead at the centre of attention. The crime that led to his death must, therefore, be solved. Since an autopsy on his body can provide important details for solving the crime, the autopsy is also part of the documentary. While the documentary portrays all of the participants, only pieces of a representative body are displayed. These pieces of a skin coloured surface are in fact, a visual fiction, as revealed in the following interview.

6.1.2. Interview with the medical examiner participant

Since the L.A. County Coroner prohibits filming real dead bodies, the documentary filmmaker chose to re-enact the autopsy scene with a body double. Though the documentary, by its very nature, claims to be authentic, the producer did not mark this particular scene in any way as fabricated. The performing medical examiner Dr. Louis A. Pena was assigned to the case of the jockey Chris Antley, whose alleged cause of death, an accidental overdose, had been determined. Pena explains that he is a forensic pathologist in the position of a deputy medical examiner for the Los Angeles County Department of Coroner. He started working there in 1996 and defines his daily work as a "determining the manner of death" job.[3] Pena has been requested for TV productions like A&E, Vantage Productions for Court TV, Discovery Channel, and MSNBC. For *North Mission Road* he, along with several others was asked to assist on the case of Chris Antley. In the following, he briefly describes what he did for the *North Mission Road* filming:

> P.: I review the autopsy thoroughly and toxicology. I know by heart major details and pertinent autopsy findings. I speak about the scene revisited and why. What I found that helped. I explained in simple terms what an autopsy is. I recreate diagrams, injuries I saw, neuropathology consult reports, and other consults. I explained why these injuries were not fatal, they were superficial. I explain why the investigator thought it was a homicide as he saw bruises he thought would be fatal. I talked about the police investigation, and how they helped by reconstructing the scene and interviewing people. I revisited the scene that night and found a large amount of blue pills that the investigator missed and it turns out these pills from the toxicology studies were the key to the case. I explained how these blue pills and the other drugs in his system are stimulants and can cause bizarre behaviour. They may have left this part out of the show. Dr. Lakshmanan and Craig Harvey review these segments before they are released out to the public for accuracy. I would often stay late after work, sometimes four or more hours.

Pena was on screen for no more than approximately five minutes. He explained the case and his involvement, re-enacted parts of the autopsy procedures, demonstrated examinations with the microscope and then summarised his findings in another interview. The few autopsy procedures in the show did not match the number of steps that occurred during the actual autopsy. The autopsy procedures shown were: filling out the report

---

3 P: We determine manner of death. How did death come about or the circumstances surrounding the death. Is it natural accident, suicide, homicide, and could not be determined? Police Agencies help us with their independent investigation and give us input about the circumstances. We are independent and solely responsible for the determination of cause and manner of death. Some other agencies, counties; sheriff-coroner systems will determine the manner of death for the pathologists. We also testify the cause and manner of death in court on usually criminal or civil cases as needed. We can testify to the identity of the decedent also.

papers, taking a scalpel, and guiding the scalpel over a surface. These actions did not take longer than two minutes, while the actual autopsy[4] took about 10 hours.[5] In addition, the actual environment of the medical examiner's lab differs from where North Mission Road shot their film. The actual autopsy suite is usually filled with other medical examiners, their cases, the involved technicians, and attending police personnel. Hence, in reality the autopsy suite is crowded with many people working instead of a solitary protagonist.

I: Which autopsy room did you use for the filming?
P: S-6. It's a smaller room used to be for sign outs.
I: And which autopsy room did you use for the actual autopsy?
P: S-24 station number one.
I: Were other people around during the autopsy?
P: Police from Pasadena and technicians, but used only at my request.
I: So usually an autopsy is performed in a bigger room, where other docs and technicians are working at the same time?
P: Yes.

Thus, the autopsy suite is by no means empty or silent as represented in the documentary. The contrary is the case; colleagues perform autopsies on corpses, talk to the technicians who prepare and clean the place constantly.

---

4 I: What kind of examination did you do?
P: I did an A-level case as required on all higher profile cases.
I: And what are in general the single steps in this autopsy?
P: Photos from death scene and police photos are reviewed before autopsy. I revisited the scene in this case after the autopsy. The body had complete photos taken with and without his clothing, he was next fluoroscoped and x-rays taken as needed at my request, then the external diagram was done as the body goes to the autopsy suite. Police are present for the complete autopsy. After this, I open the case with no technical help until the head and brain removal are needed. I open using the standard Y incision and then remove organ by organ looking carefully for trauma or natural diseases. After the dissection, I then submit tissues for microscopic study for example the heart, lungs, liver, and kidney and so on and the brain is sent separately for a neuropathology specialist to examine along with the spinal cord. A complete toxicology study of blood from the heart and femoral areas, vitreous fluid, liver tissue, stomach, bile are taken all in separate containers, labelled for chain of custody.
5 I: How much time does the examination take?
P: Approximately 4 to 4 ½ hours.
I: And how much time did you spend all together on this case? Including the examination, the field research at the location, the paperwork?
P: Approximately 10 hours, but spread out over six weeks. There are other cases going on.

However, it is not only the number of people, but the setting, including lighting, that differs:

I: At what time did the filmmaker shoot and why?

P: At night, because no work is going on and no court.

I: Did you recognise any different lighting in the autopsy room during the filming?

P: Yes, very dark and focused on myself and mock autopsy table.

I: How would you describe the usual light conditions in an autopsy room?

P: Usually bright and well lit so we can see what we are looking at during regular autopsy.[…]

I: What additional equipment was brought by the filmmakers?

P: I am not sure on this. This is film equipment, lighting, voice, sound equipment, cameras, a number of them. The autopsy subject, the dead body, is replaced by a mannequin and the procedures are then only insinuated:

I: Can you list all those details that were not authentic during the shoot? […]

P: Everything appeared authentic to me except no autopsy was done on a real dead person. I was in my scrubs, had ID badge. Time changed to seem like it is daytime but actually it is night as you now know. The microscope used on the jockey case was from another case as you see me looking at a slide. It is not the actual slide on this case of the jockey. The equipment tray is the real tray. […]

I: Do you know if they ever showed dead bodies?

P: No, they did not.

I: Why not?

P: We need to be respectful to the family of the decedent implied on the show.

[…]

I: Did the filmmaker bring additional medical tools or requested additional medical tools during filming to make it look more authentic?

P: They brought in a dummy mannequin that had skin colour so when you see me cutting on the film I am using this mannequin but going over it with the scalpel blade to mimic a real cut, but of course, I am not cutting anything. […]

I: And where did the mannequin came from?

P: The mannequin came from their own production studio, if I recall it was a half body like Rescue Randy

I: How do you know it was Randy?

P: Flat chest and it had a man's hair […]

I: And what did you do then with Rescue Randy?

P: I pretended to do the Y incision on the surface; I had a real scalpel blade but was about 1/2–1 inch away from the mannequin chest. They told me they had to have a certain depth appearance so it would look real when it came out for viewing on TV. That was real precise. The depth was quite important because it seemed when I was over an inch they would ask me to redo it at a shorter depth 1/2 inch as an example. I never touched the mannequin; they had a graphics department at the studio that would edit this stuff to the mannequin scene to make it look as real as possible.

I. Yeah?

P: They actually have full body model mannequin also for other purposes, the death scene. At this scene with jockey, they used a real actor to recreate the scene, this was critical because the initial investigator who went to the scene missed about 30 pills scattered on the floor in a room that later our tox discovered was critical to this case.

I: Why wasn't the real actor on the table?

P: I don't know but it may have to do with medical clearance on who we let on the service floor, in case of injury like the table collapses, or he slips and falls or he sees a real dead body and faints and hits his head. We are culpable.

I: Was the mannequin rubber or plastic?

P: The mannequin is plastic, [...]

I: And they take the full body model only for the crime scene?

P: I don't know if it is only for the scene, as I have seen it used for other autopsy shows but I don't know why. They did most likely because the injuries were in the extremities, not the torso. So the doctor during the filming would be at a leg cutting or arm demonstrating the injury perhaps.

I wanted to complete the coroner's experience in terms of being part of the investigation and part of the filmic re-enactment with the interpretation of the pictorial analysis answering the question which techniques are used to deal with the aspiration for authenticity in a documentary. The documentary presents a real crime case, authentic locations, and the people originally involved. However, everything about the autopsy is modified since the Coroner's Office prohibits the shooting of their dead bodies and autopsies. The setting of the autopsy suite differs; the dead body is represented by a mannequin and the autopsy procedures are re-enacted without any contact between the pathologist and the mannequin. The focus of the camera lies on the medical examiner and the artificial bluish-lit environment while the representation of the surface of a skin coloured mannequin, the supposedly dead, is shown only briefly. Hence, as only the surface of a mannequin is shown, the authenticity of the corpse representation is actually hardly distinguishable. In summary, the aspirations for authenticity, a genuine documentary trait, is presented with aesthetic media techniques. Ultimately, the question arises as to why autopsy scenes are included in a documentary. A documentary, which strives for reality, fails when the producer hints at something hidden, represented by something inauthentic, and does not render it visible. This breach of documentary practice is a direct result of the regulation of pictorial discourse by the LA County Office of Coroner, which prohibits filming of their corpses.

6.2. Producers: Interviews with the filmmaker

In this part, I want to give a brief, but due to the broad subject, incomplete insight into how television works and what kind of knowledge it provides. I will present interviews dealing with issues like gore, nudity, and censorship, as well as the dominant depiction of certain ethnicities and the distorted representation of gender and age groups, which is naturally reflected by the stereotypical representation of the dead. In order to find out what TV producers take into account when it comes to the production and broadcasting of the dead, I conducted six guideline-based interviews between 2007 and 2009 with employees of the TV show *CSI*, *NCIS* and *Dexter*.[6] I was interested in three main themes, which explain the technical background of the production and the shooting of the corpse mannequins, and respective actors, who appear as dead. I categorised these main themes as follows:

1) Money, time and censorship
2) Race, age, gender
3) Working on realism

With these three themes, I aim to present a greater insight into the intentions of the filmmaker, the factors influencing the production of dead body mannequins, and their contextual depiction. I want to demonstrate some of the reasons why contemporary media representations of the dead are broadcasted the way they are. As one will see in the following, certain time restraints affect production to a large extent, but limited budget allocations and restrictions made up by the relevant network censorship also impinge upon broadcasting. The producer tends to perform a self-censor-

6 These persons are Elizabeth Devine (Co producer, CSI), Chuck Bemis (Cameraman, CSI), Matthew W. Mungle (Producer of prosthetics and mannequins, MWM Inc.), Eddi Vargus (Employee of MWM Inc.) and Ruth Haney (Special Make-up Artist, CSI) and Joshua Meltzer (Props Manager, Dexter).

ship by shooting prettified versions of carefully decorated mannequins and pale airbrushed actors. Producing a film is a business. As the producers work for the film industry, they hesitate to shoot gratuitous scenes because they are afraid of fines by the censorship board and waste in their budgets. Since there is no way for the broad audience to review these depiction modes, which are set up under certain time, budget, and censorship restrictions, the displayed signs of death are the contemporary codes for the audience to understand that they are watching a representation of a dead body. Therefore, I not only asked all interviewees if they actually had been to an autopsy and/or seen a real dead body (most answered in the affirmative)[7], but also how they create a dead body. Special make-up effect artists Matthew Mungle and Eddi Vargus, who not only provide prosthetics for TV shows and change the appearance of an actor, but also create mannequins which are supposed to look like dead bodies at a crime scene or autopsy room, answered as follows:

I: And do they, CSI, require special bodies from you?
M: Well, depending on what the schedule is and on what the body is required to do. It's about half and a half between, if we use any actor, a real actor, or a prosthetic actual body and an actual cast that the actors hit. When we do a real actor we will use prosthetic on their faces and sometimes we use them to do the Y incision, but we have flat organs on them instead of full organs. And then, if we have to do a body if something more horrendous has happened to the person, then we do have stocked bodies that we take head casts of our actors and actresses and put them all on stocked bodies. Then maybe they are open, all their organs are out or they did mangle or anything like that.

---

7 However, the head of the special effects make-up company answered somewhat differently.
M: Never, and I will never go. Never. I got a lot of pictures. We've got tons of books of the beginning and the end, the whole process colour pictures of an autopsy, and I can look at dups, but real I don't know, I just came from when I was a kid, you know, growing up on a farm, maybe seen bulls castrated, cows having horn cut up, so I don't know, it's really weird.
I: It's interesting, because you actually kind of shape the people's image of dead bodies.
M: That's right.
I: But you have never seen them?
M: Nope. Nope. Never, and never will go.
I: The image of a whole generation.
M: Never will go too. Yeah, and never will go to an autopsy. Never go, never will. I don't want that in my psyche. I can look at it in the books and do research on it, but physically I don't want to go there.

The model for all dead body mannequins of this particular special make-up studio is the firemen dummy, the so-called 'Rescue Randy' and 'Rescue Annie'.[8]

> I: Where do you get these (touching the mannequin) from?
> E: Oh, we make them. What we did is, we bought a Rescue Randy, a real Rescue Randy, from wherever they sell them. I don't know where he bought him from, and then we mould it in all the pieces. So now, we make them ourselves.

The special make-up artist creates the body double of an actor with a 'Rescue Randy' and adds reproduced body parts such as faces or hands. The artist makes these body parts out of alginate or silicone rubber. In a live casting, the artist first applies the liquid material with a paintbrush on the desired body part of the actor and supports this by using a plaster bandage to hold the liquid. The material assumes the shape of the face. After removing the cured material, the mask turns out to be a reproduced detailed face surface of the actor. After making the body and the body parts, another artist punches the hair into the head (one hair at a time). After this is all done another artist will put make-up on the face. These procedures take a lot of time. When I interviewed the artist, he had just finished a mannequin within a day.

> E: Usually, we have more than a day, we cast it up, sculpt it up and play and then mould it and then make it, and that's the whole process involved. It takes at least two days to mould anything and on this show we cheated. I tried it, make the life cast, mould it and then paint it. All in one day before. In one day.

---

8 The product history of the 'Rescue Annie' mannequin, in turn, has another death-related background "At the turn of the 19th century, the body of a young girl was pulled from the River Seine in Paris. There was no evidence of violence, and it was assumed she had taken her own life. Because her identity could not be established, a death mask was made; this was customary in such cases. The young girl's delicate beauty and ethereal smile added to the enigma of her death. Romantic stories that speculated on this mystery were published. According to one, her death was the result of an unrequited romance. This story became popular throughout Europe, as did reproductions of her death mask. Generations later, the girl from the River Seine was brought back to life when Åsmund S. Lærdal began the development of a realistic and effective training aid to teach mouth-to-mouth resuscitation. Moved by the story of the girl so tragically taken by early death, he adopted her mask for the face of his new resuscitation-training mannequin, Resusci Anne. Because he was convinced that if such a mannequin was life-sized and life-like, students would be better motivated to learn this lifesaving procedure." Source: http://www.laerdal.com/about/default.htm, May 8, 2009

I: Must have been a long day.

E: Yeah, and it suffers for that, you know what I mean. It's never as good as we could if we had more time. For television there is no time.

According to Mungles and Vargus, a body in silicon for the TV show *NCIS* costs, for instance, about $7,000. A mannequin that actually looks like a real person can cost from $10,000 to $15,000. The price depends on how much detail the producer wants. According to Joshua Meltzer from *Dexter*, the body cost depends on the details. A full live cast, for example, would cost around $25,000 to $30,000, which is why they would never do that because it is too expensive.

To sum up, during the short introduction, when we see the dead body on a *CSI* or *NCIS* TV crime show, we are either looking at a 'Rescue Randy' with hand and face prosthetics or at an airbrushed actor, but never a real dead body. That is good news, but maybe not surprising. The subsequent themes identify the main determinations of the media business when it comes to the specific representation of these actors and prosthetics.

6.2.1. Money, time, and censorship

The determination of the pictorial production of the dead body depends generally upon three factors: money, time, and censorship. For the most part, these factors are built-in constraints when it comes to a highly competitive business like television entertainment. A. William Bluem and Jason E. Squire published a collection of articles on film industry practice by people who actually work in the film industry (Bluem & Squire, 1972). It revealed details of financing, production, screenwriting, and distribution. These articles show, in particular, that the most important factor in making a film is the return on an investment. This economic incentive limits the creative process of making a film.[9]

---

9 "Like all business, the theatrical motion picture business exists to make money. That's the only way more movies can be produced and an on-going network of production, distribution, and exhibition can be fed. Comparisons can be loosely made to other industries: Production encompasses research, development, and manufacturing; distribution can be compared to wholesaling; and exhibition to retailing. But there the comparison ends because the public's demand and use of the entertainments products such as motion pictures are unlike the demand and use of any other product. In no other business is a single example of product fully created at an investment of millions of dollars with no real assurance that the public will buy it. In no other business does the public 'use' the product and then take away with them (as Samuel Marx observed in Mayer and

"Hollywood is at the centre of the film industry and has been since 1920. The success and ubiquity of its film products across the globe from this time makes it impossible to define indigenous national film industries separately from Hollywood. [...] Our contributors show that as a business operating in a capitalist environment, the studios that made and make up Hollywood acted rationally in the pursuit of profit in response to the business environment that they found themselves in at each particular historical juncture" (Sedgwick & Pokorny 2005, p.7).

In fact, John Sedgwick and Michael Pokorny analysed the nature of film as a commodity and identified long-term industry characteristics and trends. These trends confirm the strong economic influence on filmmaking by capitalist organisations and hence their influence on the cultural drive of our society. Therefore, I will concentrate on the interview statements about the business with an industrial approach, which allows me to analyse the production of pictures from an economic standpoint since there are so many economic factors that determine the success of a movie.[10] Yet, even that determination is not as straight forward as it seems, as Anthony De Vany states:

"Anyone who claims to forecast anything about a movie before it is released is a fraud or doesn't know what he is doing. The margin of error is infinite. That does not mean that he won't ever get it right, only that he seldom will and only because of sheer luck" (De Vany, 2004, p. 275).

When I came to question the dead bodies in the TV shows, Devine replied with explicit financial concerns:

> D: So, you're not going to show if you have a body at that set injured and autopsied. You can't show them naked. They always have to be draped with a suit. At an autopsy they never drape. But the reason they are draped is that a lot of time you don't have to do make-up on the whole body. That costs a lot of money.

Thalberg) merely the memory of it. In the truest sense, it's an industry based on dreams" (Squire, 1983, p. 2f).

10 "An industry-by-industry approach to media research illuminates how each medium operates as a distinct economic endeavour. Such an intensive examination of an individual industry at a particular point in time allows a researcher to explore in depth the relationships, contingencies, and practices through which participants make the end product or service available (Mosco, 1979; Cantor, 1980; Gitlin, 1983; Wasko, 2003). It also allows researchers to see connections by tracing how companies in one industry make their products an integral part of another industry (Wasko, 1994; Kunz, 2006; Meehan, 2006)" (Meehan, 2008, p.106).

Devine then establishes a connection between the financial concern and the general idea of business behind the film-making process.

D: That's why we focus on certain things and get rid of everything else. And it's also money saving.

I: Well, that is so interesting because with your dead body representation you are actually shaping people's imagination about dead bodies.

D: It's a business. It's a business, and you don't even realise it until you actually talk to the make-up people who have a certain budget. They got a certain amount of money, and they actually have to do it in a certain way.

It is not only the limited budget determining the production and the design of a dead body, it is also time which plays an important role in the process. The mannequin artist replied as follows:

I: Is that why they have the dark blue light, so you won't see too much in the autopsy room? That is what Devine told me, the light covers some things.

E: Yeah, also a lot of things that help us, the lighting and the angles, the position it all helps, […]. Again, it comes down to time and what they want to see. Sometimes they tell us what they want to see and then, we read it there, it's completely different and we didn't make it that way, you know what I mean? So, (looking at the mannequin) that's the price. (laughing) But every eight days it's over and you got to fight for the next one. (laughing)

Obviously, he considers the timing of eight days to be too short to produce a decent mannequin. His boss mentions that TV shows like *CSI* or *NCIS* usually request a body to be produced in roughly five to eight days.

M: […] because they don't know until 5 days before what they need. It's just a normal television schedule. No time. They write and constantly change it. It goes back to the network, they change it, and then it goes back.

In addition to budget and time-related issues, the censorship restraints play an important role in the film-making process. The Federal Communications Commission (FCC) was formed in 1934 with the authority to censor the US network monopolies ABC, NBC, and CBS.[11] The task of a censor can be described as follows:

"Censors read scripts, attend every part of the production process, and often preview programs before they are aired. If a program fails to conform to a network's standards, even if they seem arbitrary, the censor can insist on changes. If a pro-

---

11 Cf. Browne, 1994.

gram producer fails to comply with the requests of the censor, the program probably will not air." (Silverman, 2007, p. 2).

A former censor of the FCC describes his profession as less authoritarian, but cites public security and quotes the Communication Acts:

"The Commission (FCC), if public convenience, interest, or necessity will be served thereby … shall grant … a station license. The 'public interest' standard defines a station operator's service requirement. Also the requirements of compliance have been eviscerated over the past several years, the mandate still contains 'public interest', which at the very least, requires the exercise of due care where children are concerned. This amorphous concept of 'public interest' retains some sense of respect for family and order in society and support for institutional values. Perhaps one can go even further. Application and interpretation of such terms as fairness, balance, truth, and dignity of the human spirit can also be attributed to its meaning." (Schneider 2001, p. 132)

According to Schneider, however, neither the "public interest", nor convenience and necessity were ever defined. Additionally, Schneider claims that a censor also needs to know about the historic power of free speech and the business structure of the industry in order to serve the FCC. Schneider, calling himself a gatekeeper rather than a censor, as a former employee of the "Standards and Practice Department", believes:

"[…] as 'censor' I had to be the 'corporate conscience', which meant I had to be a 'good citizen' within the confines of the network's legal and regulatory responsibilities to our shareholders and the public." (Schneider 2001, p. 136)

To sum up Schneider's self-description, he believes he is a person who has his fingers on the pulse of the times and knows about the needs and desires of the U.S. society at large. Assuming that other censors have the same professional ethos, this highly subjective perspective constitutes the production basis that the U.S. networks must follow. The FCC standards primarily mandate the mitigation of representations of obscenity, indecency, and profanity. They explicitly shape U.S. television culture. As Silverman states:

"If the FCC determines that a broadcast contained indecent material, then and only then can the FCC levy fines or revoke broad-cast licenses" (Silverman 2007, p. 3).

Devine explains the same context and adds the pre-emptive and anticipated censorship of her own work due to censorship restrictions and monetary considerations:

D: Well, the network looks up, because they are trying not to get fined. You can get fined if you decide to show something, you know, beside of a breast or whatever. I mean you can get fined, and the reality is, it is a business, so we don't want to film something that isn't going to make it on television. That's a waste of money. And especially when it is the body, because then you are talking about special effects, make up, certainly about an autopsy. You can't use a real actor, obviously, so you have to get, you know, really expensive models or I mean it's a big expense, to show a real autopsy would be cost prohibitive.

The presentation of a clothed dead body can be mostly tracked back to budget and censorship-related issues. According to Devine, most of the time it is a budget restriction that prohibits a nude or partially nude body. The make-up effort for the entire body would be too expensive. She also expresses concern when asked about the attractiveness of their dead bodies portrayed by Hollywood actors.

D: As far as a dead body of a beautiful woman, we try not to show the body in a sexual way. She may look sexually alive in way, but we're trying not to make her look sexual. Because I don't think that serves any purpose. I mean you can tell she was beautiful, but in the Coroner's Office they are usually not beautiful anymore. We whiten up their faces. You want them to look dead, but it shouldn't be 'Oh wow, what a babe'. I mean what would be the plan with that? On an autopsy table? We don't want people to look on the body on the table and think they are hot. That would not be good. But you know some of these women have beautiful bodies and things like that.

The response from Josh Meltzer, Showtime cable TV, of course sounds different, as they have no official censorship:

I: What about nudity? [...] I haven't seen any real bare dead bodies.
J: Oh, dead bodies aren't fun to look at if they are nude, white bodies nude we show, and we show a lot of love making.
I: Ok, but why do you wrap the dead bodies, especially the genital area?
J: That is not a censorship thing, that is for the actors comfort.
I: Yeah, I always question the other producer why they cover [...]
J: [...] no, we actually hired somebody this season, [...] I gave him a special note, there is a very specific style how he wraps the body. Dexter's kills are very virtualistic, you see a lot of skin, every person would get out of this. The guy who used to work for me was very prudish and wrapped the body completely in cellophane. You couldn't see any skin and he was doing it because of his own issues and thought the actors would be more comfor-

table […] But it also created this problem when you look at the scene all you see is bright light gleaming off from all the surroundings.

For Meltzer there is no barrier, they "… definitely want to see nipples." Also, when it comes to dead bodies. This is why even dead women with bare breasts are to be seen on *Dexter*. The decision-making here depends on the popularity of the show and an undefined self-censorship:

I: Why did Dexter become so popular?

J: Dexter is the first show that did come out really grotesque. Realistic in the portrayal of the carnage. […]Dexter shows much more. […] We really took it to the next level.

I: So you don't fight any network with any censorship?

J: No.

I: But you maybe have your own censorship?

J: Yes. Always. Always. You have to go like […] how far we think the audience will let us go?

At this point I would like to provide a few images of the portrayal of carnage from the film location of *Dexter*, which were taken by David Strick from the LA Times:

Fig. 6.7.: Dexter–LA Times report about makeup[12]

---

12 http://photos.latimes.com/backlot/gallery/makeup/2008/9/23/
   Dexter_murder_victim_makeup, September 23, 2008.

Fig. 6.8.: Dexter–LA Times report about makeup[13]

Fig. 6.9.: NCIS–LA Times report about makeup[14]

---

13 http://photos.latimes.com/backlot/gallery/makeup/2008/9/23/
   Dexter_shade_on_a_dead_man, September 23, 2008.
14 http://photos.latimes.com/backlot/gallery/ncis/2009/10/8/
   NCIS_Joe_Hailey_makeup, August 10, 2009.

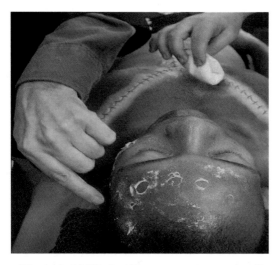

Fig. 6.10.: NCIS–LA Times report about makeup[15]

Fig. 6.11.: NCIS–LA Times report about makeup[16]

15 http://photos.latimes.com/backlot/gallery/ncis/2009/10/8/
NCIS_extra_Ezra_Masters, August 10, 2009.

16 http://photos.latimes.com/backlot/gallery/ncis/2009/10/8/
NCIS_Pauley_Perrette_red, August 10, 2009

Fig. 6.12.: NCIS–LA Times report about makeup[17]

An autopsy of a deceased infant is another crucial issue, and not only amongst coroners. This issue exists not because of emotional circumstances, but, rather, because the autopsy of an infant or child is more complicated than the autopsy of an adult. The producer is hesitant about the presentation of infant death, but cannot clearly express why this is the case.

> D: So the restrictions are just with the bodies, but there are some injures that we would just never show. […] There are some things that you just [pause] you know, especially with babies. You are not going to show an axe injury on a baby or something like that. You just cover up or you show the face, you just not even do an autopsy. I mean, we do it but talk about it.

In the same manner, Devine discusses the absence of a longer presentation of an autopsy procedure. She says that she cannot impose such inhuman shocks to the audience and the network would not tolerate it.

> D: We can't do an autopsy. I mean very rarely. The only time I have ever seen an autopsy […] even attempt to show what it's really like […] It's an inhuman shocking thing. And I think if we're ever going to turn an audience off we show them what a real autopsy looks like. But on the movie SAW IV they show an autopsy. But that's a horror film. So it's so shocking. There is no way you 're going to hold back. We have done a few things, but for the most part an autopsy is so dehumanizing. I mean they don't look human.

---

17 http://photos.latimes.com/backlot/gallery/ncis/2009/10/8/NCIS–1477, August 10, 2009

Ribs flayed all the organs off, the head pulled back and the brain out. It doesn't look real. So no, we don't even go there. I mean our boss is like[…] Look, we have got in trouble with our first season for being too graphic so we are trying not to do anything gratuitous, and I think to show real autopsies is gratuitous.

Indeed, it is the makeup artists who seems the most upset about the censorship restrictions. His entire effort on the production is rarely shown.

E: And we go through all this trouble, we make all this stuff, and then they will never show it. Yeah, I fill everything, I do everything and at the end: where did it go? 90% of what we do, they never show.

Another issue is the depiction of the uncovered corpse as an autopsy object. Different TV shows have a variety of approaches to present in the modest manner the genitals of these dead-body-mannequins:

M: I have never watched Crossing Jordan. NCIS we try to do a little different than we do on CSI because it's still CBS. What they do is, they never cover the body up with any sheets. They just put a bright light at the crotch area. When they do women, they put a hot light over here and over here (pointing at his chest.) They never use a towel, so we are always up against that, and we have to send them little crotch pieces to make them look like Barbie dolls.

For Schneider, the former censor, these restraints have a well thought-out, thorough background:

"No theme or story concept would be deemed unacceptable on the basis of subject alone. Treatment, character delineation, language, and visual depiction all would factor into the determination. In dealing with violence, showing consequences and the extent of harm and its effect on the victim would be weighed heavily. Diffusers, such as humour, and slow motion where appropriately used would also be part of the considerations. In that arena, the key word was excess. Was the portrayal too much for the viewer to digest? Was the violence extensive, overdone, exaggerated, or 'excessive'? Was it violence merely for the sake of violence" (Schneider 2001, p. 137)?

In the following example, the actual struggle with violent scenes and excessive representation can be seen:

R: Well, if somebody gets shot, got a shot into their face, it would blow-off part of your face, skin would be hanging off. So instead we mutilate the face to an extent and make it dirty and bloody. Because it's television to a point. But when the whole cheek is hanging off and the teeth and the tongue are hanging out (rolling eyes) you can't be too graphic.

This comment raises the question: What is the decisive factor that makes a scene too graphic? When exactly do the censors decide what is too graphic and what is not? Where is the turning point?

I: I have a picture in my mind like when the pathologist was taking the skin off the body, but there was no flesh attached to the skin. So they (CSI) just skipped the cutting?

M: Right, right, we have to skip all those things because for Warner that's too graphic. Cutting into skin no doubt they won't go to show that. Actually, taking a knife to skin they won't show you. Putting a gun to somebody's head you cannot throw that, you can't show somebody is getting shot. I mean, we have done it and got away with it because it's really fast, but there is a lot of things the center will not let you do.

I: And what about the viscera presentation? I mean, this is actually pretty graphic, when you put like a heart or a […]

M: Yeah.

I: This is again ok?

M: (nodding)

This statement highlights the strange limits. While cutting the skin with a knife is forbidden on *CSI* (but not on *Dexter*–cable TV), the presentation of the internal organs is permitted. I would like to provide a visual impression of the "viscera" by presenting the following images, which show actors and mannequins with autopsy make up (By courtesy of Matthew W. Mungle, W.M. Creations, Inc., 2008).

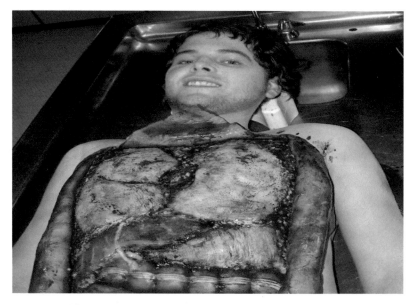

Fig.6.13.: W.M. Creations, Inc–actor with autopsy make-up

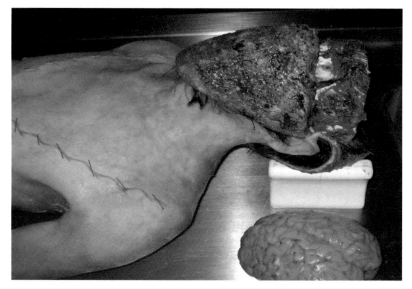

Fig. 6.14.: W.M. Creations, Inc–autopsy mannequin and brain prop

Fig. 6.15.: W.M. Creations, Inc–autopsy mannequin

The definition of what is considered unacceptable is subject to the supervision of a small group of people in each network's Standards and Practices Department. It might seem like an arbitrary negotiation of what can be shown and what cannot be shown along subjective attitudes of people in these departments. Therefore, I also asked whether any changes took place over the past few years.

I: But over the time, the censorship actually changed with certain things […]

M: I think it got worse that we can't show as much as we used to and one of that reasons is because of Janet Jackson and Justin Timberlake. You know. And I think they got worse and worse and more stringent on it. Because I wouldn't work on it, but I think that's in the first season of CSI. I remember them showing a nude woman and you saw her breast and they just flipped out. CBS just flipped out.

I: Ok, but I saw an autopsy on a woman; well you didn't see her breast but the open area.

M: Yeah, the open area and we do it in CSI, we also do it in NCIS, we do a lot of autopsies for them and they started requesting, that when we fold it down we make the breast smaller, so you don't see it from the side.

Cable TV, on the contrary, has apparently no limits according to Josh Meltzer, but when it comes down to certain scenes he reveals the hesitation present within the production party:

I: Did your own censorship scale change when you look back? Maybe you went further with some representations or did you hold back with some representations?

J: Yeah [...] when I look back to season 1 there was a trial and error period trying certain things because

I: Like what?

J: We didn't know how far we can go because we were shooting in June/July. The show wasn't on until September. So it's not like in live theatre, we're gonna try this tonight, see what happens, and if it doesn't we change it for tomorrow.

I: So what did work? What not?

J: The gorier we got, the more the audience loved it. When we would do a woman naked in a bathtub with her brain blowing out and the brains were on the wall, you know, that this is what is [...] really gross, the audience just loved it. That is what we are talking about. In CSI you would have woman in a bathtub you wouldn't see anything and you wouldn't see the blood and you wouldn't see anything, and you wouldn't see the blood spray or the brain matter or anything else on top of the wall. You know, you would see her sitting in a tub of blood but you wouldn't see anything. In Dexter, the water is shed, she is fully naked and there is blood and gore all over the wall, her brain is blown all over the wall and the audience just loves it. Because it was real, it's a horror movie with a great story. And that's really what Dexter was season one. It was a horror movie with a great story[...] the story fit is to get you from one horrific act to another act, you know, Dexter was a great story, first and foremost, that happened to be really gory.

I: Ok, so what did change? Or did something change at all?

J: We really cut back on gore in the last seasons.

I: Why?

J: Because one of the producers didn't bother. One of the producers, the one who actually found the story in the books. It starts with a series of books. She got grossed out by it, even though the audience loved it, even though the other producers loved it, even though everybody else loved it, she said she want to take it down a notch. So now, we do blood, but we don't do brains in that instance. You know, it's still pretty bloody, you know, Dexter still scares people and you know the blood flows, and it's still all about the blood, but it is not quite as grotty as it used to be.

I: And the audience did not notice anything?

J: Oh, the audience did notice, yeah, I mean, the second half of season four. I cannot give away the spoilers but the second half of season four it really takes up again. We go back to our old Dexter basically.

However, restrictions on visual representation continue to exist for Meltzer, for instance, when it comes to death struggles:

I: I was wondering, I never saw any death struggles. No agony. Why not represent this kind of…

J: Well, I don't think it's fun to watch somebody die, that's not entertaining.

I: But isn't it the same?

J: That is, bottom line, no matter what Dexter does, it still has to be entertaining. You know, watching somebody slowly die [long break] Dexter is this strange hero character with a list. You know, Dexter can't kill kids. Dexter can't kill the handicapped. Dexter can't kill the whole little list of things that crosses a line. Dexter has to kill people who are bad. The audience will accept that. Once he goes and he starts to kill people who don't deserve to die then he is just a killer. He is a bad guy. Same thing with watching somebody struggle. You know, that is why Dexter does his kills. He kills. Right into the heart. They bleed. They are dead.

The only programmes not circumscribed in their visual authority then, are those like Showtime and HBO.[18] The representations of dead bodies on HBO shows like *Six Feet Under* or *Autopsy* are, however, subject to self-censorship, and apart from graphic killing and nudity, resemble in many respects those presented on network television. As shown in chapter 4, certain taboos were broken on cable TV, but principally the common representation stays the same. Determining what precisely merits a fine by the FCC is difficult. The censors and their social background are unknown and probably changed over time. In addition, the self-regulatory forces in the networks which have also shaped the shows are usually unknown.

---

18 "Because HBO is free from commercials, advertisers threatening to pull lucrative dollars do not have to be placated. Even conservative campaign groups or those from the religious right remain reticent, accepting the fact that HBO is only available to those viewers willing to pay for the premium cable service. The station makes a virtue of its autonomy from the constraints and restrictions limiting network television" (Akass & McCabe, 2007, p. 66). It's not TV. It's HBO, which means they explicitly broadcast sex, brutal violence and profanity. According to Akass and McCabe NBC became motivated by the success of some of their shows and baldly produced shows similar to those on HBO. "But cable-standard content does not necessarily translate well on broadcast network; NBC soon fell afoul of FCC regulations and the compromises made between executives and programme makers, resulting in the cancellation of both shows after only one season" (Akass & McCabe, 2007, p. 74).

According to Silverman (2007, p. 152), it is not a government censorship, but rather a network censorship that needs to appease their advertisers. "The censor" is therefore hard to identify. Furthermore, the reasons why certain depictions are fined for "being too graphic", while others are shown, are not easily detectable either. When it comes to the depictions of the dead, the only difference between cable and network television is that the body is never presented naked on network television. This is also true for depictions of the living bodies.

6.2.2. Race, Age, Gender

Most television shows are dominated by representations of certain races (Mitchell 1987, Diuguid & Rivers 2000), a distorted representation of gender favouring men (Baur & Crooks, 2008, p.70), and age groups in which the elderly are almost not present (Healey & Ross, 2002). These proportions are then reflected in representations of the dead. Unusually, *CSI Las Vegas* has more female characters involved in crime cases than are found in the actual statistics of the Las Vegas Coroner.[19] An interview with Devine shows why the filmmaker decided to have more female characters involved:

> I: What about the statistics? When I went to the Las Vegas Coroner and got the statistics of how many people die, the age, race and gender, it was very different compared to your show. [...]You depict twice as often males than females, but in fact there are ten times more males than females.
>
> D: Yeah, but if you only got men killing men you're not gonna get the audience. [...] I mean, in reality, on our show half of the time the suspects are women. In reality one to two to three, maybe five percent of the suspects are females. Women don't commit murder that often and they don't do that violently. They usually, if they're gonna do a violent crime, they do it to their spouse or with a spouse. So it's not that interesting. I mean you

---

19 In my statistical survey of the TV show CSI: Crime Scene Investigation, the gender could not be identified in 13 cases. 104 corpses were female (35.6%), 172 corpses were male (58.9%) and three corpses were transsexual (1.0%). Therefore, male corpses are seen almost twice as often. (Seasons 1–5 of CSI Crime Scene Investigation) The statistical results of the TV show CSI still does not match the Las Vegas Coroner Homicide Statistics which I requested from their office. The male victims in homicides are represented three times more often than female victims. In these calculations all accidental, natural and suicidal deaths are excluded. A coroner's office deals with a lot more cases, which are seldom depicted on crime TV shows.

can't [...]. Our job is to sort of make the reality of it interesting. So we have to kind of twist and make a lot of stories up. And it's hard and you gonna have women in it, good looking women, when men watch and good looking men, when woman watch.

Devine explains an actual need to increase the number of female characters in the show on the grounds of attracting a male audience. Though it is not consistent with the real statistics from the Las Vegas Coroner's Office, it seems necessary to keep the male audience interested in the show by employing more good-looking women. The predominance of white actors and actresses is explained by Devine as follows:

I: And what about race, because when I looked it up there were Caucasians, Afro-Americans and Hispanics at the same level, but when I see [...]

D: We have a lot more whites. It's just, I don't know the answer to this other than we just, a lot of the time we just try to find the best actor, so many times, we don't necessarily put a character to be white or anything like that. There will be times when we just go 'Oh that will be great if we had an African American couple to do this part' and it really is how we find the actors and in reality, it's just that there are a lot less black and Latino actors. I mean when we did first look for an actor for Miami for Horatio we were looking for a Latino, of course, because it's Miami and looked and looked and looked and some of them turned us down and we couldn't just find one. So then we decided we have to look for the best actor and not just go for a particular race.

Meltzer has a slightly different idea about the representation of minorities:

I: In Dexter, like in all other TV crime shows, the victim is represented as white, young and attractive.

J: When we kill somebody he is white, but not young and not pretty looking. We don't kill a lot of minorities on the show. Dexter doesn't kill a lot of minorities. We do have a decent amount of minorities die but they are not killed, they are crime scene victims. But they are not Dexter's victims. I don't know why, to be honest with you, I would assume, and that is truly my assumption, you know, race is a delicate issue in television if it's network or cable. And all of a sudden, if we start killing a bunch of Hispanics or a bunch of African Americans, those groups would say why are you killing all the African Americans on your show, [...]like hey, wait a second, you said we ought to give jobs to African American actors and now, we are giving them jobs and you are complaining that we are killing them on the show. But when you're on the show you gotta be killed. So I mean I assume they are trying to avoid groups coming after them. And, no Germans have been killed (laughing).

To sum up, *CSI* and *Dexter* mainly represent white adult males, the media's favourite. This, however, happens not only because of the limited availability of different actors and actresses, but also because of plot. Since the show depicts crime cases, their dead body actors and actresses mostly correlate with actual homicide statistics in cities like Los Angeles or Las Vegas when it comes to the dominant age groups. Still, the gender and race depictions of corpses differ significantly from reality and, at the same time, resemble the common television figure.

6.2.3. Working on realism

In this section I will discuss the ambition of producers to make the *CSI* TV show more realistic for the viewer, yet, inauthentic in the sense of one to one representations of bodies to actual crime statistics. It is well documented that television provides audiences with a distorted view on crime. What are primarily depicted are violent crimes that are thrilling, and a distorted view of the so-called "typical crime" and the "typical criminal".[20] To abrogate these effects *CSI* and *Dexter* have hired actual investigators and detectives, who correct scripts and acting.[21] Furthermore, for *CSI*, former investigators even write scripts based on their own experiences. Thus, they claim that due to their knowledge and efforts the show itself has become

---

20 "For decades, researchers have argued that television provides us with half-truth by only reflecting crime that is interesting, exciting, or sensational (Cavender and Bond-Maupin, 1993; Pandiani, 1978). Several studies have supported this assertion and demonstrated that the 'typical criminal' and the 'typical crime' on television news and police dramas bear little resemblance to reality (Oliver, 1994; Sheley and Ashkins, 1981). Repeatedly, researchers have noted that the media tend to over represent violent crimes and underrepresent nonviolent offenses or property crimes (Graber, 1980; Oliver, 1994)" (Carmody, 1998, p. 159).

21 D: Well, I had already done some technical consulting on movies, so they were looking for someone who knew not just the information, the forensic information, but also how it works on television and movies. Because it's very different, and since I have been done already forward they have called me and asked if I can work as a consultant and so I had the Fridays off so I was able to come on one day the week initially when CSI first started to provide assistance to the actors on how to hold the instruments, you know, the equipment, the instrumentation, how they would walk into a crime scene, how big the yellow tape should be just all the aspects that they had to have for a film. What the crime scene would look like. And you know the injuries how those would look, how to make the make-up look as much as like an injury that is real. That sort of thing.

more 'real'.[22] However, reality and the representation of that reality are not necessarily identical:

"The series is distinguished by a range of post-production digital video effects, including the all but bleach bypass effect I discussed earlier. In general terms, however, the use of the 35 mm does ensure that the series' visual images provide a relatively rich, textured and 'deep' look, [...]. This does not mean that CSI looks more 'realistic' in terms of its image effect, however. In fact, the use of the colour, digital effects and lighting often mean that CSI creates an excessively expressionistic and even fantastic impression. Thus, while the use of 35 mm in CSI indicates that the quality of the image is important to the series, the fact that the image is then so explicitly manipulated in post-production rather uncannily replicates the manipulation of the visual evidence by the characters in the series itself" (Lury, 2005, p. 46).

Chuck Bemis, a cameraman, calls this specific representation the *"CSI vision"*:[23]

C: I think what we call the CSI vision, which is where you are really not in a normal visual state. You're approaching a body and then sort of the skin becomes invisible, you see the ribs and then you are going down into a lung. That's obviously not a normal status. With the lack of a better word we call it CSI world or CSI vision. That part is a fantasy. That is a view point that is not possible in reality, and I believe that is what people like.

---

22 D: I mean, when I first started with CSI, I always gave technical notes on all the scripts so I just continued to give technical notes on all the scripts because our writers are not scientists, they try to look up stuff, find twists and new evidence and new ways of doing things [...] it is my job to make sure the science is real even if it is not being used by forensics, they can't make it up. So first, you know, it was a little hard until they got ingrained and things, they wanted to be real, but now I am pretty happy that for the most parts the science in the show is real, at least our show CSI is real. I mean it may be faster, it may be, you know, obviously you can't use real blood, you can't use real body parts, you can't use real drugs. So you have to make up all the instrumentation working and all that kind of stuff, but if it is something that can't be done by something instrumental then we try to make it. We try to use the real spectra and that kind of thing.
23 "CSI has pioneered a science lab chic which depends upon computer-generated effects to make the invisible visible, to dramatise the science itself. In its deployment of, as David Callahan shows, a wholly fictional crime scene priesthood and in the dazzling reconstruction of bullet trajectories and the microscopic world of hair follicles and entry wound angles, there can be no finer example of how television constructs and disseminates its own version of reality. The arrival of CGI (Computer Generated Imaging) in prime-time TV should be of great interest to analysts of the medium. No consideration of the new realities which innovative series create or state-of-the-art sports coverage provides can be indifferent to television's aesthetics" (Barker, 2006, p. 6).

This experience is at the very core of the modern dead body representation: to look at a dead body without looking at a real dead body. It was mentioned in several interviews and touches upon the paradoxical experience with a 'real' dead and a 'media' dead body.

E   I am sure you understand. If you look at a real dead body a lot of times it looks fake, it doesn't look real, it looks wrong (…) a car accident where a face gets smashed. A lot of times that is one aim that we do achieve, is that we strive to make it look real, which is not always the reality.

I: So you try to make it look fake so it looks real for the audience?

E: Right, a lot of times you have to do that. We are using lies to tell the truth and if your head says 'Oh that's not real, that's all a lie' then it's gone. It's over. The illusion is over. So, we have to fake your mind at thinking 'Yeah, that is what is true'.

Mungle complements the statement in another interview with almost the same expression:

I: What do you think about the dead body presentation in the show?

M: Oh, I think it's great. I mean some of the pictures that we have and some of the research that we do, we look at it and go: 'If we did that they will think it's a fake'. It literally looks so fake. But it's real pictures of like a bloated body. We tried to recreate bloated bodies, but even pictures of bloated bodies look kind of comical. They are real but they are so bloated up, it looks like a fat man. That's, you know, totally different, you know. So we had to take policies in what we do and trying to scale back sometimes.

Making the authentic appear fake so that it is real for the audience is not only craftsmanship, for Mungle, it is practically art:

M: You know, not necessarily because I don't like blood, personally, but it's just, you could throw a lot of blood on something and it would look good, but there is a sense of art to this, you know, making a brain look real or something. Doing different brains for something, where you see a tumour or something taken out.

I: It's better than the real, the real looks like […]

M: Yeah, I know, see we accomplished it like that, you know, because we've gone in to redo something and make it look realistic.

Moreover, the head of the entire *CSI* TV show production, Anthony Zuiker, underlines the 'make it fake so it looks real paradox' by adding the expression 'magic of television'. In an interview with Shallon Lester in 2008 he answers the following question:

L: How do you get these bodies to look so life-like?

Z: If you use real stuff, it looks fake. If you use fake stuff, it looks real. That's
    the magic of television. We have Emmy-winning make-up artists, pros-
    thetic guys that actually do that for a living. They use rubber and goo and
    blood and paint to make it look real. You put it on film and you light it a
    certain way and it looks kind of cool. Those guys are just really talented.

The same phenomenon is described by Josh Meltzer:

I: So you also don't know if you have a test audience who is watching a scene
    and says things like this looks real and this doesn't?
J: I look at the message boards online sometimes. Yeah, there are comments
    all over the place. I mean you do something really tremendous and people
    are gonna say that looks like crap. And then you do something that looks
    like crap, I mean that really looks like crap and they are all like 'Oh that's
    wonderful', so I mean […] it's entertainment.

According to all interviewees, the body representation has to be faked with
additional arrangements because the audience will not perceive an authentic representation as authentic. The audience has learned certain media
codes to detect a dead body. If an authentic media representation does not
match this mediated knowledge about dead bodies, then the authentic
media representation will not remain in the media pictorial discourse.

However, it is not only the representation which stands for unique fake
'realism'. These new TV crime shows of the 21st century started to present
pictures of both dead bodies and their anatomy, as well as forensic medical
procedures to a much greater extent than before. Devine explains this
successful approach by comparing older TV crime shows like *Quincy* and
Columbo.

D: I think, if Quincy was on now they would be doing what we're doing. They
    would show injuries and things like that, but I think in that time it's a kind
    of an innocent period in Hollywood, where there is no way they're going to
    put that up. If you look at that time frame on TV, when someone was dead
    they just have a little blood dripping out of the mouth, maybe a little on the
    shirt. They were really afraid of putting an audience off. […] They did try
    to show that there is science behind solving a murder, but he was kind of
    like a super vamp […] But it was such a good concept. […] You have
    mystery and competing science, where people see how somebody figures it
    out, instead of having, you know, somebody like Columbo who just says
    'you know what bothers me' and somehow out of the blue he figured this
    thing out. […] The audience was always sort of in the role of the observer
    watching him being a great detective. When you watch our show, every-
    body is trying to figure out who did it. Oh, it's a blond hair, oh, remember

that first woman he talked to was blond. People are in and on the investigation. They are not supposed to just looking at it being impressed by smart detectives. So with the different way of setting up a show, so that, you know, people can start feeling like they are smart and in on it. And that's why I think people like it. They feel as if they were part of the investigation because they're seeing it happen.

The typical search for the social-psychological background of the perpetrator in order to solve the crime has changed. The new crime shows put more focus on the chemical, biological, and physical background of the crime scene and on the victim as a forensic object. In particular, the medical examination of the dead body and forensic scientific methods moved into the centre of attention. Visual mediation can provide a clearer reception of ideas and easier understanding of complex and abstract circumstances.

> D: I think what people are interested in is that there is so much information that can be gained from a corpse, a body. [...] I think that people like our shows, at least because we not only try to teach, we always want our audience to feel that they learnt something every single episode. [...] We take them into the eye, and we show them how that works, how it's done. I think people not only hear what can be done, what shows have done forever, cop shows have always said 'oh, the bullet match' the blah blah blah. People now really get how that works. So on our show we were like, the bullet matches and zoom right into the microscope and you show the straight line-up and so people go 'Oh, I get it now'. So they aren't just told the science, they are shown the science. And I think people are excited about it, they feel smart.

Indeed, that is exactly what it is. They are shown the science. A computer animated programme visualising the bullet's flight path into the body does not, however, exist in American forensic laboratories. There is no such method for following the path or course of a fatal bullet to its final destination inside the body. This computer animation entertains the audience with an enactment of the crime event in order to present the internal physical reactions arising from such fatal conflicts.

The additional forensic medical tools and procedures shown consist of elements of imaging processing techniques, such as x-ray images, electron microscope images, and single organs in the autopsy room. The visualisation of imaging techniques or medical imaging, enables diagnostic methods which deliver an interpretable pictorial construction of the inside of the body. Basic medical knowledge is needed to read or interpret abstract images like these ones. Neither the audience nor the actors know, for the most part, what they are looking at. The printout of a toxicology report, the display of an x-ray image or the gaze inside an electron microscope in a high-tech autopsy hall is a very demonstrable display of science.[24] Nevertheless, the audience follows the simplistic and superficial descriptions and explanations without any background knowledge; they cannot check or differentiate the findings. Hence, they gain a certain superficial knowledge, which cannot be applied anywhere else but to these crime shows. But this is what Anthony Zuiker, the producer of *CSI*, wants from his audience. He wants his audience to recognize the forensic science in his crime TV show. In an interview with Kristine Huntley (2005) he is quoted as follows:

"It's arguably the most important civil service this country needs, 'Zuiker says of forensic science, noting that the CSI shows feature donated equipment that is more expensive and higher tech than many labs across the country can afford. He's also familiar with the 'CSI effect' on juries in criminal cases. Juries now have a pre-existing knowledge of science,' Zuiker says, 'noting the public's increased awareness when it comes to evidence. Movies aren't exempt either'–Zuiker notes that they need to be 'more accurate in their scientific research' in order to convince audiences" (Huntley, 2005, para. 27).

Crime TV shows have no educational mandate and the knowledge obtained by the audience is rarely applicable to real life.[25] Still, the "edutainment" style moves the audience into a more active position and probably

---

24 "[…] the series (CSI) posits a Reality we can never see on screen: we may see technicians earnestly peering through microscopes (something real life CSAs–Crime Scene Analysts–do not do, incidentally, along with almost everything else on the show) and we are shown matches between bullet casings, tire treads, the scratches made by metal objects, rope cording and a host of other visual evidence, but one thing we cannot see and verify is the materiality provided or proven by DNA. The visual medium of television is largely unable to provide us with the visual reality of DNA, which is nonetheless the most conclusive speech the body can provide in the series" (Callahan, 2006, p.155).

25 In comparison to lay knowledge about "[…] other countries, past periods in history, other lifestyles, inaccessible institutions (the Houses of Parliament, law courts) or rarely encountered places (hospitals or prisons), even inside our own bodies via medical science programmes. We meet unique people (the president), unusual people (the oldest person on earth), people unlike ourselves (the aristocracy)–and so forth and so forth. Mediated knowledge is not just about recognition of the familiar or legitimating of the known, but also about the discovery of the new, about becoming familiar with the unknown, about legitimating the hitherto marginalized" (Livingstone, 1999, p.79).

wakes the desire to get to know more about the "shown science" as the growing number of forensic science students in the USA demonstrates. Following Joke Hermes, Jonathan Grays states that:

" […] since so much reality (our 'social tapestry') is constructed–map like–from the programs that entertain us, and since so much of our knowledge and experience of the world relies on television's depiction of reality, a vital component of any analysis of television entertainment must be the interrogation of its capacities and strategies for representing and creating reality" (Gray 2008, p. 104).

To sum up, in this part I aimed to deliver insight into the intentions of the filmmaker and the constraints of media representations. I wanted to examine why certain depictions remain in the pictorial discourse while others are excluded. I have shown that film making is a business, and that the film business is all about money, time and censorship. It depends heavily on the 'non-expert' audience's perspective. If, for them, the authentic looks unreal, an unrealistic dead body or organ will replace the authentic representation. That is why I will proceed with the public perspective. I will ask what the public's concerns are about the depiction of dead bodies.

6.3. Recipients: The public response to the new TV shows

What are the public responses to the new TV shows? There were certainly many articles about *CSI*, especially with a juristic and a rather humanistic background, which I will present in the following.

6.3.1. The "CSI Effect" in the juristic discourse

Nowadays in most new television crime dramas, forensic science plays a greater role than the classical work of an investigating detective. (Reiner, Livingstone & Allan, 2003) There has been a plot transformation from the social-psychological investigation of and search for the perpetrator, towards the current use of various chemical, biological, and physical evidence in order to identify them. This shift led to an emphasis on the reliance of evidence found at the scene, evidence found at the forensic laboratory and, in particular, evidence found on the corpse. This new TV phenomenon led to the so-called "CSI Effect". According to Cole and Dioso-Villa (2007) the term "CSI Effect" first appeared on the "CBS Early Show" in 2002, and by 2005 the term had spread all over the United States.

The "CSI effect" is a loose description used by the media to refer to the phenomenon that television crime dramas influence jurors in their decision-making. (Tyler, 2006) It is said that jurors watching the new crime dramas expect the same or similar scientific procedures and techniques in the courtroom which they have previously seen on TV. If these procedures and techniques are not displayed during the courtroom proceedings, the jury is more likely to not convict the accused of the crime. (Heinrick, 2006, p. 59f) This phenomenon is similar to the so-called "Perry Mason Effect". The jury in the court is expected to have a different and unreal view about how the investigation should have taken place in comparison to a real life investigation. (Heinrick, 2006)

The ensuing discourse on whether a "CSI Effect" exists is guided by the results of different surveys and various conclusions. The study "The CSI Effect and Its Real-Life Impact on Justice" of the Maricopa County Attorney's Office (MCAO) in 2005 has often been quoted in media articles to support the claim that the "CSI Effect" has a significant influence on the jurors.[26] However, this study consists of a survey that concentrates on the perceptions of prosecutors and the perceptions of an actual jury were never investigated. Hence, the study only reveals the assumptions of prosecutors and cannot examine the claim as regards the jurors' TV habits and the influences on them. (Boudreau 2008) It was even argued that the "CSI Effect" could turn out to be an urban legend because other studies have not supported a CSI TV show based tendency by the jury leading to the accused being acquitted. (Boudreau 2008)[27] Cole and Dioso-Villa categorised six different "CSI Effects" in order to draw conclusions about the most important "CSI Effect", which is if jurors who watch CSI are influenced by the show and would acquit the accused due to an unrealistic view of the forensic evidence. Therefore, four types of evidence were discussed in order to prove their tenableness. This evidence included anecdotes, surveys of legal actors, simulated jury decision-making studies, and acquittal rates in criminal cases. Cole and Dioso-Villa concluded that there was little support for the influence of the "CSI Effect" on the jury.

---

26 The study consist of a survey of 102 prosecutors with jury trial experiences.
27 Nick Schweitzer, Ph.D. student and Michael Saks, ASU professor of law and psychology, conducted a survey with 48 jury-eligible students on the CSI Effect and did not find a significant effect on verdicts.

The other "CSI Effects" concern the anticipated educational aspect for the audience (which includes, of course, jurors-to-be and perpetrators-to-be) which was suggested by the CSI creator himself.

"But experts agree that much of the forensic science depicted on 'C.S.I.'–40%, according to forensic scientist Thomas Mauriello–does not even exist. And even when the techniques are real, the neatly perfect depictions of collecting, processing and analyzing evidence are not" (Cole & Dioso, 2005, para. 12).

As can be deduced from the numerous articles, the CSI TV show obviously sparked interest and concomitant fears. There was also an enormous and measurable change of interest in forensic science amongst students. According to Jeffrey Heinrick (2006), there were four forensic science students who graduated at the West Virginia University in 1999, while the number increased to 400 in 2004. It can clearly be seen as a sign that the investigation of a crime, including the examination of a dead body, attracts more attention and interest than ever. At the same time, there are voices in the humanistic discourse who warn against the too explicit display and examination of a dead body.

6.3.2. The "CSI Effect" in the humanistic discourse

Lately, the media representations of dead bodies in the TV crime shows have often been connected with the concept of pornography. In the following, I would like to scrutinise the applicability of these comparisons and ask why this comparison has gained so much popularity. Therefore, I will first of all introduce those authors who have made these comparisons and later discuss their approaches. I argue that the media representations of dead bodies are not comparable with representations of actors from the pornography genre, though others have done so; these comparisons, however, obviously define the normative borderline of the present pictorial discourse of the media representation of the corpse.

In 1955 Geoffrey Gorer was the first to claim in the essay "The pornography of death" that the society of the twentieth century suppresses the subject of 'death' in the same way, the society of the nineteenth century did with the subject of 'sexuality'. He explains death as a taboo that carries the ambivalent disposition of 'guilt and pleasure'. According to Gorer, this disposition is also the significant characteristic of Pornography, which is why he compares the tabooing of death with the tabooing of sexuality: "At present, death and mourning are treated with much the same prudery as sexual impulses were a century ago" (Gorer, 1955, p. 128).

Lately, more and more scientists have taken up this comparison, referring to the media representations of corpses. In 2005 Karen Lury describes the representations of dead bodies in the new TV crime show '*CSI Las Vegas*' as stylistically pornographic, which is taken up by Karen Boyle and Elke Weissmann (2007) who confirm this description. Sue Tait (2006) calls the distinctive camera technique of the TV show *CSI* a "carnographic gaze", while Jacque Lynn Foltyn (2006) even claims: "In many ways, death is replacing sex as the taboo to be challenged by television, so the corpse has become the porn star of popular culture." Elizabeth Klaver (2006) draws a different picture, stating that the cultural necrophilic desire to look at the dead body has shifted to the desire for a certain pictorial representation rather than for the dead body per se. Most of these scientists refer first to Gorer's thesis and then to an inflated context of new media representations of dead bodies.[28] These rather unusual theses raise questions about the propriety of such comparisons, if not, in general, about the necessity of these comparisons. I will proceed with three approaches.

Pornographic Iconography

The film and television scholar Karen Lury (2005) describes the mode of representation in *CSI* as follows[29]:

"At times, the presentation of the image in the series verges on the obscene. Many images in CSI reveal things that are gruesome and disgusting or explicitly sexual, yet I would suggest that even when they are not obscene in terms of content, they are stylistically pornographic" (Lury, 2005, p. 56).

Lury states an evident connection between the 'infamous, money shot' in the pornographic movie and the 'CSI shot'. The television scholars Karen Boyle and Elke Weissmann further Lury's theses and explore the question of connection between the distinctive *CSI* camera mode and the pornography mode. They compare pictures representative of the pornographic

---

28 The authors do not quote each other which probably has to do with publishing at the same time, yet they come up with the same kind of comparisons between death and pornography.

29 For her general thesis about CSI, Lury analysed one episode out of nine seasons of CSI (Las Vegas, not CSI Miami or CSI New York), which was about a prostitution crime ("Snuff").

genre with those of *CSI* produced wounds and simulations of fatal bullets' flight paths and equate them with physical penetration. This kind of shot:

"[…] apparently recreates, through the use of prosthetics, models and computer generated images, the impact of criminal (and, less often, accidental) violence on the body of the victim" (Boyle & Weissmann, 2007, p. 90).

Of course, a comparison between the entire pornography genre and one single *CSI* TV show does not provide the possibility to conduct a precise comparative analysis. Still, they distinguish the cinematic pornography based on studies from Linda Williams (1999). According to Williams, hardcore pornography shows "real sex", while soft-core pornography relies on the suggestion of intercourse and climax.

"What, and how, hardcore shows has varied over time, but in the contemporary context the signatures of hardcore would include close-ups of aroused genitals and other body parts, penetration shots and the so-called 'money shots' of male ejaculation" (Boyle & Weissmann, 2007, p. 91).

Both authors also refer to Williams (1990, p. 48) when it comes to the "principle of the maximum visibility" of the staging of bodies.

"Achieving this visibility requires artifice–the selection of the sexual positions that shows the most of bodies and organs; the over-lighting of easily obscured genitals; the emphasis on external ejaculation (ibid: 49)–but the visible is offered as a guarantee of authenticity […]" (Boyle & Weissmann, 2007, p. 91).

In their opinion, the maximum of the physical visibility in *CSI* is similar to the pornographic depiction of bodies. They come up with three significant signs for their comparison, namely the pornographic body as a body of proof; second, the disembodiment of the pornographic body; and third, the physical reaction of the viewer. They argue that *CSI* shots create a scientific authenticity. These authentic shots and the use of the dead body by the investigator as a 'work station' for crime detection, presents the corpse as a disembodied object of evidence. However, both authors see the connection between the physical reaction of the pornographic viewer and the physical reaction of the *CSI* viewer. They are more critical than Lury and put "physical reactions" in connection with the so-called CSI effect. In their conclusion Boyle and Weissman state that:

"[…] the 'pornographic' qualities that have been widely attributed to CSI in academic and popular responses relate not only to the penetrating camera and its graphic exposure of bodily injury and decay, but also, as we have argued in this essay, to the equation of maximum visibility with 'truth'" (Boyle & Weissman, 2007, p. 80).

Gothic eroticism and the necrophilic gaze

The communication scientist Sue Tait (2006) analyses the construction of the scientific appearance of the staging of the forensic corpse in *CSI*. She argues that the corpse offers an ideal representational surface for the constitution and performance of scientific expert's assessment and:

"[…] this instrumentalized view of the corpse enables the performance of a Gothic eroticism and the conceit that a rational imperative frames our looking and authorizes a necrophilic gaze" (Tait, 2006, p. 46).

Following Sawday (1995), she explains the connection from the forensic representation to the gothic eroticism with the history of anatomical corpse representation with pedagogic context.

"Science offers a refuge for the pornography of death. I describe the gaze this offers the viewer as necrophilic because we are positioned to take pleasure from imagery of death, imagery which often penetrates the flesh" (Tait, 2006, p. 51).

These tabooed views of and insights into the nude body were previously left to the horror genre or the pornography genre alone. According to Taits, they represent the "secrets of the flesh" and with the carnographic insight into the body they break the taboo. The new camera techniques generate different views of the body such as the "[…] carnographic spectacle of the ruined body" (Tait, 2006, p. 51). Following Pinedo (1997), Tait describes CSI scenes showing an open corpse and relates it to the carnality which degrades the hard-core and horror genre, to disreputable genres because it causes physical reactions like excitement or disgust. Moreover, Tait states that the victims in *CSI* are often illustrated in a violent erotic context.[30] For this argument, she finds two shows ("Slaves of Las Vegas"

---

30 "On CSI the performance of science, the pursuit of truth and solution, and the apparent realism enable an explicit engagement with the erotics of violence and death. Victims on CSI frequently meet their end in violently eroticized contexts such as being smothered during sex, while watching a peep show, following rape, to conceal incest, in the course of sex work or upon discovery during a three-way of an unexpected penis"(Tait, 2006, p. 52).

and "Spring Break"), which are concerned with fatal sex crimes.[31] This leads her to the following conclusion:

"This positivist milieu authorizes a necrophilic imaginary, whereby visual pleasure is produced through carnographic imagery, the eye's penetration of the body (a body often ruined in sexual circumstances) and a gendered gaze upon the corpse (death is more interesting when it happens to somebody beautiful). The depiction of the female corpse on CSI continues a history of representation which relies on the female body to signify the sexual, and reiterates the modernist theme of erotics made possible only through death" (Tait, 2006, p. 59).

The media dead as the new porn star

The sociologist Jacque Lynn Foltyn describes in a lecture entitled "Dead sexy: post-disaster/terrorism voyeurism and the corpse, pop culture's new porn star" that the dead are the media's new "porn stars". Following Gorer she states:

"In many ways, death is replacing sex as the taboo to be challenged by television, so the corpse has become the porn star of popular culture" (Foltyn, 2006).

She also analyses the media representation of the dead in modern pop culture and notes that the dead have become the centre of media attention not only in the USA, but also in European countries:

"While the images of death are not new I noticed the corpses become the star of our visual culture challenging taboos around death and dead in modern society from CSI [...] in our youth and beauty obsessed culture dead celebrities are dead sexy [...]" (Foltyn, 2006).

Not only celebrities, but also the dead in the new crime shows like *CSI* receive more attention:

"The corpse becomes a sex symbol, pop culture's latest porn star. The new body we voyeuristically explore. In the 21st century death is replacing sex as a taboo to be challenged by TV, cinema and the internet" (Foltyn, 2006).

Yet, according to Foltyn the dead body appears in different media types and enactment modes, which are not always "sexy", but authentic like in

---

31 "That one of the looks the corpse may draw is an erotic gaze is confirmed by the act of necrophilia on 'Spring Break'. The perpetrator represents his rape of a dead woman as an honest mistake: 'It's spring break, I'm not the first guy to find a girl passed out on the beach'" (Tait, 2006, p.52f).

the funeral parlour documentary-soap *Family Plots*, which features real corpses as main characters.[32]

"Clearly we are of two minds about the dead body. Attracted to and repulsed by it, regarding it as sacred and profane" (Foltyn, 2006).

According to Foltyn, "death is the new sex" and a demand for more authentic corpse depiction has risen. She argues that older TV shows like *Quincy* presented the corpses with privacy and discreetly covered under towels, while degradation and the voyeuristic gaze came with the new TV shows. Today, the dead body in the crime genre has a lot in common with the body in the pornographic one. She argues that both bodies are presented in close-ups in order to examine parts of the body, surfaces, and how they function in detail. Foltyn elaborates on bodies which are prodded, poked, penetrated, and presented as an outraging sight. Pointing towards an exploitation of the young and beautiful instead of presenting the old and ugly, she also states that both bodies are presented undressed or half-dressed. She concludes that socially appropriate emotions such as love or grief are absent.

In summary, Foltyn concludes that since there is no meaning attached to this kind of representation of the dead, these representations turn decadent. The eroticised corpse is the ultimate taboo body. The dead become an entertainment product and the drive for higher viewership ratings supports the "[…] increasingly macabre representation of dead bodies or decomposition and dissection appearing in our culture" (Foltyn, 2006).

Necrophilic desire

Klaver (2006) also concentrates on necrophilic desire when it comes to dead body representations, but follows Fromm by saying:

"[…] the culture has become *necrophilous in character*, mainly due to this collective drive to reify which, promoted by technology, gives rise to the consumer imaginary so prevalent in the West today" (Klaver, 2006, p. 133f).

Following Fromm,[33] Klaver also describes that the necrophilous desire for the dead body has turned into a desire for a sanitised object that is sup-

---

32 Furthermore, Foltyn also observes this in other shows, (e.g. Desperate Housewives, Ghostwhisperer, Dead like Me, Real Autopsy) as well as in new video games, on the Internet, in music, and art as an increase in the treatment of the dead.
33 Corpses appear as "clean, shining machines" (Fromm, 1973, p. 350).

posed to substitute the corpse. (Klaver, 2006, p. 134) Respectively, she also refers to Jean Baudrillard's hyperreality term, which stands for the image taking over the real:

"Watching an autopsy on television or in the movies, then, would better be described as watching the substitution of the image for the real, the scene of an autopsy whereby an actor or dummy stands in for the dead body" (Klaver, 2006, p. 134).

While observing the media representation in *Crossing Jordan* or *The Silence of the Lambs* she finds that great care is taken when representing the dead body on television. The body is never uncovered, and the dissection is shown only to the smallest extent. She also notes that she never knew how sanitised the dead body on television was until she attended a real autopsy:

Rather than seeing the corpse with our own eyes (or smelling it), the audience is seeing a substitute, the body objectified to an image. In fact, in both shows, the camera even does the work of dismemberment for us, allowing us to gaze at the image of a body fragmented into camera shots without actually having to do or watch any of the cutting or opening ourselves. Quite a difference. Necrophilous desire to gaze at the dead body has indeed been transferred from desire to look at the dead body itself to a much more sanitized version. (Klaver, 2006, p. 136f)

According to Klaver, the viewer can be located as a voyeur who watches scenes usually happening behind closed doors from a secure private place. This position enables the viewer to possess the body on screen, while the "[…] looked-at body becomes the reified object of sexual desire, the sanitized and superficial image […]" (Klaver, 2006, p. 140). Just like Ariès and Foltyn, she argues that through the remoteness of death in the postmodern West, death has become a spectacular object, especially in the visual media.

"But note how the discourse of autopsy is already lending itself to sexual imagery in the desire of the voyeur to know the hidden recess of the dead body by entering the hidden recesses of Western culture. We speak of autopsy as deploying a penetrating or piercing gaze, made possible by phallic instruments that expose the interior of the body for the benefit of our knowledge. Indeed, this particular habitus of Westerners, arguably in place since the Renaissance, towards the dead body as a sexual object has been unpacked in many interpretations of representations of the corpse" (Klaver, 2006, p. 140f).

According to Klaver it is not only this voyeuristic view that generates the sexual aestheticisation of the cadaver but also the highly iconic quality of television images which are charged with a sexual display. At this point, the taboo turns visible. As the sexual charge seems immanent in television images, Western culture prohibits this kind of display at all costs. Even though real autopsies are performed on uncovered corpses, the media censors forbid a total nude/naked person in an autopsy scene.

"In a sense, autopsy scenes end up with fascinating, built-in fort/da mechanism, where the image of the cadaver is pushed and pulled, attracting and repulsing, at the same time. And of course, the action of fort/da is essentially what underpins Ariès' explanation of how death can so easily become spectacular. Something invisible and prohibited as the all-too-deviant Real is suddenly made visible and available as the reified image, mediated for our consumption [...] The necrophilous subject responds by being utterly fascinated" (Klaver, 2006, p. 141).

The approach of Klaver differs from the previous approaches. She determines the necrophilous desire to view an image of a sanitised, clean object that stands in for a dead body representation on television. Thus, she draws an important line between her arguments and those of the previous authors. She notes the difference between watching dead body dummies and fake autopsy on television and actual necrophilic behaviour which describes the desire for a real corpse.

Conclusion and discussion

To sum up, I found that the authors examining this subject attach their respective comparisons of corpse representations to different levels, for instance, the recipient's (viewer's) level as well as the film production level. Additionally, the common characteristic of these approaches is that they are based upon a normative argumentation structure. Gorer's thesis seemed already hardly plausible if one takes into consideration that the concept of "sexuality" was generated only in the nineteenth century, while death was always picked out as a central theme, as a concept and problem. From the nineteenth century onwards, the term "sexuality", i.e. what we presently define as sexuality, was not at all available. Hence, the terms "death" and "sexuality" have a very different historical context. Therefore, it should be called into question whether the suppression of sexuality in the nineteenth century is substantial before proceeding with this thesis. Foucault (1977), for instance, demonstrated in his analysis of sexuality that displacement actually creates what should be suppressed. In particular, the generation of the concept of "sexuality" and forcing this concept into a discourse, contrast with the thesis of a suppression of sexuality in the nineteenth century. Hence, it should be examined, first and foremost, why these comparisons of the pictorial representation of the dead with the concept of pornography are so popular? Respectively, what, in particular, causes the combined use of both taboo contexts. What can be deduced from these discussions?

Linda William described pornography as a genre which explicitly aims to excite its audience with the enactment of sexual acts. (Williams, 1999) Dolf Zillmann defines pornography as a pictorial representation of human sexual behaviour of every kind and in every connection. (Zillmann, 2004). These definitions, of course, are based on the assumption that pornography is always just what society considers to be pornography at a certain time, which also generates the classical topos of social-scientific research of pornography.[34] This means that pornography is subjected to temporal transformations of cultural norms. Sexual taboos are always dependent on a culture, which is why pornography is also always defined as normative.(Kendrick 1996, Marcus 1979) Hence, according to Herbert Selg, textual or graphic documents, which are classified as pornographic, illustrate the shift towards a negative connotation because "good pornography" is a contradiction in itself. (Selg, 1997, p. 48) The categorisation "pornography" contains, therefore, a degradation of primarily female characters which defines what a specific society understands at a certain time as "obscene". The categorisation of the new media representation of corpses as pornography, even if portrayed as "aesthetic pornography"[35], rather describes the depreciation of these representations through these authors than of the representation itself. For this reason, I asked earlier for the necessity of such comparisons. This conclusion, however, is not supposed to disavow the descriptive comparison of media phenomena, but the list of normative arguments insinuates that producers have of certain TV series and thus their recipients as having a necrophilic, carnal or even pornographic gaze. At this point, the question arises what else can be compared if the least common denominator is the "maximum visibility of the truth"? In fact, the "penetrating camera and its graphic exposure of bodily inju-

---

34 I would like to thank Sven Lewandowski for the discussion on this topic and for the draft of his paper "La femme machine? Pornographische Inszenierungen von Sexualität und Körperlichkeit" in 2008.

35 Unfortunately, the above mentioned authors refrain from explicitly defining "pornographic aesthetic", which makes it difficult to follow the comparison.

ries" can also be applied to the new medical TV shows[36] because these shows also concentrate on wounds and medical techniques. In a metaphorical sense, the "penetrating camera" can also be applied to all 'real life' TV shows[37] or 'real life' game shows[38] in which the camera explores the privacy of the actors to an ever greater extent. Yet, at the recipient's level the authors anticipate certain physical reactions which seem to support their theses:

"As a consequence, the body does not only appear as the object of the medical gaze; it is also invested with the iconography and, more importantly, the acoustics of the slasher film. This shares with pornography an emphasis on carnality […] the 'CSI shot', because of its speed and its emphasis on gore is able to engage the viewer's body" (Boyle & Weissmann, 2007, p. 97).

Shootings from other genres (comedy, drama, action, etc.) can, of course, animate the body of the viewer, too. There is still no research which studies possible physical reactions from viewers of shows like *CSI*. These assertions are just assumptions which should be empirically scrutinised first, before they develop into just another so-called CSI effect.

A significant difference between the new crime show genre and pornography is, above all, the production and the reception which concentrates on a primarily male dominated sector. (Selg, 1986, p. 56) The reality of the production and reception of *CSI* does not reflect this dominance. For instance, the fictive victims of the show are twice as often male characters than female ones. This, of course, stands in contrast to classical pornography films in which female stereotypes are at the centre. (Selg, 1986, p. 56) Another significant difference is that *CSI* never shows real naked dead bodies in erotic poses. The censorship regulations for American series categorically exclude a naked body that is entirely visible. Though *CSI* can simulate "insight shots" it does not justify the categorisation as "penetrating camera". In *CSI*, the inside of the body is presented either by computer animations or by a preserved mannequin.

In spite of the shortened representation of the arguments of the different authors, a few but essential differences already appear at the different levels which is why a comparison cannot be held between pornography and the new media representations of corpses, except at the subjective

---

36 E.g.: ER, Grey's Anatomy, Chicago Hope, Dr. House, Nip & Tuck
37 E.g.: Big Brother, The Bachelor/ette, The Osborns or Cops
38 E.g.: America's got talent, Dancing with the stars, American Idol

normative level. Even if it seems acceptable to compare different techniques of visualisation from a truth-authenticity approach in television studies, these approaches indicate the limits of the pictorial discourse: Which corpse representations are acceptable, and which representations are classified as pornographic, and thus negatively. This public discourse reflects the mechanism of inclusion and exclusion within the pictorial discourse.

6.4. Summary

My aim in this chapter was to reveal the broader context of the production and the effects of the representations, which generate and shape restrictions of the pictorial discourse of dead bodies in contemporary TV shows. I asked how the context of the pictorial discourse is organised and if any perspective about the dead body was preferred. I argued that restrictions made by medical officials, producers and recipients altogether clearly shape the audiences' idea of how a dead individual appears.

As I first demonstrated in the forensic documentary, it is in fact forbidden by the Los Angeles County Coroner officials to film dead bodies in the pathology department. Instead, the participating medical examiner re-enacted an autopsy on a mannequin. Subsequently, I presented interviews with people working in the film industry which demonstrated various factors of restriction on visual production, such as money, time, and censorship, which are set in the course of a TV show production. The third approach pointed to the restriction demands coming from the public side. I reflected the academic discourse about the viewers' response to the new representation of corpses and showed that the public discussions indicated the limits of the pictorial discourse. Some corpse representations are acceptable, and some representations are negatively classified as pornographic, reflecting the mechanism of inclusion and exclusion within the pictorial discourse.

Part 4–Conclusion

7 Conclusion

In the beginning, I cited Thomas Macho and Hans Belting, who argued about whether there is a new visibility of death or an accomplishment of an invisibility of death. I argued that since the 21st century, there is an emergent visibility of death representation that is entirely new. Prior to 2000, crime shows rarely showed crime victims at the crime scene and only rarely in pathology, with the exception of *Quincy, M.E.* With the turn of the century and the rise of many new TV shows that revolved around a corpse, the dead were also shown in the morgue, embalming room or in pathology. My thesis synthesises the arguments of Macho and Belting and expands them by including a "sophisticated system of death representation", coined by Hallam, Hockey and Howarth. The representations refer to death and obscures death at the same time. Producers still hesitate to produce representations of death of a significant other like in *Family Plots*. Meanwhile, older representation systems compete with new and manifold sophisticated representation systems in contemporary TV.

In order to prove my hypothesis of whether there has emerged a new representation system of death and if so how it is characterised, I subdivided my research into two major parts. Part 1 included film analysis (chapter 3) and pictorial analysis (chapter 4) and Part 2 included statistical inquiries (chapter 5) and field research and interviews (chapter 6). Part 1 disclosed how much of the dead body is shown and how this done and Part 2 disclosed what is not shown and why. The two chapters served to research if there is a new system of representation and if so, how it is constituted. For the analysis, I selected 13 new TV shows, all of which were produced in the 21st Century. The selection was based on the corpse representation, i.e. the dead body remained in the plot and, after being represented as a crime victim at scene, recurred in the course of a show in pathology, the morgue or embalming room or 'killing room'.

In Part 1, I verified the emergence of a new system of death representation in new TV shows by introducing thirteen TV shows with corpse representations. These representations differ from previous death representations in TV shows. Furthermore, the images disclosed a changing attitude towards death, from denial to rapprochement and domestication. With the help of the generation of four consecutive depiction models and a list of conducted representation trends, I demonstrated the main discourse of new depiction models. The list included: (1.) a trend towards aestheticisation, seen in the dominant representation of embellished dead (bodies), (2.) a trend towards sterility, like the dominant representation of clean dead (bodies), (3.) a trend towards subjectifying, like representing the dead as a partner for interactions, (4.) a trend towards objectifying the dead as objects of anatomical knowledge and (5.) the trend towards more violation against the corpse. The stronger the trend was present in a TV show; the higher the images were classified into depiction models. Therefore, these depiction models are consecutive and can be listed as follows:

1) The simulation of the authentic contains images of real decedents
2) The traditional depiction contains no images of dead or images with covered-up dead
3) The modern depiction contains plain images of aesthetic corpses, and finally
4) The breach of style contains rather abstract images of corpses

Thereafter, I conducted a film analysis for Part 1, which was based on a comparison between two autopsy scenes. I wanted to specify the aesthetic trend that was mentioned in the previous chapter because the trend seemed to be the most striking common denominator. The autopsy scenes were selected from a fictional TV show and an autopsy documentary, which served as a contrast for the fictional TV shows. The findings revealed that the producer for the popular crime TV show made use of massive media aesthetic techniques on a visual and audio level. Due to the exhaustive use of media aestheticisation techniques, the typical characteristics of a dead body during an autopsy were neglected in the popular TV show. These typical characteristics were, however, displayed in the documentary. They showed an atonic body with signs of old age, barely covered on a messy wet table, sometimes sliding back and forth due to the autopsy procedures. During the procedure, every step of the destructive opening of the upper body and the head was clearly visible. The camerawork and the lighting revealed every step of the procedure and every organ, which was removed and examined for approximately half an hour. In the popular TV show, a prettified and pleasing body, young, tight and athletic, was represented, which afterwards also displayed a visible large opening in its chest but for approximately two minutes. The depiction of prettified bodies with disgusting traits constitutes the new aesthetic image of the dead. The film analysis proved that a massive media aestheticisation of material and social reality was used in the popular crime show. At the end, I concluded five evident differences between the fictional TV show and the documentary:

1) The plot and the amount of time the autopsy procedures were shown for,
2) The different dead body figures
3) The setting, which differed in terms of arrangement, cleanliness, privacy and style,
4) The visual level and the use of different light and colour effects, and
5) The audio level, the use of different communication, noises and sounds.

To summarise, the substantial differences between the documentary and the fictional TV show indeed support the hypothesis that a massive aestheticisation effort for staging corpses has taken place in fictional TV shows.

In Part 2, I first statistically specified in chapter 5 what is not shown and why. Here, I introduced the common theories on taboo and death and applied them to the new TV shows. This is why I then distinguished between general TV show representation restrictions and specific representation taboos regarding the dead body. I contrasted the new representations of the dead in a documentary soap with the representation of the dead in a drama / black comedy show and concluded that the fictional TV show omits detailed representations of the embalming. The selected TV show provided images of the dead that statistically most often looked like this: a covered, clean and tidy, white, middle-aged man seemingly resting on a clean and tidy table in a clean and tidy environment, always surrounded by other figures that seem to care about his appearance. The dead were seldom represented in an old age group and if they were, then it was without any age marks or signs of decay. The dead were never shown dirty, on a messy table or in an untidy embalming room. The dead were also never shown in any kind of motion when uncovered. Thus in 63 episodes with

210 corpses, not a single lifting of a corpse into a coffin was shown. These strong restrictions, concerning age, disorder and motion can, therefore, be seen as actual manifestations of taboos in Western culture, where death has always been viewed as a peaceful sleep and a releasing rest. In contrast, the docu-soap "Family Plots" violated all these restriction and was cancelled soon after the second season.

In chapter 6, I represented interviews with film participants and film-makers, in order to reveal the broader context of the production and effects of the representations. I questioned how the context of the pictorial discourse is organised and if one's perspective on the dead body would be more favourable. I argued that medical officials, producers and recipients explicitly shape media representations of the corpse.

I demonstrated, with a forensic documentary, that it was in fact not only forbidden by Los Angeles County Coroner Officials to shoot their dead bodies in pathology, but also that the participating medical examiner instead had to re-enact an autopsy on a mannequin.[1] Thereafter, I presented interviews with people working in the film business, demonstrating various factors of restriction like financial restraints, time limitations and censorship, which are set in the course of the TV shows' production. The third approach pointed to the restriction demands, which come from the public side. I reflected the academic discourse surrounding the viewers' response to the new representation of corpses, and showed that the public discussions marked out the borders of the pictorial discourse. According to them, some corpse representations are acceptable and some representations are negatively classified as pornographic, which reflects the mechanism of inclusion and exclusion within pictorial discourse. I concluded that I could clearly show certain trends of the new representations of death and found explanations in the interviews of why the corpses are represented the way they are.

---

1 Meanwhile, the Coroner participated in a penalty program for D.U.I convicted civilians which included, amongst other things, a tour through the coroner's office service floor (autopsy suites) for the convicts, in order for them to see what might happen to them if they were involved in a fatal accident.

7.1. Visual knowledge and communicative genre

In my research, I demonstrated the various characteristics of the sophisticated systems of representation in contemporary TV shows. Most of us have never actually seen a real dead body on television, much less in reality. We in fact see actors re-enacting death, or dead actors when they were still alive and soon to be dead actors. The representation of the death of a significant other has been neglected in TV show history, however, old representation systems, which did rarely show dead figures have lost the competition to the increasing number of new and actually visible representations of corpses. There is a new visibility of new representation systems, which refer to death but refuse the death of the significant other. When working on the emergence of the new death representation system since the 21st century, this research should not conclude without offering possible reasons for the emergence of this new phenomenon. That is why I will offer a sociological superstructure for the explanation of the findings. In the following, I will apply the sociology of knowledge, especially the 'communicative genre' approach of Hubert Knoblauch on my findings.

Regula Valérie Burri (2009, p. 24f) argues that in contrast to other academic disciplines, sociology paid only little attention towards depictions in the past. This changed when the sociology of media and communication started to focus on depictions. Burri refers to Stefan Mueller-Doohm's research, in which he developed a cultural-sociological depiction hermeneutic, an approach that I used in my research. Visual sociology (Raab 2008, Knoblauch & Schnettler 2007) also discovered images and focussed on the use of them in new media. According to Burri, sociology of knowledge is another discipline, which took interest in the meaning of images when it comes to the production, distribution and reception of knowledge. As one can see, the importance of images has been recognised and Burri claims that a visual turn in sociology started.

According to Bernt Schnettler (2007), the main challenge of sociology of visual knowledge is the empirical research on the influence of visualisation techniques on the transformation of action, communication and knowledge. This means that sociology of visual knowledge has to determine the forms and functions of visual representations. (Schnettler & Pötzsch, 2007) Analysing the approaches of how to determine visual representations, Jürgen Raab (2008) refers to 'Gattungsanalyse' (Luckmann & Knoblauch, 2000) which could be applied to my research if its focus was to be extended. At the core of my research stands the question: "has a new system of death representation emerged and if so, how can it be described?" I have proven that there is a new representation system of death, which displays specific representation codes. Discourses are stable and defined processes of attribution of meanings. They are chronological and socially structured, and reflect specific knowledge about social problems regarding interpretation and action (Keller, 2005, 231). At this point, by applying 'Gattungsanalyse', I will investigate further as to why this new system of representation has emerged, and why these representation codes are structured the way they are. Afterwards, I will draw conclusions about the causes by analysing the effect. Since the cause usually takes place before the effect, in this case before the turn of the 21st century, many causes could come into consideration. However, the term 'kommunikative Gattung', translated as 'communicative genre' supports the possibility to separate these causes. Thomas Luckmann (1988) provided the term for communication analysis. Hubert Knoblauch and Jürgen Raab (2001) also applied the communicative genre to media phenomena. They describe the communicative genre as follows:

"Communicative genres are defined as historically and culturally specific, socially fixed and modelled solutions to communicative problems which serve to cope with, mediate and transmit intersubjective experiences of the life-world. They differ from more spontaneous communicative processes in that actors orientate their reciprocal actions by means of predictably typified patterns. The more fixed these patterns become, the more predictable the course of action becomes for those involved–speakers and listeners respectively" (Knoblauch & Raab, 2001, p. 197).

Hence, in this sub-chapter I will use two different kinds of genres. The media genre term, used here in the traditional sense for TV formats, distinguishes, for instance, fantasy and crime representation codes. The communicative genre term is characterised by genre crossing, family resemblances of corpse representations. Hence, the TV crime show is media genre and the new representations of corpses can be defined as in the communicative genre. Both genre forms originate from fixed and predictably typified patterns. However, the genre term is used here in the traditional sense for different types of media narratives and the communicative genre term can be applied to media narratives but also other phenomena with fixed patterns. Fixed patterns of the new representations of the dead are the recurring narratives (e.g. the corpse remains visible), cast formations (e.g. new figures like the embalmer or pathologists), actions (e.g. dealing profession-ally with the dead body), camera, light, colour and audio settings and also requisites (specific media aesthetic representation codes). Applied to my research findings, the new representations of corpses constitute a genre crossing family resemblance, the communicative genre, which functions to solve communicative problems. (Knoblauch, 2005)[2]

"The function of genre-like conventionalisations may be seen as relieving actors from the task of coping with subordinate action problems, such as the coordina-tion of turn taking. Communicative genres are constituted in those situations where communicative actions have to cope with typical and recurring problems, particularly if these problems are of some relevance. Since they concern social actions between typical actors, communicative genres therefore reflect the current social action problems and the relevance systems of certain types of actors" (Knoblauch & Raab, 2001, p. 198).

Therefore, the communicative genre insinuates a communicative problem, which can be solved, according to Knoblauch (1995, p. 105), in referring to Luckmann (1990), by routine communicative genres, which allow coping, knowledge transfer and consolidation of intersubjective experiences. (Günther & Knoblauch, 1995, p. 5) Hence, I want to ask: what is the communicative problem that has to be solved by new representations of death in new TV shows? In the following, I will introduce the possible explanations for the why, and then the possible explanations for the how. I propose that new genre developments require the figure of the dead and that typical media body images have inspired these representations.

7.1.1. Changing Genres

In order to find out why these new TV shows dealing with death repre-sentations emerged, I searched for references in interviews with producers

---

2 "Kommunikative Gattungen sind also nicht nur Mittel zur Koordinierung von Handlun-gen, die sich von einem Institutionsbereich zum nächsten, von einer Epoche zur ande-ren und von Kultur zu Kultur unterscheiden können. Sie sind Muster und Vorfertigung kommunikativer Abläufe, die als solche im Wissensvorrat abgelegt sind. (Im Wissens-vorrat enthalten ist auch das Wissen über die Art der kommunikativen Gattungen und ihrer Verwendung.) Es geht in ihnen jedoch nicht nur um den äußeren Ablauf der Kommunikation. Vielmehr besteht ihre Grundfunktion ja in der Lösung immer wieder-kehrender kommunikativer Probleme–und das sind auch die der Wissensvermittlung" (Knoblauch, 2005, p. 175).

and in media related articles. However, these sources rarely question why there are so many new corpse representations. They usually ask why, for instance, crime TV shows like CSI and its two spin-offs were such an instant success and usually the reasons put forward ranged from new cast formation, new visual effects (VFX), different camera work, as well as new narratives. The cast, for instance, consists of not only a team of two police officers or a genius detective or a convincing lawyer or a moral scientist but in fact, consists of all of them in one episode; a team skilled in different fields of expertise whose members pull on bulletproof vests at the crime scene, medical scrubs in the laboratory and suits in the courtroom. Hence, a fusion of genre-crossing figures can take place in one TV show, with a single figure or a team performing different tasks, which were before constituents of different genres. The adoption of narratives, tasks and uniforms from different genres might indicate a reference to the success of forensic crime shows.

Furthermore, new visual effects support the understanding of case-solving medical aspects, while providing the audience with images from the alleged "inside" of a corpse. With the help of computer-generated imagery (CGI), most of the time a simplified animation of biological procedures is used so that the audience can visually follow the trace of the fatal bullet to its final destination. Science is made easily accessible for the audience. At same time, the camera position during conversations remains in the observer position, which usually offers the audience the "being-involved-at-the-scene" perspective. Along with a new cast formation and new visual effects, new narratives are inevitable. Beside the fact that due to faster camera work now two plots are told in one episode, the narrative has also changed distinctively from the "who done it" concept to the "how was it done" concept, i.e. from a social-psychological search for the perpetrator, to the biological-chemical-physical-evidence-based search to prove somebody guilty of a crime. This shift is most probably a side effect of the rise of educational television and in general, the increasing number of TV shows being produced that across genres. It is often stated, that this new cast formation, consisting not only of attractive but smart characters, who vigorously and virtuosically use new kinds of technical support, are actually making science exciting.[3] Hence, these reasons seem to explain the success

---

3 CSI Miami follows different representation modes. Although they work with the same cast formation, CSI Miami is rather old fashioned and uses special effects and car chasing scenes instead of laboratory scenes are to be seen.

of the TV show but not that of the corpse. One can argue here that the representations of corpses are just a side effect. I, however, have faith in the claim that the corpse is the base of the three reasons. For instance, in pathology, a medical examiner has no purpose without a corpse, visual effects from the inside of a body are detached from the context and without a corpse as the object of examination, the new narrative of "how was it done" is not applicable. The corpse, consequently, plays a vital role in constituting these new genre elements and, therefore, most importantly, for the success of these new TV shows. I propose this is why the corpse became a constant part of these new TV shows. However, while *Crossing Jones* and *Bones* adopt the same pattern, *Castle* references old police show narratives, still using corpses the way *CSI* does. *Dexter* even combines case and murder solving. Due to the fantasy genre, the shows *Dead like me*, *Tru Calling* or *Pushing Daisies* work with dead characters, who are "not yet really dead", as well as ghosts or the temporarily awoken. The corpse, and especially its representation codes, has turned into a communicative genre within these different new TV shows. At this point, one could object that there are TV show genre modifications all the time. Some are successful and some are not. The question remains as to whether there might be a better explanation in answering the success of the dead as represented in TV shows.

In the course of my research, I came upon an idea, which is virtually impossible to prove empirically within the scope of this thesis. This idea is connected to the history of death representation. At the beginning, I described Ariès' research regarding the history of death. He studied attitudes towards death across different centuries up until the 20th century. He observed changing attitudes towards death, for example, with the help of images. In his pictorial research, he found out that images about death changed over the centuries expressing different attitudes toward death. I stated in chapter 1 that in history, the depiction of death occurred in cyclic periods. I argued that the confrontations with realistic depictions of the corpse are always only temporarily acceptable in society. This is why modification of death representation took place from ancient times to the early Middle Ages, from the High Middle Ages to the Late Middle Ages, from early modern times to the middle of modern times, and from the middle of modern times to late modern times. The alternating changes can roughly be determined into explicit and threatening representations as well as into mourning and comforting representations. The last representation trend was characterised by a sentimental post-mortem photography style in late modern times. Hence, cyclic alternating periods of explicit and implicit representation systems might indicate that contemporary history will most probably see another rise of explicit and threatening representations. This, in fact, started with the new art of death photography, art installations and "Body Worlds" in the 20th century. Moreover, with the invention of television, a steadily increasing amount of corpses can be seen at any time in any place where a television is found. I believe that nowadays we are surrounded by an increasing amount of dead representations. Especially corpse representations with forensic medical context in TV shows at the turn of the 21st century signify the return of the realistic corpse. I suggest that the new proliferation of death images was a periodic return caused by a pictorial discourse since the very beginning of the Common Era. To summarise, I believe that the development of new genres with new casts and narratives create a carrier, namely the dead, who serve all the new requirements for the success of these new forensic TV shows. The dead give the opportunity to employ a bigger staff of characters, additional horror elements and low-budget pathology scenes. With the help of the audiences' curiosity and fascination with the corpse, generated by historical cycles, these forensic TV shows have been a major success and the corpse has become a standard element for death representations, even for TV shows, which deal with different narratives other than crime. They have just adapted the popular communicative genre of the dead. This might explain then why the dead are used, but not why the dead are represented the way they are. I will try to explain this by referring to changing body images seen in the media.

7.1.2. Changing body images

Bodies are changing. Especially since the 19th century, external bodily design turned into the design of the "social self" (Villa, 2008, p. 8). According to Villa, the urge to design the body is never only a subjective, private and individual matter for free and self-confident persons. Against all media claims in this matter, she states that this work is highly normative, and that audio-visual media especially not only influences, but also produces attitudes towards the body. Media conveys body ideals and the feasibility of ideal bodies. Bodies have to appear healthy, young and fit to indicate willpower, discipline and control. Being obese, lacking personal hygiene or a beauty regime indicate people who are unhealthy, weak-minded and have careless attitudes. (See also: Annette Geiger et al. 2000, Gabriele Klein 2001, Karola Weber 2006 and Sabine Merta 2008). Norbert Elias, has already described in "The Civilizing Process" (1968), the historical transformation of relations between structures and individuals concerning the control of emotions and appropriate behaviour in Western Europe up to the 19th century. He detected a long-term transformation of personalities due to the transformation of social structures. Over time, a modern social structure developed alongside a society whose individuals were more connected and dependent upon one another. Based on these new interdependencies, Elias identified a greater sensitivity regarding our own and other individual's actions and reactions. The changes accelerated the advancement of shame and embarrassment regarding our own and others' bodies (Elias, 1980, p. 397). The awareness of the body's appearance and bodily functions gradually increased over time, and turned from external constraints into highly controlled and internalised self-constraints (Elias, 1980, p.366). The media produces and reflects the urge for perfect bodies by presenting role models with the required characteristics. I will claim in this closing chapter that the drive for the standardisation and civilisation of body appearances and the bodily functions of living individuals represented in the media has also been extended to the dead. The dead body continues to be a body of symbolic staging. Hence, I assume that since body images in the media change, our media representations of the dead change too, and therewith the image our society has of a dead person.[4] Although the dead are invisible in society almost everyone has an idea about what a dead person looks like, as they watch television. According to Hubert Knoblauch (2005, p.210) the increasing pervasion of new information and communication technologies caused sociology to bring up terms like "knowledge-based society" or "information society". He assumes that under the influence of new communication techniques, the common relation of experience and knowledge alternates. Knowledge and communication consist of not only texts and words but of also images and certainly movies. The visual knowledge reflects the order of a pictorial discourse. In

---

4 At this point, one may wonder why Foucault's disciplinary self-techniques (Foucault, 1976, 176) were not applied as well, since the dead in the media is often represented by a living actor. The focus of this work is based on the representation of corpses and since the internalization of discipline techniques requires a living character, Elias' description of the advance of embarrassment concerning "the other" seemed rather appropriate.

this thesis, I have shown that the new representation system of dead bodies consists of certain codes in order for them to be recognised as such by the audience. The process of representation and approval or disapproval of the codes reveals the pictorial discourse within a social group for a certain time, i.e. which images of the dead can be represented, which enter and which leave the pictorial discourse. What does the pictorial discourse reveal about contemporary social symptoms in coping with death? Here, a comparison of the contemporary media representation trend of bodies in general would be worthwhile. While this might be the first thesis concerned with the representation of the dead body, there has been a proliferation of research on body images represented in the media, especially when it comes to its effects on an audience. How can contemporary media body images be characterised in contrast to dead body images in the media?

In general, academic discourse about media body images makes the media responsible for body dissatisfaction amongst its audience, especially where young women are concerned. However, according to Maggie Wykes and Gunter Barries (2005), body obsession has historical precedents pointing towards religious ascetism and fasting, however, the most influential body obsession has come from contemporary Western culture. The authors argue, that:

"[...] the media works on the body in much more subtle and broad ways than simply the promotion of a thin aesthetics and that the pursuit and promotion of slenderness is in many ways a metaphor and sometimes a disguise for a whole range of perceived gender norms within the agenda of sexual politics" (Wykes & Gunter, 2005, p. 10).

Studies about body images in media are most often connected with a growth of eating disorders amongst young women and the media is usually seen as being responsible for this development.[5] Sarah Grogan (1999), was concerned with body dissatisfaction caused by media images in not only women, but also men and children. She investigated the impact of the media on body images and the social pressure that comes with media-

---

5 "The modernity of apparent expansion of 'fasting' and its focus on the body rather than on the soul appears to parallel the explosion of the mass media over the past 40 years. Consequently, causal or probable relationships between media representations and body image have been regularly, theoretically posed since Orbach (1978), who briefly noted the tendency for the media to produce a picture of ideal femininity as 'thin, free of unwanted hair, deodorised, perfumed and clothed... They produce a picture that is far removed from the reality of everyday loves' (1978:20–21)" (Wykes & Gunter, 2005, p. 2).

formed ideas of shape and size. She discovered that there are differences between male and females body images concerning weight and shape. According to her, women are more often portrayed as slim. (Grogan, 1999, p. 94) Men on the contrary, are portrayed as being of standard weight, and as being young, handsome and muscular. (Grogan, 1999, 97) Moreover, youthfulness and bodily control are also typical features of media representations. Liz Schwaiger (2006) argues that:

"[….] the deep-seated cultural valorisation of youth and bodily control and culturally ingrained intolerance of ambiguity in body performance marks (and perhaps masks) a historically contingent, ageist perspective on older age, one that is informed by the same patriarchal value system that privileges the masculine over the feminine" (Schwaiger, 2006, p. 35f).

Mike Featherstone (1991) claims that it is consumer culture that urges the individual to fight against physical decay[6], and that it emphasises that the body must be youthful, healthy and beautiful.[7] Kathleen Woodward (1991) describes the media representation of ageing and defines youthfulness as a masquerade:

"In a culture which so devalues age, masquerade with respect to the aging body is first and foremost a denial of age, an effort to erase or efface age and to put on youth. Masquerade entails several strategies, among them: the addition of desired body parts (teeth, hair), the removal or covering up of unwanted parts of the body (growth, grey hair, 'age spots'); the 'lifting' of the face and other body parts in an

---

6 "Consumer culture latches onto the prevalent self-preservationist conception of the body, which encourages the individual to adopt instrumental strategies to combat deterioration and decay (applauded too by state bureaucracies who seek to reduce health costs by educating the public against bodily neglect) and combines it with the notion that the body is a vehicle of pleasure and self-expression. Images of the body beautiful, openly sexual and associated with hedonism, leisure and display, emphasis the importance of appearance and the 'look'. Within consumer culture, advertisements, the popular press, television and motion pictures, provide a proliferation of stylised images of the body" (Featherstone, 1991, p. 170).

7 "[…] with effort and 'body work' individuals are persuaded that they can achieve a certain desired appearance. Advertising, denature articles and advice columns in magazines and newspaper ask individually to assume self-responsibility for the way they look. This becomes important not just in the first flush of adolescence and early adulthood, for notions of 'natural' bodily deterioration and the bodily betrayals that accompany ageing become interpreted as signs of moral laxity (Hepworth and Featherstone 1982). The wrinkles, sagging flesh, tendency towards middle-age spread, hair loss, etc., which accompany ageing should be combated by energetic body maintenance on the part of the individual—with help from the cosmetic, beauty, fitness and leisure industries" (Featherstone, 1991, p. 178).

effort to deny the weight of gravity; the molding of the body's shape (exercise, clothing)" (Woodward, 1991, p. 148).[8]

I suppose that these specific representation features of the living body influence the representation features of the dead body. If television defines the ever-changing body images of a culture, images of the dead body are influenced as well. In the previous chapters, I could find the same characteristics, which were covered, respectively, not represented. These characteristics include signs of age (such as folds and wrinkles), signs of disorder (such as bodily hair and hair in disarray), flawless skin (without age spots, pimples or warts) and dirt as well as bodily deficits or inconsistencies.

It seems obvious that the social monitoring of the body in the media outlives the death of the body. Not only the living body, but also the dead have to facilitate compliance with social regulations on TV promoting the youthful, healthy and beautiful role model in contemporary Western societies. Just like funeral services that offer embalming and enable corpse viewings[9], the vast majority of the analysed TV shows present dead figures in pathology and embalming rooms, morgues or at the scene of the crime, looking their best. In general, it can be stated that there is no difference between living bodies and dead bodies, only the fatal wounds or Y incisions mediate the actual status of the body. The dead body reflects the living body with all its representational taboos. In fact, here it comes down to the accomplishment of the invisibility of death in the sense of the real individual death. An increasing amount of death representational systems exclude old or messy bodies. However, the representation codes of the distinctive new communicative genre are not yet complete.

When Bronfen held a lecture in Zurich 2007[10] about the visibility of death, she noted a contradiction; the more Western culture denies death, the more it is to be seen in the media, talked about, and the more it is theorised. She also noted a certain aesthetic in the depiction of death that

---

8 Although the author analysed representation of bodies in literature a comparison shows conformity of the listed traits.

9 This is also reflected by the TV show Six Feet Under and lately even in an episode of Nip & Tuck, a show about plastic surgery. The embellishment aspects were issued in a grotesque situation. An extremely rich client, Hedda Grubman who is terminally ill, wants the surgeon to make her the best-looking funeral star ever. (Nip & Tuck: Original Air Date 24.10. 2006, Season 4, Episode 8: Conor McNamara) I would like to thank Thomas Macho for this note.

10 Title of the Zurich Sociology Colloquium: Zum Leben erweckt! Tod in der Soziologie. November 16, 2007

serves the purpose of hiding death, while the narrative of victims and privation carries the idealisation and stylisation of deceased heroes.[11] Bronfen (1992) analysed the depiction of the dead body with gender-based theories and elaborated on the idea of female corpses in the depiction of male artists and authors. She examined the depiction of the beautiful female corpse and claimed that social and psychological conflicts, as well as norms of art and culture, can be mediated through the depiction of a female corpse. (Bronfen, 1987, p. 378) She concluded that through the female corpse, the most poetic of all subjects, the anxiety of death and the longing for death can be stated and banned. The mere body of a beautiful female corpse offers an empty and endless space for projections. According to Bronfen (1987, p. 379) it is a mirror for all the fantasies and anxieties of the male viewer. The female body disturbs the male order, but then functions as an affirming mirror, which supports a patriarchal worldview. (Bronfen, 1987, p. 406)

Menninghaus (2007, p. 62), however, questions Bronfens' phantasm of the beautiful female corpse. He refers to written records from ancient times and states this phantasm does not only entail an implication of the male beautifying gaze on the woman. In ancient times, the gaze is first directed on male beauties and their depiction. The obsession, as Menninghaus calls it, now with living male beauties has made a comeback in contemporary audio-visual media. According to Menninghaus, not only female but also male models in television generate peculiar gender equality when it comes to the pressure of aesthetic evaluation. (Menninghaus, 2007, p. 267) The return started with the invention of photography. According to Menninghaus, the connection of photography to modern print media pro-

---

11 According to Bronfen people can deal with death in a very indirect way namely through the death of the other in visual or narrative representations. For Bronfen these representations are based on a ambivalent insurance as the depictions of death insists on the one side on the acknowledgement of death in life, a frightening knowledge, and on the other side the depictions of death affirm a belief in immortality, which is caused by the entertaining and moral edification depictions about death. Depictions of the death fascinate the viewer with its frightening knowledge about death. Then again aesthetic depictions allow suppressing the knowledge about death because they show the fictional death of somebody else in a picture or in a story. Bronfen maintains that depictions of death always express an anxiety of but also desire for death. "Provoking the spectator or reader to hover between denial and acknowledgement, narrative representation of death (whether visual or textual) serve to show that any 'voyeur' is always also implicated in the field of vision and that the act of fragmenting and objectifying the body of another ricochets back by destabilising the spectator's position as well" (Bronfen, 1992, p. 54).

vided a worldwide presence of images of beautiful bodies. With the increasing development of photography techniques and retouching techniques, images of models, actors and other prominent persons, are becoming more and more edited. This causes even higher expectations on the perception of bodily attractiveness. According to Menninghaus (2007, p. 257), it is the beauty product branch that is interested in these extremely edited images because they underline the gap between real and ideal appearance and profit from culture's desire for perfection.

As already mentioned, the representation of the dead body mirrors the high standards for the representation of living bodies. However, it is not only beautification that characterises the body and dead body representation. Since Romanticism, the relationship between art and beauty has changed dramatically. The ideal of beauty became less important within the system of art and non-beautiful stimuli were set to warrant art's characteristic urge for novelty and difference. This new course of art occurred at the same time. The drive to beautify started to spread into everyday life. New communicative inclusion and exclusion mechanisms covered the areas of the body, fashion and lifestyles. This new art is still beautiful whilst borrowing inspiration from the interesting, grotesque and repellent.[12] The same is true for the representation of dead bodies in contemporary TV shows. Just like art, the media also urges for novelty and difference instead of only beautification. Filmmakers, especially from the most famous TV show *CSI*, produce images in which the corpse is represented as a disgusting object. The representations are not only determined by the beautiful corpses, which mirror societies drive for the ideal body. The representations consist of ugly and repellent elements and this novelty and difference evokes attention instead of weariness. These are the new representation codes which, following the logic of art and combining beauty and disgust, form the topoi of the "aesthetic dead". This development resulted in the producers creating an entirely new image of the dead. Usually the deceased are represented as artificial and beautiful, displaying horrifying traces of

---

12 According to Menninghaus, in contrast to the ubiquitously affirmation of the beauty in fashion, design, advertisements and cosmetics, beauty in art is no longer important. This, however, does not mean that artwork is no longer beautiful or that advertisement stops to use grotesque or repellent elements. Menninghaus detects a shift which is characterised by beauty moving from art to everyday life culture. Even where advertisement or fashion strategists purposefully focus on the "broken", "sick", "sloppy" or just the ordinary look, the desired effect is accomplished through increased attention. (Menninghaus, 2007, p. 270f)

violence, and sometimes also as a dissected and disgusting, usually unidentifiable, piece of art object. The beautiful dead body with the Y incision on
the chest is a new representation topos but also the unidentifiable decomposing object placed in a stylish laboratory. Menninghaus (1999) writes that
a book about disgust is always also a book about the decomposing corpse,
which he claims to be the cipher of disgust. The term "disgust"[13], according to Menninghaus, refers to Aurel Kolnai, based on a normative evaluation, which is used rather inflationary and hyperbolically in contemporary
society. He states that there are three essential characteristics of disgust.
Firstly severe defence, secondly, the physical presence of a close phenomenon, which, thirdly, provokes simultaneous attraction and fascination. (Menninghaus, 1999, p.13) This conforms to all authors mentioned
before, who also described the corpse as fascinating and repellent at the
same time. The term disgust does not only a composite of the opposite of
beauty or the over-saturation of beauty, it is also a supporting contrast, as
Menninghaus puts it. The supporting contrast provides beautiful art with
novel stimuli, which is needed within the system of art to attract attention.
(Menninghaus, 1999, p. 74) However, it seems necessary to elaborate on
the term "disgust", as it seems that even the disgusting representations of
dead bodies in these new TV shows still fail to show the actual opposite of
the embellished body, namely the opposite of svelte and athletic bodies
with juvenile proportions, smooth skin and trimmed, respectively, shaved
body hair. This avoidance on the side of the production is only determined
by the representation of the opposite of the ideal dead body model. The
disgusting dead body, however, is most of the time, represented as the
complete other non-human object: bloated, dismembered, decomposed,
completely burned or skeletonised. These representations are hardly identifiable with former human beings and cross the line of unpleasant repre-

---

13 "Everything seems at risk in the experience of disgust. It is a state of alarm and emergency, an acute crisis of self-preservation in the face of an unassimilable otherness, a
convulsive struggle, in which what is in question is, quite literally, whether "to be or not
to be". This accounts, even in apparently trivial cases, for the peculiar gravity of the distinction at issue in disgust, the distinction between digestible/wholesome/appetizing
and unpalatable, between acceptance and rejection (vomiting, removal from proximity).
The decaying corpse is therefore not only one among many other foul smelling and disfigured bjects of disgust, meets with such a decisive defence, as measured by its extremely potent register on the scale of unpleasureable affects. Every book about disgust
is not least a book about the rotting corpse. The fundamental schema of disgust is the
experience of nearness that is not wanted" (Menninghaus, 2003, p. 1).

sentations of dead bodies. The actual disgusting representation is put into an embellished context to such an extent that the representation becomes beautiful again. This aesthetically staged transgression shows clearly the still extant and static taboos.[14] The producer creates disgust by staging a slimy dripping organ removal or the boiling of a scull in pathology with corresponding sfx acoustic effects. These scenes, again, hardly ever appear in a documentary. While images of actors working on the dead body permeate these new TV shows, other realities of the dead become invisible. The ideal dead body, therefore, provides an empty projection screen for the spectator and hides, at the same time, the many different realities of a dead body. That means, the most destroyed bodies can be shown but the audience is hardly ever confronted with, for instance, a dead body of an elderly, hardly covered woman, as seen in the autopsy documentary. It seems as the combination of old age and death and illness cannot be inflicted on the spectator. The droopy and non-natural, bearing deformed or strained facial expression and in general, movements, which would evoke the association of mere dead meat, are avoided, as well as any staging of leakage of bodily fluids. These fixed omissions clearly mark the communicative genre as well. The dead, not taking into account deadly wounds, are either pretty and clean, well-positioned and covered in a stylish environment or they are an unidentifiable disgusting bunch of human remains in a stylish environment. The aesthetic representations of beautified and disgusting corpses cover the reality of death, the actual taboo.[15] To summarise, in these new TV shows the typical deceased is not normally an elderly person but instead most of the time a young to middle aged victim of crime represented mainly by attractive actresses and actors, reflecting society's drive for the body to look healthy, athletic and clean. However, since pure beauty always bears the risk of monotony and weariness in itself, the filmmakers blend in new stimuli. Bit by bit the number of also disgusting representations of corpses is being increased. Therefore, dead body representation in these new TV shows reflects society's compulsion for bodily civilising, and at the same time, the art-inherent mechanism of mixing beautiful and disgusting

---

14 According to Menninghaus taboos based on disgust are indestructible and 'wear-resistant, which is why, for instance, Abject Art will always attract attention.
(Menninghaus, 1999, p. 565)

15 According to Menninghaus the classical establishment of aesthetics in disgust taboos and in the beautiful surface of a disgust-free ideal body continues to appear even in rather drastic forms of its transgression. He expects more, different and new conjunctions of beauty and disgust in future. (Menninghaus, 1999, p. 566f)

stimuli. The blunting effect causes the production to represent the dead as beautiful but at the same time disgusting. According to Menninghaus, purified beauty can lead to over-saturation. Pure disgust, however, can also have a negative effect: namely the alienation of the audience. I assume that this is why a composition, the aesthetic corpse, is portrayed. These representational consolidations generate the communicative genre of the "aesthetic dead"–beautified and disgusting.

Belting (2001) argues media images of the body influence the viewer. The human body in pictures creates a disciplining effect on the contemporary viewer. Further research should, therefore, take into account the effects of these new dead body images.

7.2. New Representations of Death in other Audio-Visual Media

In this work, I detected the new media trend of representing corpses as constant and processual elements of new TV shows on television within the last decade. Where else can one spot a corpse on television?

Besides the crime shows with short victim-at-scene representations, there are also news channels, for instance, the US local station KTLA, which provides plenty of film footage. When an event of death, like a fatal accident or homicide occurs in Los Angeles, the newscast correspondents can report live from the crime scene. Sometimes the coroners are still at work and the covered dead are to be seen. Another way to see the dead on television is in horror movies. New subgenres like splatter (for instance, the SAW series) and slasher films (for instance, the "A Nightmare on Elm Street" series) also supply various sightings. Both subgenres have in common that they focus on graphic violence against the human body, like torture or manslaughter. Apart from television, new interactive media phenomenons like online video platforms also offer the chance to view corpses. A new addition is YouTube (2005),[16] which trumps television in

---

16 YouTube is a video website, which was founded in February 2005 by Chad Hurley and Steve Chen (since 2006 owned by Google). YouTube offers a platform for video upload, free service and free access to anyone with internet access. Some countries block YouTube. According to its website company history information, it is the leader in online video. Source: www.youtube.com/t/company_history, access: 02.02.2010

so far that representations of death on these platforms are sometimes real. The flood of representations is overwhelming.[17] In the following, I will give some illustrations of recent examples of how YouTube represents the dead. I put forward that YouTube videos cross the line from fictional death to the death of a significant other. Whilst one can argue that the experience of the death of the significant other can never be experienced in fictional TV shows, the experience of the death of others and significant others is very well possible on YouTube. Furthermore, while the crime TV show represents actors and mannequins as dead, YouTube videos cannot be traced back or confirmed as to their validity regarding dead representations. The boundary between fake and original footages blurs. On the one side, actors apply for playing the dead in TV shows and on the other side victims, who did not choose if they wanted to die, are recorded and placed on YouTube.

I would like to start with three recent public killings. Several videos were uploaded on YouTube in December 2006, which showed the execution of Saddam Hussein, former president of Iraq, who was sentenced to death. One video is called "Saddam Hussein Execution–Execucao completa"[18], which I will quickly summarise. The execution takes place by hanging. Saddam Hussein is showed as the executioners put a rope around his neck. When the trap door opens, Saddam Hussein falls down and disappears. Only a few seconds later, the face of the strangled man is to be seen again. This incident is of the public death of a well-known perpetrator who was seen many times before on television. A similar case of a public death is the shooting of Neda, a young Iranian woman. Several videos on YouTube in June 2009 showed how she collapsed and died on the street after a fatal Basij bullet hit her. Both videos were recorded with cell phones and uploaded within hours of the incidents. The visibility of a public death on the internet, no matter if of an unknown victim or of a well-known perpetrator, has caused many reactions. The Youtube's user community decided to block the videos of Neda due to its inappropriate content shortly after their emergence. The video of the hanging of Saddam Hussein

---

17 According to the company "People are watching hundreds of millions of videos a day on YouTube and uploading hundreds of thousands of videos daily. In fact, every minute, 20 hours of video is uploaded to YouTube." Source: www.youtube.com/t/fact_sheet, Access: 02.02.2010

18 User: agangster, uploaded December 31, 2006, www.youtube.com/watch?v0AfJrZSRj-fE Access: 02.02.2010

is still online.[19] Another visible killing on YouTube is the so-called taser incident in Vancouver in 2007. Robert Dziekanski, died after the use of a taser gun by the police. The video emerged on YouTube in November 2007, a month later after the killing, and shows the tasering and subsequent collapse of the man. According to CBS news, the ambulance attendants arrived only minutes later and declared his death after unsuccessfully reviving him.[20] In all three cases, the source and, therefore, the validity of the uploaded YouTube videos cannot be traced back other than to an email address; however, authorities in all three cases proved the incidents of death. Such YouTube videos, uploaded from unknown public witnesses come up with an authenticity request, while TV shows, on the other hand, display in the closing credits who played the dead or who provided the mannequin for the dead representation. When I claimed in the beginning that the death of a significant other disappears behind the new representation system of death, I focused on television. YouTube as another audiovisual entertainment and information source sets new landmarks by sharing videos, which represent the real death of the unknown other and for friends and family the death of a significant other. However, when Nodar Kumaritaschwili died in a luger crash on the first day of the Olympic Games, on the 14th of February 2010, 26 videos were uploaded within a few hours after the incident. The YouTube community flagged the videos due to inappropriate content and stopped the broadcasting of the fatal accident.

I am crossing a line, going further with the videos of the "soon to be dead but still alive person" videos posted on YouTube. Well-known examples are Randy Pausch's last lecture: "Really Achieving your Childhood Dreams" in 2007[21], Jade Goody fighting cancer in 2009[22] or surveillance videos of the Columbine shooting in 1999[23], uploaded in 2006.[24] While

---

19 Several other videos, for instance "Saddam Hussein Execution–Best Version" are blocked from the YouTube community too. Some videos are accompanied by music; some videos omit showing the complete version.

20 Taser video shows RCMP shocked immigrant within 25 seconds of their arrival, November 15, 2007, http://www.cbc.ca/canada/british-columbia/story/2007/11/14/-bc-taservideo.html, Access: 02.02.2010

21 Randy Pausch's last lecture, Uploaded: December 20, 2007, http://www.youtube.com/watch?v=ji5_MqicxSoReally_achieving_your_childhood_dreams, Access: 14.02.2010

22 Jade Goody Exclusive Interview–Jade Goody Cancer Battle, March 06, 2009, http://www.youtube.com/watch?v=9O6r9iNGODc, Access: 14.02.2010

23 Zero Hour: Massacre at columbine high is a documentary based on the columbine high school shootings

these videos, presenting identifiable personalities, are available without any restriction, other videos called "Autopsy" are restricted with sign up requests.[25] In particular, some of the autopsy videos, which are blocked now, consisted of the same content as the earlier described *Autopsy* documentary. In July 2009, however, a video of the forensic pathologist Dr. Michael Baden conducting an autopsy was uploaded and is still not blocked.[26] I suppose that since these recordings are from actual TV shows, they were not blocked because they have already been broadcasted.

YouTube videos cross the line from fictional death to the death of a significant other. While TV shows provide actors and mannequins for death representations and avoid the representation of real decedents, it is very possible to experience of the death of other and significant other on YouTube. Here, the distinct line is crossed several times. The audience can experience the death of other people on the internet and, although there are attempts to restrain crucial footage of dead people, it is in the nature of a highly used upload platform that more footage is always about to be produced. Apart from these most explicit differences, in TV shows the dead are used as working tools for solving a case. A strict representational system with certain codes offers images of the dead, either as identifiable prettified corpses or as unidentifiable objects of disgust. In these blocked YouTube videos, however, the dead appear with unpleasantly disturbing looks as in the documentary *Autopsy*. These autopsy videos showed the dead with distorted faces, and uncontrolled bodies, moved and opened up by others in loud and crowded places. Unlike TV shows, in which status, age and gender of the decedents play a role, possible repulsive elements were not covered or prettified.

---

24 Columbine shooting cafeteria footage Harris Klebold, http://www.youtube.com/watch?v= UJ13CZ4Hekg&feature=fvw, Access: 14.02.2010

25 Videos entitled "medical dissections of human scalps" however can be found without restriction,http://www.youtube.com/watch?v=IoD4vg9Ddag&feature=PlayList&p=3FA4DDE21AF2FA83&index=0 ., Access: 14.02.2010

26 Autopsy presents. An autopsy with Dr. Baden Pt1 of 3,http://www.youtube.com/watch?v=mJAGBY13O4Q, Access: 14.02.2010

Works Cited

Akass, K. & McCabe, J. (Eds.). (2005). *Reading Six Feet Under: TV to die for.* London: I.B. Tauris.

Akass, K. & McCabe, J. (Eds.). (2007). *Quality TV: Contemporary American Television and Beyond.* London: I.B. Tauris.

Allen, J., Reiner, R. & Livingstone, S. (2003). From law and order to lynch mobs: crime news since the second world war. In Mason, P. (Ed.), *Criminal visions: media representations of crime and justice.* Cullompton: Willan.

Anders, G. (2002). *Die Antiquiertheit des Menschen 1: Über die Seele im Zeitalter der zweiten industriellen Revolution; Die Antiquiertheit des Menschen 2: Über die Zerstörung des Lebens im Zeitalter der dritten industriellen Revolution.* (3. ed.) München: Becksche Reihe.

Anders, G. (1956). Ikonomanie. In Kemp, W. (Ed.), *Theorie der Fotografie 1945–1980,* (pp. 108–113) München: Schirmer/Mosel.

Ariès, P. (1975). The reversal of death: changes in attitudes towards death in western societies. In Stannard, D. E.(Ed.), *Death in America.* Pennsylvania: University of Pennsylvania Press.

Ariès, P. (1981). *Studien zur Geschichte des Todes im Abendland.* (2. ed.) München, Wien: Hanser.

Ariès, P. (1984). *Bilder zur Geschichte des Todes.* München, Wien: Hanser.

Baur, K. & Crooks, R. (2008). *Our sexuality.* (10 Ed.) Belmont: Wadsworth Publishing.

Belting, H. (1996). Aus dem Schatten des Todes. In Barloewen, C. (Ed.), *Der Tod in den Weltkulturen und Weltreligionen.* München: Diederichs Verlag.

Belting, H. (2000). Vorwort zu einer Anthropologie des Bildes. In Belting, H. & Kamper, D. (Ed), *Der zweite Blick: Bildgeschichte und Bildreflexion.* München: Fink.

Belting, H. & Kamper, D. (Ed). (2000). *Der zweite Blick: Bildgeschichte und Bildreflexion.* München: Fink.

Belting, H. (2000). Bild und Tod. Verkörperung in den frühen Kulturen. In Belting, H. (Ed.), *Bildanthropologie. Entwürfe für eine Bildwissenschaft,* München: Fink.

Belting, H. (Ed.). (2001). *Bildanthropologie. Entwürfe für eine Bildwissenschaft,*: München: Fink

Belting, H. (2007). *Bildfragen: Die Bildwissenschaften im Aufbruch.* München: Fink.

Barloewen, C. (1996). *Der Tod in den Weltkulturen und Weltreligionen.* München: Diederichs

Barthes, R. (1989). *Die helle Kammer: Bemerkung zur Fotografie.* Frankfurt/M.: Suhrkamp.

Barthes, R. (1964). *Mythen des Alltags.* Frankfurt/M.: Suhrkamp.

Batchen, G. (2004). *Forget Me Not: Photography and Remembrance.* Architectural Press, Princeton.

Barker, A. (2006). *Television, Aesthetics and Reality.* Cambridge: Scholar Press.

Baudrillard, J. (1978). *Agonie des Realen.* Berlin: Merve.

Baudrillard, J. (1993). *Symbolic Exchange and Death.* London, New York: Sage.

Baudrillard, J. (1994). *Simulacra & Simulation.* Michigan: University of Michigan Press.

Bideau, A., Desjardins, B., Brignoli, H. & Perez (Eds.). (1997). *Infant and Child Mortality in the Past.* International studies in demography. New York: Clarendon Press Oxford.

Bignell, J. (1997). *Media Semiotics: An Introduction.* Manchester: University Press, Manchester.

Blanchot, M. (2007). Die zwei Fassungen des Bildlichen. In. Macho, T. & Marek, K. (Eds.): *Die neue Sichtbarkeit des Todes.* München: Fink.

Boehm, G. (1994). *Was ist ein Bild?* München: Fink.

Bostnar, N., Pabst, E. & Wulff, H. J. (Eds.). (2008). *Einführung in die Film- und Fernsehwissenschaft.* (2 ed.), Stuttgart: UTB.

Bogner, A. & Menz, W. (2005). Das theoriegenerierende Experteninterview. Erkenntnisinteresse, Wissensformen, Interaktion. In Bogner, A., Littig, B. & Menz, W. (Eds.). *Das Experteninterview: Theorie, Methode Anwendung.* 2. Edition. Wiesbaden: VS Verlag für Sozialwissenschaften.

Bordwell, D. & Thompson, K. (2003). *Film Art: An Introduction.* New York: McGraw-Hill.

Boyle, K., Weissmann, E. (2007). Evidence of Things Unseen: The Pornographic Aesthetic and the Search for Truth in CSI. In Michael A. (Ed.): *Reading CSI.* London, New York: IB Tauris.

Bredekamp, H., Fischel, A., Schneider, B. & Werner, G. (2003). Bilderwelten des Wissens. In: Bredekamp, H., Werner, G. & Bruhn, M. (Eds). *Bilderwelten des Wissens. Kunsthistorisches Jahrbuch für Bildkritik.* Berlin: Akademie Verlag.

Bredekamp, H. (1997). Das Bild als Leitbild, In Hoffmann, U., Joerges, B. & Severin, I. (Eds.), *LogIcons. Bilder zwischen Theorie und Anschauung,* Berlin: Sigma.

Bruzzi, S. (2001). Observational ('Fly-on-the-wall'). In Creeber, Glen (Ed.). *The Television Genre Book.* London, Bfi Publishing.

Bruzzi, S. (2001). Docu-soap. In Creeber, G. (Ed.): *The Television Genre Book.* London, Bfi Publishing.

Burda, H. (2004). Icomic turn weitergedreht–Die neue Macht der Bilder. In Burda, H., Maar, C. (Ed.). *Iconic turn. Die neue Macht der Bilder.* Köln: DuMont.

Burns, S. & Burns, E. A. (2002). *Sleeping Beauty II: Grief, Bereavement in Memorial Photography American and European Traditions.* New York: Burns Archive Press.

Burns, S. (1990). *Sleeping Beauty: Memorial Photography in America.* Santa Fe: Twelvetrees Press.

Buschhaus, M. (2005). *Über den Körper im Bilde sein. Eine Medienarchäologie anatomischen Wissens.* Bielefeld: Transcript.

Bradbury, M. (1999). *Representation of Death. A Social Psychological Perspective.* London: Routledge.

Bronfen, E. (1992). *Over Her Dead Body: Death, Femininity and the Aesthetic.* Manchester: University Press, Manchester.

Browne, N. (1994). *American Television. New Directions in History and Theory.* Harwood: Academic Publishers.

Callahan, D. (2006). DNA, Surveillance and bodily realities in CSI. In: Barker, Anthony (Ed.). *Television, Aesthetics and Reality.* Newcastle: Cambridge Scholars Press.

Carmody, D. C. (1998). Mixed Messages: Images of Domestic Violence on "Reality" Television. In Cavender, G.; Fishman, M. (Eds.). *Entertaining Crime. Television Reality Programs.* New York: De Gruyter.

Corner, J. (2001). Form and Content in Documentary Study. In: Creeber, Glen (Ed.). *The Television Genre Book.* London, Bfi Publishing.

Corner, J. (2001). Documentary Realism. British Film Institute, London p. 126–127, In: Creeber, Glen (Ed.). *The Television Genre Book.* London, Bfi Publishing.

Corner, J. (1991). "Meaning, genre and context: the problematics of 'public knowledge' in the new audience studies". In Curran, J. & Gurevitch, M. (Eds.): *Mass Media and Society.* London: Edward Arnold.

Chandler, D. (2001). *Semiotics: The Basics.* London, New York: Routledge.

Creeber, G. (2001). *The Television Genre Book.* London, Bfi Publishing.

Debord, G. (1996). *Die Gesellschaft des Spektakels.* Berlin: Edition Tiamat.

Dolinak, D., Matshes, E. & Lew (2005). *Forensic Pathology: Principles and Practice.* Elsevier: Academic Press.

Dovery, J. (2001). Reality TV. In. Creeber, G. (Ed.): *The Television Genre Book.* London, Bfi Publishing.

Douglas, M. (2002). *Purity and Danger. An analysis of concepts of pollution and taboo.* (First published 1966). London: Taylor & Francis Inc.

Eco, U. (2002). *Einführung in die Semiotik.* (9 ed.) München: Fink.

Eco, U. (2004). *History of beauty.* New York: Rizzoli.

Eco, U. (2007). *On Ugliness.* New York: Rizzoli.

Elias, N. (1985). *The Loneliness of the Dying.* Oxford: Blackwell.

Elias, N. (1997). *Über den Prozess der Zivilisation. Soziogenetische und psychogenetische Untersuchungen. I. Wandlungen des Verhaltens in den weltlichen Oberschichten des Abendlandes.* Frankfurt/M.: Suhrkamp.

Elias, N. (1980): *Über den Prozess der Zivilisation. Soziogenetische und psychogenetische Untersuchungen. II 2: Wandlungen der Gesellschaft. Entwurf zu einer Theorie der Zivilisation.* 7. Aufl. Frankfurt/M.: Suhrkamp.

Esser, E., Hill, P. & Schnell, R. (Eds.). (1999). *Methoden der empirischen Sozialforschung.* (6 ed.) München, Wien: Oldenbourg.

Esser, A., Groß, D., Knoblauch, H. & Tag, B. (Eds.). (2007). *Tod und toter Körper. Der Umgang mit dem Tod und der menschlichen Leiche am Beispiel der klinischen Obduktion.* Kassel: University Press.

Faulstich, W. (1994). *Grundwissen Medien.* München: Fink.

Faulstich, W. (2003). *Einführung in die Medienwissenschaft.* München: UTB.

Featherstone, M. (1991). The Body in Consumer Culture. In Featherstone, M., Hepworth, M. & Turner B. S. (Eds.). *The Body: social process and cultural theory.* London: Sage.

Felix, J. (2002). *Moderne Film Theorie.* (Filmforschung. 3) Mainz: Bender.

Flick, U. (2007). *Qualitative Sozialforschung. Eine Einführung.* Hamburg: Rowohlt.

Fiske, J. & Hartley, J. (1978). *Reading Television.* London: Methuen.

Fiske, J. (1987). *Television Culture.* London: Routledge

Fischer-Lichte, E. (2007). *Semiotik des Theaters. Eine Einführung: Semiotik des Theaters: Semiotik des Theaters 1: Das System der theatralischen Zeichen. Eine Einführung.* Vol.1, (5 ed.) Tübingen: Narr.

Foucault, M. (1976): *Ueberwachen und Strafen.* Frankfurt/M: Suhrkamp.

Foucault, M. (1977). *Der Wille zum Wissen - Sexualität und Wahrheit 1.* (14 ed.) Frankfurt/M: Suhrkamp.

Foucault, M. (1994). *The order of things. An Archaeology of the Human Sciences.* (1966 french version) New York: Vintage Books

Foucault, M. (2005). *Die Geburt der Klinik. Eine Archäologie des ärztlichen Blicks.* (7 ed.) Frankfurt/M.: Fischer.

Fromm, E. (1973). *The Anatomy of Human Destructiveness.* New York: Holt, Rinehart and Winston.

Gennep, A. (1999). *Übergangsriten.* (Les Rites De Passage 1981) Frankfurt/M, New York: Campus

Gittings, C. (1984). *Death, Burial and the Individual in Early Modern England.* London, Sydney: Croom Helm.

Goffman, E. (1959). *The Presentation of Self In Everyday Life.* New York: Doubleday.

Goodman, N. (1995). *Sprachen der Kunst. Entwurf einer Symboltheorie.* Frankfurt/M.: Suhrkamp.

Goodall, J. (2000). Grieving Parents, Grieving Children. In: Avery, G. & Reynolds, K. (Eds.): *Representations of Childhood Death.* New York: St. Martin's Press Inc.

Gorer, G. (1967). *Death, Grief, and Mourning.* Garden City: Doubleday-Anchor.

Gorer, G. (1965). *Death, Grief and Mourning in Contemporary Britain.* (first published in Encounter, 1955) London: Cresset Press.

Gugutzer, R. (2004). *Soziologie des Körpers.* Bielefeld: Transcript.

Gray, J. (2008). *Television Entertainment.* New York: Routledge.

Gray, H. (2004). *Watching race: Television and the struggle for blackness.* Minnesota: University of Minnesota Press.

Grogan, S. (1999). *Body Image: Understanding Body Dissatisfaction in Men, Women, and Children.* London, New York: Routledge.

Hallam, E., Hockey, J. & Howarth, G. (1999). *Beyond the Body: Death and Social Identity.* London, New York: Routledge.

Hickethier, K. (2003). *Einführung in die Medienwissenschaft.* Stuttgart: Metzler.

Hickethier, K. (1993). *Film- und Fernsehanalyse.* Stuttgart: Metzler.

Hickethier, K. (2001). *Film- und Fernsehanalyse.* (3 ed.) Tübingen: Narr.

Hickethier, K. (2002). Genretheorie and Genreanalyse. In Felix, J. (Ed.). *Moderne Film Theorie.* (Filmforschung. 3) Mainz: Bender.

Howarth, G. & Jupp, P. C. (1996). *Contemporary Issues in the Sociology of Death, Dying and Disposal.* New York: St. Martin's Press Inc.

Howarth, G. & Leaman, O. (2001). *Encyclopaedia of Death and Dying.* London, New York: Routledge.

Hüppauf, B. & Weingart, P. (2009). *Frosch und Frankenstein. Bilder als Medium der Popularisierung von Wissenschaft.* Bielefeld: Transcript.

Imdahl, M. (1980). *Giotto, Arenafresken. Ikonographie, Ikonologie, Ikonik.* München: Fink.

Kaoru, I. (2008). *Landscape with a Corpse.* Hatje, Cantz

Keller, R. (2005). *Wissenssoziologische Diskursanalyse. Grundlegung eines Forschungsprogramms.* Wiesbaden: VS-Verlag.

Kendrick, W. (1996). *The Secret Museum. Pornography in Modern Culture.* Los Angeles, London: University of California Press Berkeley.

Keppler, A. (2006). Die Einheit von Bild und Ton. Zu einigen Grundlagen der Filmanalyse. In: Mai, M. & Winter, R. (Eds.). *Das Kino der Gesellschaft–die Gesellschaft des Kinos. Interdisziplinäre Positionen, Analysen und Zugänge.* Köln: Halem.

Keppler, A. (2006). *Mediale Gegenwart. Eine Theorie des Fernsehens am Beispiel der Darstellung von Gewalt.* Frankfurt/M.: Suhrkamp.

Klaver, E. (2005). *Sites of Autopsy in Contemporary Culture.* Albany, N.Y.: State University of New York Press.

Kleiber, G. (1993). *Prototypensemantik: Eine Einführung.* Tübingen: Narr.

Klemme, H. F., Pauen, M. & Raters, M. L. (2006). *Im Schatten des Schönen. Die Ästhetik des Hässlichen in historischen Ansätzen und aktuellen Debatten.* Bielefeld: Aisthesis.

Knoblauch, H. (1995). *Kommunikationskultur. Die kommunikative Konstruktion kultureller Kontexte.* Berlin, New York: De Gruyter.

Knoblauch, H. (2000). Topik und Soziologie. Von der sozialen zur kommunikativen Topik. In: Ueding, G. & Schirren, T. (Ed.). *Topik und Rhetorik. Ein interdisziplinäres Symposium.* Tübingen: Niemeyer.

Knoblauch, H. & Luckmann, T. (2000). Gattungsanalyse. In Flick, U., Kardorff von, E.& Steinke, I. (Ed): *Qualitative Forschung. Ein Handbuch.* Hamburg: Rowohlt.

Knoblauch, H. & Raab, J. (2001). Genres and Aesthetics of Advertisement spots. In: Knoblauch, H. & Kotthoff, H. (Eds.) *Verbal art across cultures: the aesthetics and proto-aesthetics of communication.* Tübingen: Narr.

Knoblauch, H. & Schnettler, B. (2007). *Powerpointpräsentationen. Neue Formen der gesellschaftlichen Kommunikation von Wissen.* Konstanz: UVK.

Kolnai, A. (2007). *Ekel Hochmut Hass. Zur Phänomenologie feindlicher Gefühle.* Frankfurt/M.: Suhrkamp.

Korsmeyer, C. & Smith, B. (2004). *Visceral Values: Aurel Kolnai on Disgust. On Disgust.* Peru, Illinois: Open Court Publishing Company, a division of Carus Publishing Company.

Kuchenbuch, T. (2005). *Filmanalyse. Theorien–Methoden–Kritik.* Wien: UTB.

Lamneck, S. (2005). *Qualitative Sozialforschung. Lehrbuch.* 4. Edition. Beltz: PVU.

La Rocca, C. (2006). Das Schöne und der Schatten. Dunkle Vorstellungen und ästhetische Erfahrung zwischen Baumgartner und Kant. In: Klemme, Heiner F.; Pauen, M., Raters, M.L. (Eds.). *Im Schatten des Schönen. Die Ästhetik des Hässlichen in historischen Ansätzen und aktüllen Debatten.* Bielefeld: Aisthesis.

Lewandowski, S. (2010). La femme machine? Pornographische Inszenierungen von Sexualität und Körperlichkeit. In: Dörre,K. & Lessenich, S. (Eds.). *Unsichere Zeiten. Herausforderungen gesellschaftlicher Transformationen.* Wiesbaden: Westdeutscher Verlag.

Livingstone, S. (1999). Mediated knowledge, recognition of the familiar, discovery of the new. In: Jostein, G. (Ed): *Television and Common Knowledge.* London, New York: Routledge.

Luckmann, T. (1992). *Theorie des sozialen Handelns.* Berlin, New York: De Gruyter.

Luckmann, T. (1988). Kommunikative Gattungen im kommunikativen Haushalt einer Gesellschaft, In Smolka-Kordt, G., Spangenberg, P. M. & Tillmann-Bartylla, D. (Eds.) *Der Ursprung der Literatur.* München: Fink.

Lury, K. (2005). *Interpreting Television.* Bloomsbury: Hodder Arnold Publication.

Maasen, S., Mayerhausen & T., Renggli, C. (2006). *Bilder als Diskurse–Bilddiskurse.* Velbrück: Weilerswist.

Macho, T. (1987). *Todesmetaphern–Zur Logik der Grenzerfahrung.* Frankfurt/M.: Suhrkamp.

Macho, T. & Marek, K. (2006). *Die Neue Sichtbarkeit des Todes.* München: Fink.

Macho, T. (2008). Was tun Sie, wenn Sie einen Menschen lieben? In Hofer, M. & Leisch-Kiesl, M. (Eds.) *Evidenz und Täuschung. Stellenwert, Wirkung und Kritik von Bildern.* Bielefeld: Transcript.

Marcus, S. (1979). *Umkehrung der Moral. Sexualität und Pornographie im viktorianischen England.* Frankfurt/M.: Suhrkamp.

Mayer, R. G. (2005). *Embalming History, Theory and Practice.* Fourth Edition. New York: McGraw-Hill.

Mead, M., Métraux, R. (1962). The Image of the Scientist among High-School Students—A Pilot Study. In Hirsch, W. & Barber, B. (Eds.) *The Sociology of Science.* New York: Free Press of Glencoe.

Meehan, E. R. (2008). Ancillary markets–television: From challenge to safe haven. In McDonald, P. & Wasko, J. (Eds.): *The contemporary Hollywood film industry.* Victoria: Blackwell Publishing, Malden Oxford.

Menninghaus, W. (2003). *Disgust. The Theory and History of a Strong Sensation.* Albany, N.Y.: State University of New York Press.

Menninghaus, W. (2002). *Ekel. Theorie und Geschichte einer starken Empfindung.* Frankfurt/M.: Suhrkamp.

Menninghaus, W. (2003). *Das Versprechen der Schönheit.* Frankfurt/M.: Suhrkamp.

Metz, C. (1974). *Film Language: A Semiotics of the Cinema.* New York: Oxford University Press.

Metz, C. (1982). *The Imaginary Signifier.* Bloomington: Indiana University Press.

Mersch, D. (2006). *Medientheorien zur Einführung.* Hamburg: Junius.

Merta, S. (2008) *Schlank!. Ein Körperkult der Moderne.* Stuttgart: Franz Steiner Verlag:.

Meuser, M. & Nagel, U. (2002). ExpertInneninterviews–vielfach erprobt, wenig bedacht. Ein Beitrag zur qualitativen Methodendiskussion, in: Bogner, A., Littig, B. & Menz, W. (Eds.): *Das Experteninterview. Theorie, Methode, Anwendung.* Opladen: Leske & Budrich.

Mikos, L. & Wegener, C. (2005). Qualitative Medienforschung. Ein Handbuch. Konstanz: UVK.

Mitchell, W. J. T. (1994). *Picture Theory: Essays on Verbal and Visual Representation.* Chicago: University of Chicago Press.

Mitchell, W. J. T. (1986). *Iconology: Image, Text, Ideology.* Chicago: University of Chicago Press.

Mitchell, W. J. T. (1997). Der Pictorial Turn. In Kravagna, C. (Ed.): *Priviligierter Blick. Kritik der visuellen Kultur.* ID Berlin: Archiv.

Monaco, J. (2000). *Film verstehen.* Hamburg: Europa Verlag.

Murdock, G. (1999). *Television and Common Knowledge.* London, New York: Routledge.

Mueller-Doohm, S. (1993). Visuelles Verstehen–Konzepte kultursoziologischer Bildhermeneutik. In Jung, T. & Mueller-Doohm, S. (Eds.) *"Wirklichkeit" im Deutungsprozess. Verstehen und Methoden in den Kultur- und Sozialwissenschaften.* Frankfurt/M.: Suhrkamp.

Mueller-Doohm, S. (1997). Bildinterpretation als struktural-hermeneutische Symbolanalyse. In Hitzler, R. & Honer, A. (Eds.): *Sozialwissenschaftliche Hermeneutik. Eine Einführung.* Opladen: Leske & Budrich.

Mueller, H.P. (1992). Sozialstruktur und Lebensstile. Der neuere theoretische Diskurs über soziale Ungleichheit. Frankfurt/M.: Suhrkamp.

Neale, S. (1980). *Genre.* London: British Film Institute.

Neale, S. (1995). 'Questions of genre'. In Boyd-Barrett, O. & Newbold, C. (Eds.) *Approaches to Media: A Reader.* London: Arnold.

Panofsky, E. (1975). Ikonographie und Ikonologie. Eine Einführung in die Kunst der Renaissance, In Panofsky, E. (Ed.) *Sinn und Deutung in der bildenden Kunst.* Köln: Dumont.

Panofsky, E. (1970). *Meaning in the Visual Arts.* Harmondsworth: Penguin.

Prokop, D. (2009). *Ästhetik der Kulturindustrie.* Marburg: Tectum.

Rod, M. A. (2007). *The Psychology of Humor: An Integrative Approach.* Elsevier: Academic Press.

Raab, J. (2008). *Visuelle Wissenssoziologie. Theoretische Konzeption und materiale Analysen.* Konstanz: UVK.

Rosenkranz, K. (1853). *Aesthetik des Haesslichen.* Königsberg. Verlag Gebrüder Bornträger, (Faksimile Neudruck der Ausgabe Königsberg 1853, Ed. Walther Gose & Walter Sachs. Stuttgard–Bad Cannstatt 1968) Friedrich Frommann Verlag (Günther Holzboog).

Ruby, J. (1999). *Secure the Shadow: Death and Photography in America.* Cambridge: The MIT Press.

Sachs-Hombach, K. (2003). *Das Bild als kommunikatives Medium. Elemente einer allgemeinen Bildwissenschaft.* Köln: Halem.

Sachs-Hombach, K. (2005). *Bildwissenschaft zwischen Reflexion und Anwendung.* Köln: Halem.

Sachs-Hombach, K. (2005). *Bildwissenschaft.*, Frankfurt/M.: Suhrkamp.

Sachs-Hombach, K. (2006). *Bild und Medium. Kunstgeschichtliche und philosophische Grundlagen der interdisziplinären Bildwissenschaft.* Köln: Halem.

Sappol, M. (2003). *Dream Anatomy.* Washington, Bethesda, Md.: U.S. Dept. of Health and Human Services, National Institutes of Health, National Library of Medicine.

Schaaf, M. (1980). Theorie und Praxis der Filmanalyse. In Silbermann, A., Schaaf, M. & Adam, G. (Eds.). *Filmanalyse: Grundlagen, Methodik, Didaktik.* München: Oldenbourg

Schirra, J. (2006). Begriffsgenetische Betrachtungen in der Bildwissenschaft: Fünf Thesen. In Sachs-Hombach, K (Ed.). *Bild und Medium: Kunstgeschichtliche und philosophische Grundlagen der interdisziplinären Bildwissenschaft.* Köln: Halem.

Schmidt, B. (2002). *Die Macht der Bilder: Bildkommunikation–menschliche Fundamentalkommunikation.* Aachen: Shaker.

Schneider, A. R. (2001). *The Gatekeeper. My thirty years as a TV censor.* Syracuse New York: Syracuse University Press.

Schulze, G. (1997). *Erlebnisgesellschaft. Kultursoziologie der Gegenwart.* (7 ed.) New York, Frankfurt: Campus Verlag.

Schwan, S. (2005). Film verstehen–Eine kognitionspsychologische Perspektive. In. Sachs-Hombach (Ed.). *Bildwissenschaft zwischen Reflexion und Anwendung.* Köln: Halem.

Schweppenhaeuser, G. (2007). *Ästhetik. Philosophische Grundlagen und Schlüsselbegriffe.* New York, Frankfurt: Campus.

Schweinitz, J. (2006). *Film und Stereotype. Eine Herausforderung für das Kino und die Filmtheorie. Zur Geschichte eines Mediendiskurses.* Berlin: Akademie Verlag.

Schnettler, B. & Pötzsch, F. (2007). Visuelles Wissen. In Schützeichel, R. (Ed.). *Handbuch Wissenssoziologie und Wissensforschung.* Konstanz: UVK.

Seer, U. (1992). *Was Farben uns verraten.* Stuttgart: Kreuz-Verlag.

Selg, H. (1986). *Pornographie. Psychologische Beiträge zur Wirkungsforschung.* Bern, Stuttgart, Toronto: Hans Huber.

Sedgwick, J. & Pokorny, M. (2005). The characteristics of a film as a commodity. In. Sedgwick, J. & Pokorny, M. (Eds.). (2005). *An Economy History of Film.* London, New York: Routledge.

Silverman, D. (2007). *You Can't Air That. Four cases of controversy and Censorship in American Television Programming.* Syracuse University Press, Syracuse New York

Silbermann, A., Schaaf, M. & Adam, G. (1980). *Filmanalyse: Grundlagen, Methoden, Didaktik.* München: Oldenbourg.

Squire, J. E. (1983). *The movie business book.* New York: Touchstone Books.

Squire, J. E., & Bluem W.A. (1972). *The Movie Business.* New York: Hastings House.

Sykora, K. (2009). *Die Tode der Fotografie 1: Totenfotografie und ihr sozialer Gebrauch.* München: Fink.

Timmermans, S. (2006). *Postmortem. How Medical Examiners Explain Suspicious Deaths.* Chicago: Chicago Press.

Turner, V. (1995). *The ritual process: structure and anti-structure.* (First published 1969), New York: Aldine Transaction.

Todd, M.E. (2003). *Der Körper denkt mit.* Bern, Göttingen, Toronto, Seattle: Hans Huber.

Trebess, A. (2006). *Metzler Lexikon Aesthetic: Kunst, Medien, Design und Alltag.* Stuttgart Weimar: Metzler.

Vany De, A. (2004). *Hollywood Economics. How extreme uncertainty shapes the film industry.* London, New York: Routledge.

Villa, P. I. (2008): Schoen normal. Manipulationen am Körper als Technologien des Selbst. Bielefeld: transcript.

Weber, K. (2006): *Koerperkult und -inszenierung.* Saarbruecken: VDM Verlag.

Weber, T. (2006). Filmische Codierungen des Todes. In: Macho, T. & Marek K. (Eds): *Die neue Sichtbarkeit des Todes.* München: Fink.

Weber, T. & Moebius, S. (2007). Die mediale Repräsentation des Todes. Der Tod in den Kulturen der Moderne am Beispiel des Films. In: Schroer, M. (Ed). *Die Gesellschaft des Films.* Konstanz: UVK.

Weber, T. (2008). *Six Feet Under: Die Domestizierung des Todes.* In: Seiler, S. (Ed.). Was bisher geschah. Serielles Erzählen im zeitgenössischen amerikanischen Fernsehen. Köln: Schnitt – der Filmverlag.

Weber, T. (2010). Tote in den Medien unter dem Vorwurf der Pornographie. In: Glahn, J., Groß, D. & Tag, B. (Eds): *Die Leiche als memento mori. Interdisziplinäre Perspektiven auf das Verhältnis von Tod und totem Körper.* Reihe Todesbilder (Vol.3) Frankfurt/Main, New York: Campus.

Welsch, W. (1996). *Grenzgänge der Ästhetik.* Stuttgart: Philipp Reclam.

Weiss, M. (2002). *The chosen body. The politics of the body in israeli society.* Stanford: Stanford University Press.

Williams, L. (1999). *Hard Core: Power, Pleasure, and the "Frenzy of the Visible"*. Berkely: California University Press.

Woollacott, J. (1981). *Popular Television and Film*. London: Bfi Publishing.

Woodward, K. (1991). *Aging and its discontents: Freud and other fictions*. Bloomington: Indiana University Press.

Wykes, M. & Gunter, B. (2005). *The media and body image: if looks could kill*. London: Sage.

Zettl, H. (2002). The essentials of media aesthetics. In Dorai, C. & Venkatesh, S. (Eds.): *Media Computing: Computational Media Aesthetics*. Boston, Dordrecht, London: Kluwer Academic Publishers.

Zettl, H. (2008). *Sight, sound, motion; applied media aesthetics*. 5th edition. Belmont: Wadsworth Pub. Co.

Articles published in Journals

Ariès, P. (1974, December). The Reversal of Death: Changes in Attitudes Towards Death. *Western Societies*. Special Issue: Death in America. American Quarterly, Vol.26, No.5, pp. 536–560.

Ariès, P. & Murchland, B. (1974, May). Death inside out. Facing Death. *The Hastings Center Studies*, Vol.2, No.2, pp. 3–18.

Blum, G., Sachs-Hombach, K. & Schirra, J. (2007). Kunsthistorische Bildanalyse und allgemeine Bildwissenschaft: Eine Gegenüberstellung am konkreten Beispiel - Die Fotografie Terror of War von Nick Ut (Vietnam, 1972) In: Frücht, J. & Moog-Grünewald, M. (Eds.) *Sonderheft 8 der Zeitschrift für Ästhetik und Allgemeine Kunstwissenschaft: Ästhetik in metaphysikkritischen Zeiten -- 100 Jahre Zeitschrift für Ästhetik und Allgemeine Kunstwissenschaft*. pp.117–152.

Cole, S.A. & Dioso-Villa, R. (2007). CSI and Its Effects: Media, Juries, and the Burden of Proof, *New England Law Review*, Vol. 41, No. 3, pp. 435–469.

Csaszi, L. (2003). World Trade Center Jokes and Their Hungarian Reception, *Journal of Folklore Research*, Department of Folklore and Ethnomusicology, Indiana University. Vol. 40, No. 2, pp. 175–210.

Diuguid, L. & Rivers, A. (2000). The Media and the Black Response. *Annals of the American Academy of Political and Social Science*, The African American Male in American Life and Thought, Vol. 569, pp. 120–134.

Healey, T. & Ross, K. (2002). Growing old invisibly: older viewers talk television. *Media, Culture & Society*, Vol. 24, No. 1, pp. 105–120.

Honneth, A. (1992). *Eine Kolumne - Ästhetisierung der Lebenswelt*, Merkur; Soziologie. Eine Kolumne. Ästhetisierung der Lebenswelt." *Merkur* Vol. 46, No. 519, pp. 522–527.

Luckmann, T. (1986). *Grundformen der gesellschaftlichen Vermittlung des Wissens: Kommunikative Gattungen.* Kölner Zeitschrift für Soziologie und Sozialpsychologie, Sonderheft 27, pp.191–211.

Porter, R. (1999). Classics revisited: The hour of Philippe Ariès, *Mortality*, Vol. 4, No.1, pp.83–90.

Schnettler, B. (2007). Auf dem Weg zu einer Soziologie visuellen Wissens. *Sozialer Sinn*, Lucius, Stuttgart, Vol. 8., No.2, pp.189–210.

Schwaiger, L. (2006). To Be Forever Young? Towards Reframing Corporeal Subjectivity in Maturity. International Journal of Ageing and Later Life, Centre for Social and Community Research, Murdoch University, Western Australia 2006 1(1): p.11–41.

Selg, H. (1997). Pornographie und Erotographie. Psychologische Vorschläge zur Sprachregelung. *Freiwillige Selbstkontrolle Fernsehen e. V.: TV Diskurs–Verantwortung in audiovisellen Medien*, Baden-Baden: Nomos Verlagsgesellschaft, Vol 1, pp. 48–51.

Smyth, W. (1986, October). Challenger Jokes and the Humour of Disaster. In *Western Folklore*, Western States Folklore Society Stable, University of California Los Angeles, Vol. 45, No. 4, pp. 243–260.

Tait, S. (2006). Autoptic vision and the necrophilic imaginary in CSI. *International journal of cultural studies*. University of Canterbury, New Zealand, Vol. 9(1), pp.45–62.

Videka-Sherman, L. (1987): Research on the Effect of Parental Bereavement: Implications for Social Work Intervention. *The Social Service Review*, The University of Chicago Press, Chicago, Vol. 61, No. 1, pp. 102–116.

Walter, T. (1991). Modern Death: Taboo or not taboo. *Sociology* 25(2), pp. 293–310.

Information from the world-wide-web

Boudreau, D. (2008). CSI effect: Not guilty! Retrieved from http://researchmag.asu.edu/2008/03/csi_effect_gets_a_not_guilty_v.html, March 25, 2008

Chandler, D. (1997). 'An Introduction to Genre Theory'. Retrieved from http://www.aber.ac.uk/media/Documents/intgenre/chandler_genre_theory.pdf, June 5, 2007

Chandler, D. (2003). Television and Gender Roles. Retrieved from http://www.aber.ac.uk/media/Modules/TF33120/gendertv.html, August 19, 2008

Cole, S. & Dioso, R. (2005). The Wall Street Journal: Law and the Lab. Do TV shows really affect how juries vote? Let's look at the evidence. Retrieved from http://www.truthinjustice.org/law-lab.htm, March 25, 2008

Guthmann J. (2002). Dem Tod ins Gesicht sehen–Bilder aus dem Leichenschauhaus in der zeitgenössischen Fotografie. Retrieved from http://www.jensguthmann.de/zürich.pdf, May 5, 2008

Huntley, K. (2005). CSI Files - Anthony E. Zuiker, Retrieved from http://www.csifiles.com/interviews/anthony_zuiker.shtml, January 12, 2008

Heinrick, J. (2006). Arizona State University: Everyone's an Expert: The CSI Effect's negative Impact on Juries. The Triple Helix Fall, pp.59–61. Retrieved from http://www.cspo.org/documents/csieffectheinrick.pdf. March 25, 2008

Lester, S. (2008). The Body Behind CSI: Anthony Zuiker–The shows executive producer and writer gets gory with FHM. Retrieved from http://www.fhmonline.com/articles-3208.asp, February 12, 2008

Lovgren, S. (2004). CSI Effect is mixed blessing for Real Crime Labs. National Geographic News, Retrieved from http://news.nationalgeographic.com /news/2004/09/0923_040923_csi.html, May 5, 2008

Lynn-Foltyn, J. (2006). Dead sexy: post-disaster/terrorism voyeurism and the corpse, pop culture's new porn star. Retrieved from http://www.bath.ac.uk/ podcast/lectures/002-podbath-Deadsexy.mp3, June 23, 2009

Maricopa County Attorney's Office (2005). CSI: Maricopa County: The CSI Effect and Its Real-Life Impact on Justice, Maricopa County, AZ, Retrieved from http://www.maricopacountyattorney.org/Pressdefault.asp, March 24, 2008

Mitchell, R. (1987) "…And the Company President Is a Black Woman", Retrieved from http://www.medialit.org/reading_room/article234.html, September 2, 2008

Schweitzer, N. & Saks, M. (2007). CSI effect gets a not guilty. Spring issue of the law and science journal Jurimetrics. Retrieved from http://researchmag.asu.edu/2008/03/csi_effect_gets_a_not_guilty_v.html, January 18, 2009

Spier, R. H. (1987). We Are What We Watch: We Watch What We Are. New research study explores WHY we watch and WHAT we choose. Retrieved from http://www.medialit.org/reading_room/article274.html, September 2, 2008

The Laerdal Foundation for Acute Medicine: History in brief. Helping saves lifes. Retrieved from http://www.laerdal.com/about/default.htm, May 8, 2009

Tyler, T. R. (2006). Viewing CSI and the Threshold of Guilt: Managing Truth and Justice in Reality and Fiction. Yale Law Journal, Retrieved from http://www.yalelawjournal.org/pdf/115-5/Tyler.pdf, March 25, 2008

Walter, T. (2006). Morbid Fascinations - our obsession with death. A Battle in Print. Retrieved from www.battleofideas.co.uk/C2B/document_tree/ViewADocument.asp?ID=266&CatID=42, 7 July 2009

List of LA Time photos from the world-wide-web

(All pictures were taken by David Strick and published in the LA Times online)

http://photos.latimes.com/backlot/gallery/makeup/2008/9/23/Dexter_murder_victim_makeup, September 23, 2008

http://photos.latimes.com/backlot/gallery/makeup/2008/9/23/Dexter_shade_o n_a_dead_man, September 23, 2008

http://photos.latimes.com/backlot/gallery/ncis/2009/10/8/NCIS_Joe_Hailey_m akeup, August 10, 2009

http://photos.latimes.com/backlot/gallery/ncis/2009/10/8/NCIS_extra_Ezra_ Masters, August 10, 2009

http://photos.latimes.com/backlot/gallery/ncis/2009/10/8/NCIS_Pauley_Perret te_red, August 10, 2009

http://photos.latimes.com/backlot/gallery/ncis/2009/10/8/NCIS-1477, August 10, 2009

List of TV show information from the world-wide-web

Dr. G: Medical Examiner: http://www.imdb.com/title/tt0364314/ Access: July 5th, 2008,

Autopsy–Confessions of a Medical Examiner: http://www.imdb.com/title/ tt0430897/ Access: July 5th, 2008,

North Mission Road: http://www.imdb.com/title/tt0381788/ Access: July 5th, 2008,

Autopsy Through the eyes of death detectives: http://www.autopsyvideo.com Access June 5th, 2008

CSI: Crime Scene Investigative Service: http://www.imdb.com/title/tt0247082/ Access: June 15th, 2008,

CSI: Miami: http://www.imdb.com/title/tt0313043/, Access: October 10th, 2009,

CSI: NY: http://www.imdb.com/title/tt0395843/ , Access: October 10th, 2009,

Law & Order: http://www.imdb.com/title/tt0098844/ , Access June 15th, 2008

Family Plots:http://www.imdb.com/title/tt0407390/ Access: July 5th, 2008,

Crossing Jordan:http://www.imdb.com/title/tt0284718/ Access: June 15th, 2008,

Bones:http://www.imdb.com/title/tt0460627/ Access: June 15th, 2008,

Navy NCIS: Naval Criminal:http://www.imdb.com/title/tt0364845/ Access: June 15th, 2008,

Castle:http://www.imdb.com/title/tt1219024/, Access: January 5th, 2010,

Dead Like Me:http://www.imdb.com/title/tt0348913/ Access: June 25th, 2008,

Pushing Daisies:http://www.imdb.com/title/tt0925266/ Access: June 25th, 2008,

Tru Calling:http://www.imdb.com/title/tt0364817/ Access: July 2nd, 2008,

Heroes:http://www.imdb.com/title/tt0813715/ Access: July 2nd, 2008,

Dexter:http://www.imdb.com/title/tt0773262/ Access: April 9th, 2009,

Emergency Room:http://www.imdb.com/title/tt0108757/ Access: April 9th, 2009

House, M.D.:http://www.imdb.com/title/tt0412142/ Access: December 6th, 2009

Grey's Anatomy:http://www.imdb.com/title/tt0413573/ Access: April 9th, 2009

Interviews

- Elizabeth Devine (Co producer, CSI), Los Angeles, July 28, 2008
- Chuck Bemis (Cameraman, CSI), Los Angeles, August 24, 2008
- Matthew W. Mungle (Head of MWM Inc.), Los Angeles, August 29, 2008
- Eddi Vargus (Employee of MWM Inc.), Los Angeles, 2008, August 24, 2008
- Ruth Haney (Special Make-up Artist, CSI), Los Angeles, 2008, August 24, 2008
- Joshua Meltzer (Props Manager, Dexter), Los Angeles, 2009

List of Figures

Chapter 4

Chapter 5

Chapter 6

Index

Social Science

Tsypylma Darieva, Wolfgang Kaschuba,
Melanie Krebs (eds.)
Urban Spaces after Socialism
Ethnographies of Public Places in Eurasian Cities
2011, ca. 330 pages, ISBN 978-3-593-39384-1

Jörg Feuchter, Friedhelm Hoffmann, Bee Yun (eds.)
Cultural Transfers in Dispute
Representations in Asia, Europe and the Arab World
since the Middle Ages
2011, ca. 300 pages, ISBN 978-3-593-39404-6

Stefan Malthaner
Mobilizing the Faithful
Militant Islamist Groups and their Constituencies
2011, 273 pages, ISBN 978-3-593-39412-1

Elahe Haschemi Yekani
The Privilege of Crisis
Narratives of Masculinities in Colonial and
Postcolonial Literature, Photography and Film
2011, 320 pages, ISBN 978-3-593-39399-5

Hubert Heinelt, Eran Razin, Karsten Zimmermann (eds.)
Metropolitan Governance
Different Paths in Contrasting Contexts:
Germany and Israel
2011, 352 pages, ISBN 978-3-593-39401-5

Mehr Informationen unter
www.campus.de/wissenschaft

Frankfurt · New York